LEGAL PATH DEPENDENCE
and the
LONG ARM
of the
RELIGIOUS STATE

LEGAL PATH DEPENDENCE
and the
LONG ARM
of the
RELIGIOUS STATE

Sodomy Provisions and Gay Rights
across Nations and over Time

VICTOR ASAL
AND
UDI SOMMER

Both authors contributed equally to this work and their names appear in alphabetical order.

Published by State University of New York Press, Albany

© 2016 State University of New York

All rights reserved

Printed in the United States of America

No part of this book may be used or reproduced in any manner whatsoever without written permission. No part of this book may be stored in a retrieval system or transmitted in any form or by any means including electronic, electrostatic, magnetic tape, mechanical, photocopying, recording, or otherwise without the prior permission in writing of the publisher.

For information, contact State University of New York Press, Albany, NY
www.sunypress.edu

Production, Jenn Bennett
Marketing, Fran Keneston

Library of Congress Cataloging-in-Publication Data

Names: Asal, Victor, author. | Sommer, Udi, author.
Title: Legal path dependence and the long arm of the religious state : sodomy provisions and gay rights across nations and over time / Victor Asal and Udi Sommer.
Description: Albany, NY : State University of New York Press, 2016. | Includes bibliographical references and index.
Identifiers: LCCN 2016007708 (print) | LCCN 2016007838 (ebook) | ISBN 9781438463230 (hardcover : alk. paper) | ISBN 9781438463247 (paperback) | ISBN 9781438463254 (e-book)
Subjects: LCSH: Gays—Legal status, laws, etc. | Homosexuality—Law and legislation. | Homosexuality—Religious aspects. | Gay rights.
Classification: LCC K3242.3 .A83 2016 (print) | LCC K3242.3 (ebook) | DDC 345/.02536—dc 3
LC record available at http://lccn.loc.gov/2016007708

10 9 8 7 6 5 4 3 2 1

The history of the past is but one long struggle upward to equality.
—Elizabeth Cady Stanton

*We will never have true civilization until we have
learned to recognize the rights of others.*
—Will Rogers

CONTENTS

	List of Figures	ix
	List of Tables	xi
	Acknowledgments	xiii
Chapter 1:	Introduction	1
Chapter 2:	The History of Sodomy Laws and the Theory of Legal Path Dependence	33
Chapter 3:	The Religious State and Death Penalty for Sodomy	63
Chapter 4:	Sodomy Provisions and Their Repeal	79
Chapter 5:	Equalization of Rights	107
Chapter 6:	The Gay Rights Index	123
Chapter 7:	Conclusions	141
Appendix A:	Descriptive Statistics	149
Appendix B:	A Correlation Matrix	150
Appendix C:	Supporting Analyses and Robustness Tests	151
Appendix D:	Supporting Analyses and Robustness Tests	153
Appendix E:	Supporting Analyses and Robustness Tests	156

Appendix F:	Illustrations	158
	Notes	161
	References	167
	Index	191

FIGURES

Figure 1.1. Distribution of Sodomy Laws around the World and over Time (1975–2005) — 3

Figure 1.2. Number of Countries Legalizing Homosexual Relations — 27

Figure 5.1. Distribution of Sodomy Laws around the World and over Time (1975–2005) — 108

Figure 6.1. Distribution of Gay Rights around the World and over Time (1975–2005) — 125

Figure 6.2. Distribution of Levels of Gay Rights — 128

Figure 6.3. Variation in Gay Rights in Different World Regions (Percent of countries in Region with GRI Score) — 129

Figure 6.4. Criminalization and Legal Equality (Change over Time) — 130

Figure 6.5. Variation in Levels of Legal Protection for Gays (Change over Time) — 131

Figure 6.6. Protection of Women under International Law (CEDAW) and Level of Protection for Gay Rights — 132

Figure 6.7. GDP Per Capita and Levels of Protection for Gays — 133

Figure 6.8. Democratic Conditions and Variation in Legal Protection for Gays — 134

TABLES

Table 1.1. The Types of States in the Dataset (1970–2008)   25

Table 3.1. Variables and Data Sources   73

Table 3.2. Results of the Selection Model   74

Table 4.1. Analyses of the Predictors of Repeal of Sodomy Laws (GEE Models)   88

Table 4.2. Analyses of the Predictors of Repeal of Sodomy Laws (1990–2003)—with Alternative Measures for the Effects of Religion   90

Table 4.3. Institutional Contexts of Sodomy Provisions (1972–2008)   100

Table 4.4. Repeal of Sodomy Provisions via Judicial and Non-judicial Institutions   103

Table 4.5. Multinomial Logistic Regression Model: Analyses of Repeal of Laws Criminalizing Same-Sex Sex (1972–2002)   105

Table 5.1. Analyses of the Predictors of Prohibitions on Legal Discrimination   120

Table 6.1. Analyses of the Predictors of Gay Rights Index (Ordered Logistic Regression Models)   136

Table 6.2. Analyses of the Predictors of Gay Rights Index (GEE Models)   138

Table 6.3. Predicted Probabilities   139

ACKNOWLEDGEMENTS

Udi: I am indebted to many who supported me over the years it took to write this book. Risking the possibility of missing some, I would like to take this opportunity to thank those individuals and organizations by name. First, I'd like to thank my coauthor, Professor Victor Asal of the University at Albany, State University of New York. It has been a pleasure working with such a prolific scholar over the years, and this book is the culmination of collaborative work of nearly five years. In addition, I would like to acknowledge my research team: Maayan Ravid, Adi Grady, Oren Regev, Elliot Talbert-Goldstein, David Bimbat, and Tom Gur. Their work in data collection, compilation, and visualization was vital. Funding support has been invaluable in making this project possible. I would like to thank the Marie Curie Grant for their support. Additionally, two internal grants at Tel Aviv University supported some of the research assistance necessary for this project.

At SUNY Press I have benefitted from the enthusiasm, efficiency, and wit of Michael Rinella. The reviews of the manuscript by anonymous readers were astute, constructive, and extremely useful. This book will, I hope, live up to their recommendations, and it was surely improved thanks to their efforts. Earlier versions of some of the analyses in this book appeared in various conference papers as well as in the *Comparative Political Studies* piece "Original Sin" and in the *Law and Society Review* article "Institutional Paths to Policy Change." I am grateful to the editors and the reviewers at the journals for their invaluable help and insightful comments. Likewise, elements in the GRI index presented in Chapter 6 appeared in an article in *International Political*

Science Review. I would like to thank the editor and the reviewers for their help and comments.

My colleagues were a source of support and inspiration and, when necessary, had the critical perspective that allowed me to refine and improve my work both at Rockefeller College of Public Affairs and Policy at the University at Albany, State University of New York and at the political science department at Tel Aviv University. In particular, I would like to thank Julie Novkov, David Rousseau, Sally Friedman, Anne Hildreth, Rey Koslowski, Peter Breiner, Azar Gat, Yossi Shain, Michal Shamir, and Yael Shomer. I would also like to thank the Royal Norwegian Embassy in Israel, the Norwegian Ambassador, and Mr. Henrik Width for the Norwegian-Israeli Research Grant in the Social Sciences, which supported the presentation of parts of this research at the World Conference on Constitutional Law at the Department of Public and International Law at the University of Oslo.

I am deeply grateful to my parents, Pnina and Zvi Sommer, for their support of various sorts. I am indebted to Yael (Jane) Yahil, who bigheartedly adopted us as if we were her own. Stan and Iris Salomon are our closest relatives in America. Their kindheartedness and material and moral support were crucial. Our friends Michal(s), Idan, Guy, Dana, Ron, Hila, Kelly, Daniel, Ayala, and close family Amity, Amnon, and Olga all gave me the supportive community I so vitally needed when working on this book. Without my three kids, Talia, Ori, and Inbal, this project would probably have been much easier but then again utterly unimaginable. Last but certainly not least, I would like to thank Michali, the love of my life. Without her this would not have been possible.

Victor: I would like to thank my coauthor Udi Sommer who has shown admirable patience with me over the course of years. I would like to thank Michael Rinella and the team at SUNY Press without whom this book would not exist. I would like also to thank my family, Nadav, Gilad, and Barbara for their support. Finally, I would like to thank my parents, Ruth Asal and Tsvi Asal (Z"L), who worked hard to instill in me the belief that everyone should be treated fairly and that prejudice is never okay.

1

Introduction

In 1998, while responding to a report of a shooting in a private dwelling, the Houston police entered the apartment of John Lawrence. Upon entering the residence, the Texan policemen found Mr. Lawrence, an adult man, engaging in consensual homosexual sex with another adult male by the name of Tyron Garner. Lawrence and Garner were arrested and convicted on charges of violating a legal ban on sodomy in the state of Texas. The state court of appeals upheld the provision, prohibiting two adults of the same sex from engaging in certain sexual acts. The Texas court used a 1986 decision of the United States Supreme Court, *Bowers v. Hardwick* (478 U.S. 186) as controlling precedent. In *Bowers*, the court had recognized the constitutionality of prohibitions on same-sex sexual relations, which in some states had been in place for centuries. However, when the United States Supreme Court later reviewed *Lawrence v. Texas* (539 U.S. 558) in 2003, the justices handed down a 6 to 3 decision, not only reversing the decision of the state court but also overruling their own court's precedent in *Bowers*. The resolution in *Lawrence* effectively legalized consensual same-sex intercourse in the United States (Pedriana, 2009).

The United States is not the only country that has witnessed a sea change in the legal status of homosexuals in the recent past. In an opinion concurring in the judgment of the Constitutional Court of South Africa repealing the sodomy provision of this country, Justice Albie Sachs intimated:

It is important to start the analysis by asking what is really being punished by the anti-sodomy laws. Is it an act, or is it a person? Outside of regulatory control, conduct that deviates from some publicly established norm is usually only punishable when it is violent, dishonest, treacherous or in some other way disturbing of the public peace, or provocative of injury. In the case of male homosexuality, however, the perceived deviance is punished simply because it is deviant. It is repressed for its perceived symbolism rather than because of its proven harm. . . . Thus, it is not the act of sodomy that is denounced . . . but the so-called sodomite who performs it; not any proven social damage, but the threat that same-sex passion in itself is seen as representing to heterosexual hegemony. (*National Coalition for Gay and Lesbian Equality v. Minister of Justice and Others*, 1998, p. 188)

Since the 1960s the legal and societal environment facing the LGBT community (Lesbian, Gay, Bisexual and Transsexual—used interchangeably with LGBTI (Intersex) and LGBTIQ (Queer) throughout the book)—has changed dramatically in many countries. The number of countries that do *not* outlaw sodomy has almost doubled from 60 countries in 1975 to 103 countries (or a little more than 50 percent of the countries in the world) today. Yet, in various countries sodomy provisions remain on the books, prescribing in certain cases as harsh a penalty as capital punishment in case of their violation.

For a graphic illustration of this momentous change, examine the maps in Figure 1.1. The maps show the progression over time of one of the key aspects of gay rights examined in this book—sodomy laws and their repeal. The top left section of the first map indicates the distribution of sodomy laws in the world in the year 1975. The distributions in each consecutive decade until 2005 appear in the other three maps in the figure. In all four maps, the countries in grey are those where sodomy laws are in effect in that year; the countries in white are the ones where no sodomy provisions are on the books. We go into greater detail and discuss sodomy laws later on in this book (predominantly in Chapters 3 and 4). Yet, even a cursory glance at the maps will clearly indicate one important global trend over time; at least since 1975, an increasingly greater share of the countries in the world do not have sodomy provisions on the books. First, several countries in Europe repealed previously established laws (e.g., Spain). Later on, countries in Africa, Asia, and North and South America joined them. Overall, this trend toward more progressive

Figure 1.1. Distribution of Sodomy Laws around the World and over Time (1975–2005)

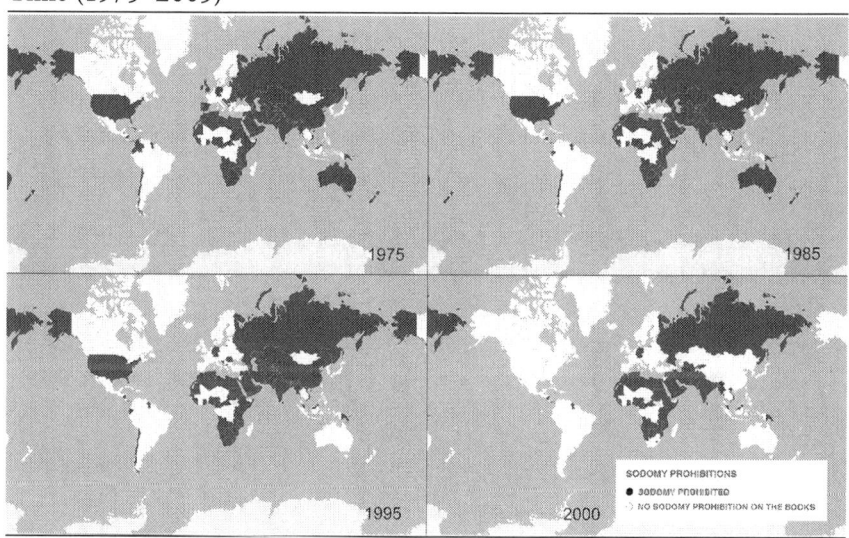

legal conditions for gay individuals, at least as far as same-sex legal prohibitions and their repeal are concerned, is clear. In the four decades since the 1970s, a diminishing number of countries posed any type of legal barriers for members of sexual-minority groups to engage in sexual activity in line with their sexual orientation. As we discuss at length in Chapters 5 and 6, such a trend toward more liberal conditions for homosexuals in certain parts of the world was true not just for sodomy laws but applied as well—particularly since the 1990s and early 2000s—to a broader range of legal rights for LGBT individuals.

In some countries the legal conditions have improved to such an extent that the state is now actively obligated to protect LGBT individuals and communities. Fourteen countries—including the United States of America—have legalized same-sex marriage, which is also true for some regions in Mexico. Furthermore, several countries now prohibit employment discrimination against LGBT individuals.

In many countries—particularly in the West—homosexuality is not just legal but visible: openly LGBT individuals are elected to public office (Saunders, 2009). In Germany, Guido Westerwelle was the first openly gay candidate to serve as foreign minister and vice-chancellor, and the capital city of Berlin had an openly gay mayor for 12 years (Reddy, 2012). In 2013 there were six declared members of the LGBT community in the United States Congress (Peters, 2013). Some countries are even taking measures to punish other countries for their discrimination against homosexuals (Gjorgievska, 2014; Williams, 2009). By any measure, this is a broad transformation in the United States, when one compares the present reality where there are now states that protect the work rights of members of the LGBT community to the situation that has existed in most of American history when people in all states would be fired for being gay. As bad as those circumstances were, of course, the American situation was good when compared to actions of certain other countries where people who were gay could lose even their lives.

The progress is particularly notable given the largely acrimonious environment just a few decades earlier, when, as Peters (2013) notes with respect to the United States, for instance:

> [f]or decades, the words "gay" and "Congress" were usually seen together only in stories of scandal and shame: an arrest after an illicit proposition in an airport bathroom, accusations of trawling for sex on a phone service. When Gerry E. Studds came out 30 years ago, the first congressman to do so, it was only after an affair with a 17-year-old Congressional page was revealed. (p. 13)

At the same time, in the United States there has still never been an openly gay individual nominated for the cabinet in the executive branch (Johnson, 2014) or the Supreme Court of the United States.

The variance in sexual-minority rights is true not only within the same country over time, but also cross nationally; variance among countries around the world is still substantial, with gay rights still being severely abused in certain places. For example, despite the improving worldwide trend, legal conditions for sexual minorities in Gambia deteriorated considerably in the summer of 2014. In this country, provisions imposing life imprisonment became law. It was no coincidence that six months earlier, the Gambian president, Yahya Jammeh, had articulated his contempt for this minority group. In a statement in February of that year, the African leader announced:

> Homosexuality will never be tolerated and in fact will attract the ultimate penalty since it is intended to bring humanity to an inglorious extinction. We will fight these vermins called Homosexuals or gays the same way we are fighting malaria-causing mosquitoes; if not more aggressively. We will therefore not accept any friendship, aid

or any other gesture that is conditional on accepting Homosexuals or L.G.B.T. as they are now baptized by the powers that promote them. As far as I am concerned, L.G.B.T. can only stand for Leprosy, Gonorrhoea, Bacteria and Tuberculosis; all of which are detrimental to human existence. (Hannon, *Slate*, September 8, 2014)

The first goal of this book is to describe those different types of variance—first, between countries in the rights they afford LGBTIQ individuals and groups; and second, how those rights change over time within the same country. Such variance consists of trends towards improved legal terms for sexual-minority groups as well as cases where such trends fall short. After all, the story of gay rights worldwide is not merely a rosy tale of liberalizing conditions, since in a considerable number of countries different variants of the Gambian case have transpired. Upon describing such diametrically opposed trends, the second goal of this book is to offer explanations for the reasons why we see different legal treatments of sexual minorities in different countries and the factors that impact how these treatments change temporally.

The broad theoretical framework we offer here attempts to explain the causes that lead some countries to have sodomy laws on the books while others either never had such laws or have decided to repeal said provisions. We delve into questions concerning the causes for the prescription of the death penalty for homosexuality. Furthermore, we examine what leads certain countries to prohibit discrimination against homosexuals in the workplace. The theoretical framework offered in this book argues that there are systematic explanations for these trends rooted in legal systems, colonial heritage, and religion. Those roots are also influenced by other variables such as systems of government, political institutions, levels of globalization, ethnic heterogeneity, and geographical locations.

It is important to note right at the outset that we do not purport to argue that an identical set of processes and institutions leads to all changes in the legal status of sexual minorities. This book examines a range of such rights—from the right not to lose one's life because of one's sexual orientation, through the right to freely live one's sexual desires, to the right not to be discriminated against based on sexual orientation. While several common threads run through the frameworks we offer to analyze those various legal rights, those frameworks do differ. For instance, as we show in Chapter 2, religion plays a major role in explaining the variance between countries that prescribe the death penalty to citizens violating a sodomy prohibition and countries that do not. While religion is still critical for explaining the mere presence of such provisions on the books, in Chapters 3 and 4 we demonstrate that legal path dependence since colonial times is at least equally important. Furthermore, when we examine issues of equality under the law in Chapters 5 and 6, the importance of international law and international institutions come to the fore. Those explain a good deal of the variance in equality under the law for LGBT. The connections between those predictors and the different types of sexual-minority rights examined in this book are probabilistic and not necessarily deterministic; legal path dependence, or the influence of religion within state affairs, influences the likelihood of certain legal circumstances for sexual minorities.

Thus, while it makes perfect sense to examine different types of gay rights in the same book—it is a set of legal provisions that pertain to sexual minorities—there are aspects of those political phenomena that differ. Put another way, the dependent variables in all chapters are clearly related to each other; they concern the rights denied or granted sexual-minority groups over time and in different jurisdictions around the world. Yet, the sets of predictors offered to explain variance in those outcome variables somewhat differ.

In sum, the first valuable insight from this book is probably the notion that while the political and legal issues examined all fall into the category of gay rights—and while obviously there is a *prima facie* hierarchy where abolition of death penalty for sodomy is at the most basic level, sodomy repeal is next, and equality under the law is at the top—in fact, moving up this apparent ladder of rights (which we measure using the Gay Rights Index in Chapter 6) is a result of a combination of legal and political processes. Both legal and political institutions and the work of legal and political agents explain the phenomena we study here. It might be tempting to argue that since they are all considered rights of a minority group defined by sexual orientation, there is some cumulative nature by which similar predictors explain all. In reality, however—we argue and demonstrate—no one set of independent variables could satisfactorily account for all. Yet, taken together, the analyses and accounts developed in this book for the different types of sexual-minority rights shed new light on legal provisions protecting gays in different parts of the world and on the ways those provisions evolve over time.

Our research provides substantial insight into the factors that contribute to the legal conditions framing and defining same-sex relations. In addition, it offers important lessons about how legal and political institutions develop and change over time, and how those institutions interact with economic conditions and with global trends to influence the very private lives of individual citizens. The liberty of individuals to engage in the type of sexual activity they desire, and the right of members of a minority group not to be discriminated against, are determined by institutional evolution, which in some cases is centuries old. What is more, it is global forces and economic trends well beyond the bedrooms of individual citizens that determine their political rights and liberties, including the types of activity they are allowed to engage in within those very bedrooms (Cook, 1999).

The Importance of de jure Provisions

This book is focused on the description and analysis of the variance in laws, which is done for a reason. While in countries where homosexuality has been legalized there can still be high levels of discrimination and violence, the abolition of the death penalty for same-sex relations—or alternatively the legalization of homosexuality—are still crucial steps. As Stone Gledhill (2013) notes:

> While there is still an alarmingly high level of homophobic violence (and violence in general) in South Africa (Msibi, 2009), sexual minorities interviewed in Goodman's (2001) research spoke of feeling safer being openly homosexual in public, as well as being able to go to the police for any discrimination or harm perpetrated against them. Vitally, they saw decriminalization as a first step to attaining further freedoms in expressing their sexuality. (Goodman, 2001)

Conversely, in places where anti-LGBT provisions are still on the books, such as in India, members of sexual-minority groups may be in real danger. Even if Section 377 of the Indian Penal Code—on which we expand extensively later in the book—is not rigorously enforced, the reality is that it can still create a situation of oppression and abuse (Khosla, 2011). The law can provide a "fig leaf of legitimacy for the harassment of queer people by families, friends, the medical establishment and other official institutions" (Narrain, 2009, p. 138). It can also provide a platform for abuse given the shame and social ostracism that individuals might face if they are exposed as being gay (Patel, 2010). Nasir, a 27-year-old self-described *kothi*—a term used in India to describe men, often homosexual with feminine characteristics, who do not conform to traditional gender roles—intimates:

> The Sampangi-Ramanagar police filed a false case against me under a wrong name [. . .] and put me in the lock-up. When I protested against this confinement, they told me we cannot do anything with you, so just be here. I was made to be there until 11pm and after approximately an hour, three policemen came to me and asked me whether I have a penis or not: "let us see". When I didn't listen to them, they started hitting me in order to make me take off my clothes [. . .], put a stick into my arsehole [. . .] and forcibly inserted [their] penises in my mouth and the other in my arse [. . .] till they all came out and left me. (Narrain, 2009, p. 138, citing Bhan, 2005, p. 8)

Such treatment, particularly likely in the absence of legal protections, is neither limited to India nor to low-level government employees and officials. President Robert Mugabe of Zimbabwe in 1997 at the national independence celebrations declared, "[i]f dogs and pigs do not do it [homosexual acts], why must human beings? We have our own culture, and we must re-dedicate ourselves to our traditional values that make us human beings" (cited in Hepple, 2012). Mugabe, however, as chief executive, was not alone. Other branches of the Zimbabwean government left little in the way of hope for gay rights. Quansah (2004) summarizes the ruling in *Banana v. the State*:

> The appellant was a former non-executive president of Zimbabwe. He was convicted, *inter alia*, on two counts of sodomy by the High Court. He appealed against the conviction to the Supreme Court. The Court had to decide whether, amongst others, the Common Law crime of sodomy was in conformity with Section 23 of the Zimbabwean Constitution, which guaranteed protection against discrimination on the ground of gender. The [Court] held that Section 23 of the Constitution did not include an express prohibition against discrimination on the ground of sexual orientation. That provision prohibited discrimination between men and women, not between heterosexual men and homosexual men. The latter discrimination was prohibited only by a constitution, which proscribed discrimination on the grounds of sexual orientation. The real complaint by homosexual men, in the majority's view, was that they were not allowed to give expression to their sexual desires, whereas heterosexual men were. Insofar as that was discrimination, the majority thought it was not the sort of discrimination, which was prohibited by Section 23

of the Constitution. [. . .] The real discrimination was against homosexual men in favor of heterosexual men, which was not discrimination on grounds of gender. Consequently, the majority concluded that the criminalization of consensual sodomy was not discrimination under the Constitution. (pp. 213–214)

In Jamaica—another country where legal provisions prohibit same-sex sexual relations—as recently as 2013, Dwayne Jones, a 17-year-old, was chopped to death when he was identified as "a cross-dressing teen" (Brathwaite, 2013). That same year in Jamaica, there were nine murders of LGBT individuals targeted for being gay. Likewise, members of sexual-minority groups have received death threats (Lavers, 2013). A painfully clear example of the existing level of discrimination against homosexuals that is socially acceptable can be seen in a recent article in the *Jamaica Observer* with the blunt title "Thousands rally against tossing out buggery act; shout out for clean, righteous living" and subtitled "Stand up for families, fight against greed, selfishness, speakers urge" (Skyers, 2014). In Saudi Arabia in as late as 2014, 35 individuals were arrested for attending a "gay party" (GayAsiaNews, 2014); and in 2003 the country executed three men because they were homosexual (Arab News, 2002). In Egypt, where homosexuality is illegal and LGBT members have been regularly arrested, there are reports that sexual-minority rights are not better protected since the military seized control again in 2013 (Trew, 2014).

In sum, laws on the books may have pernicious effects even when they are seldom enforced. As Justice Kennedy of the United States Supreme Court noted in the ruling that invalidated sodomy laws in the United States, if "homosexual conduct is made criminal by the law of the State, that declaration in and of itself is an invitation to subject homosexual persons to discrimination both in the public and the private spheres" (*Lawrence v. Texas*, 539 U.S. 558 [2003]). Along the same lines, Narrian notes that the expectation of heterosexual marriage in India is fierce; and with no legal alternative, suicide may become a real outlet (2009, p. 139). Lastly, in South Africa, before the repeal of anti-sodomy laws, the journalist Mark Gevisser said that to live their lives the way they wish when the law makes criminal their behavior created a situation for the LGBT community where "[w]e exercise the freedom we think we might have in South Africa not by right but by favor, by indulgence. We are dependent on, at best, the goodwill of the police to meet and act as we do; and at worst we are dependent on their blind eye, their lack of knowledge or their inefficiency" (2013, p. 61).

This Book's Argument

Beyond the specific examples above, our data show that prohibitions against sodomy still exist in some 80 nations and territories worldwide. In seven of those, individuals may pay with their lives for engaging in homosexual activity. This book offers a comprehensive analysis of the legal conditions for lesbian, gay, bisexual, and transsexual individuals with a large sample of countries over a period of several decades. Three major issues concern us in this book: the death penalty prescribed to same-sex sexual behavior (Chapter 2); the decriminalization of sodomy or the repeal of sodomy laws as in the examples from the United States and South Africa, as well as the institutions (judicial or non-judicial) through which decriminalization happened (Chapters 3 and 4); and legal provisions against discrimination of sexual minorities (Chapters 5 and 6). Of those three issues, the one that has lasted the longest and had the most far-reaching implications is the decriminalization of sodomy. We examine capital punishment for sodomy and thoroughly analyze it here; yet, it is important to bear in mind that with few exceptions, in the overwhelming majority of countries and jurisdictions where such a penalty had been on the books, it was repealed long ago. Only recently has equality under the law for sexual minorities (e.g., equality in the workplace) made the political agenda for some countries. Sodomy clauses, on the other hand, are legal provisions that remained on the books for decades in the case of some countries, and centuries, in the case of others. While most countries prescribing death for same-sex sexual relations repealed this provision during the 19th or early 20th centuries, the sodomy provisions remained on the books well into the 20th and 21st centuries. Accordingly, in recent decades it was the repeal of such laws that was typically the first legal obstacle on the way to legal equality for sexual-minority groups.

Our explanations for those legal trends concerning sexual minorities are based on legal path dependence and the influence of religion and the religious state. On the legal side, we contend that the legal inheritance from colonial times has had long-lasting effects on sexual-minority rights around the world. Nations with legal systems based on English Common Law inherited a prohibition on homosexual acts, which influenced gay rights, in some cases, for centuries to come. Common Law sodomy prohibitions, which find their origins in colonial times, were entrenched in the system, with vested interests of various types and of different parties, rendering legal change quite unlikely. Thus, due to path dependence, where the legal system originates from English Common Law the likelihood of decriminalization declines precipitously.

When legal institutions prohibiting homosexual activity are in place from the nation's founding, the costs associated with changing the legal status quo are high. Likewise, when religion plays a key role in the state's politics (large religious constituencies, legal limitations on minority religions, religious courts with extended jurisdictions, etc.), the likelihood that homosexual activity is legal decreases (Eastman, 1997).[1] For instance, under the British Empire, homosexual intercourse was made illegal in New Zealand in 1840. The prohibition against any type of sexual relations between men was expanded in this country later in the 19th century; and it was not until 1986, with the amendment of the Crimes Act and the passage of the Homosexual Law Reform Act, that consensual sex between men over the age of sixteen became legal. Other examples include—but are not limited to—Australia, India, and Israel (Frank et al., 2010; Joseph, 1996; Sanders, 2009). As we will elaborate in great detail, the prototypical alternative legal system—Civil Law structures (of various types)—again due to legal path dependence, did not have the effect of increasing the likelihood of sodomy provisions. The reason is that such provisions had been annulled shortly after the French Revolution in the late 18th century, in most cases never to be reinstated.

We identify three major pillars that supported such a path-dependent nature of the legal evolution of sodomy provisions: codification efforts by the British Empire that transported much of the legal setup of the motherland to colonies and territories all over the world and, with it, transported the sodomy provisions; legislation by local legislatures that preserved the spirit of English law; and rulings by constitutional courts and supreme courts in the different nations that articulated constitutional or statutory interpretations largely along the lines of original English law. Using original data in addition to data drawn from several existing sources, we examine those questions cross nationally over time, as well as while using case studies.

As for the religious aspects, in Judeo-Christian traditions and later on in Islam, the death penalty for homosexuality was divinely prescribed (Eron, 1993). Indeed, in response to the Human Rights Council of the United Nations, Nigeria defended capital punishment for same-sex relations using religious justifications and contended that it was a "just" penalty (Strasser, 2010). States that limit religious freedom are more likely to frame sodomy as a sin and to take religious texts as guides on how to punish such acts. The Jewish bible spells out that sodomy is evil when it reports on the efforts by the people of Sodom to rape Lot's guests (Genesis 18:17).[2] While there are numerous interpretations of the scripture, it is the traditional interpretation that is of particular interest for us here, as we believe it is key for the link between the involvement of the state in religion and its likelihood to employ the death penalty as punishment for sodomy. One might argue that the evil of Sodom was attempted rape and not homosexuality. However, in Leviticus 18:22 God tells Moses: "Do not have sexual relations with a man as one does with a woman; that is detestable." Traditional Christian analysis strongly agrees that homosexuality is evil (Gagnon et al., 2001; Olyan, 1994). For example, see Jude 1:7.[3] Certain views in the Qur'an are not dissimilar (Sura 26:165–167).

Traditional Islamic interpretations continue to this day to see male same-sex sex as prohibited by God (Duran, 1993; Habib, 2009; Wafer, 1997). While non-Abrahamic religions have had more ambivalent attitudes (and sometimes much more positive views) towards homosexuality in the past, many religious conservatives even in these faiths, either through Western influence or other factors, have also come to define homosexuality as evil (Bacchetta, 1999; Crompton, 2006; Dynes, 1992; Sharma, 1993). This link with a religious view that sodomy is evil—while not true everywhere, for every religion, or every religious authority within different religions—is key.

Indeed, even the prohibition in 16th century English law, which later influenced sodomy legislation around the world, finds its origins in a political dispute around religion. As we elaborate, it was the English Reformation and the assumption of a religious leader replacing the papacy that was the key motivation for King Henry VIII to pass his anti-sodomy legislation. As we also show, in some cases the influence of religion has indeed come full circle. This was the case in Sudan, for instance, as well as in Nigeria and Pakistan in recent years. In those countries, the origins of sodomy prohibitions were in English law. The Sudanese Penal Code, for example, was adopted in 1899 with some changes from the Indian Penal Code. It was only nine decades later that the Sudanese government added legal prohibitions on sodomy, this time pursuant to Sharia law. Replacing language largely echoing the provisions mostly in Section 377 of the Indian Penal Code, Section 148 of the new Sudanese provision reads:

> Sodomy: (1) Any man who inserts his penis or its equivalent into a woman's or a man's anus or permitted another man to insert his penis or its equivalent in his and is said to have committed Sodomy; (2) (a) Whoever commits Sodomy shall be punished with flogging one hundred lashes and he shall also be liable to five years imprisonment; (b) If the offender is convicted for the second time he shall be punished with flogging on hundred lashed and imprisonment for a term which may not exceed five years. (c) If the offender is convicted for

the third time he shall be punished with death or life imprisonment. (Human Rights Watch Report 2005, 21n)

Another example for the long arm of the religious state is Uganda, where current religious ideology has proved to be influential in the context of LGBT rights and their denial. Homosexuality was outlawed in Uganda when Uganda was under control of the British Empire, based on the Indian Penal Code (Sanders, 2009, p. 12). Many current African politicians and religious leaders have argued that homosexuality was "imported from the West" (Awondo et al., 2012, p. 148), and so the Common Law origin of criminalizing homosexuality is irrelevant. There is, however, strong evidence to the contrary. Epprecht (2009) points out that in general in Africa, until colonialism and the imposition of Christianity, same-sex relations were much more acceptable. Hoad (2007) argues that same-sex relations were something that, in various parts of Africa, was an accepted practice at least in some periods within the life cycle. Specifically related to Uganda, Msibi (2011, p. 99) points to the acceptance of same-sex relations among many of the peoples of the country before colonialism. One historical event that underlines both the different attitudes towards homosexuality in the country before colonialism and the impact of colonialism is the story of King Mwanga II:

> It is no secret that King Mwanga II, the Baganda monarch [. . .] engaged in sexual relations with other men: he made sexual demands upon his male servants and was enraged when they started refusing [. . .] to his advances on the grounds of their Christianity; his response was to order the killing of those who were converting to the new religion, and these slain servants are now called the "Uganda martyrs" [. . .]. The King's same-sex activities were falsely presented by Western colonialists to show that the Baganda were disgusted at them; this was in keeping with the West's imposition of homophobia in Africa. (Msibi, 2011, p. 99)

At the time of this book's printing, circumstances in Uganda have gone from bad to worse as far as legal rights for LGBT are concerned. The current religious and political leadership in Uganda is extremely hostile to homosexuality, and the situation has deteriorated due to outside influences based on religious ideologies. In the last decade there has been a concerted effort to enhance punishments for homosexuality and to punish not just sodomy but any homosexual "propaganda" (Awondo et al., 2012). One of the key factors is the lobbying and support efforts funded by International House of Prayer, an evangelical organization based in the United States (Lowder, 2014). The Campus Crusade for Christ, one of the largest charities in the United States, is another organization that uses its resources to coordinate anti-homosexual workshops in Africa and to support efforts to outlaw homosexuality or make existing laws more stringent. This includes imposing the death penalty for homosexuality (Michaelson, 2014).

While the death-penalty bill was being debated, a Ugandan gay-rights activist was killed after being identified by a Ugandan newspaper as someone who deserved to die. Both the bill and the advocacy for killing gay-rights activists were conspicuously framed in religious terms (Gettleman, 2011). Largely due to international pressure, the president stifled attempts to pass the capital-punishment bill, despite strong support in parliament (Awondo et al., 2012, p. 147). Though the bill failed, the general atmosphere towards homosexuals in the country has only deteriorated (Feder, 2014).[4]

As important as the Ugandan, American, Indian, and South African examples are, this book aims to go beyond case studies and specific illustrations from particular countries and complement those with research drawing on large-N databases and cutting-edge quantitative, analytical approaches. As such, it makes important contributions to the literature. While we have scholarship on the legality of homosexual relations in particular countries (Healey, 2002; Schmid, 2000), particularly within the states of the United States (Eskridge, 2008; Kane, 2003; 2007; Pinello, 2003; Robertson, 2006), and some comparisons between countries in the West (Ben-Asher, 1989; Hensle, 2009; West & Green, 1997), there has been very little cross-national inquiry of LGBT rights outside of the West (Frank et al., 2009; Sanders, 2009). With quantitative research limited to a relatively small number of nations and to cross-sectional snapshots, there also exists a paucity of time-series cross-national quantitative analysis beyond the United States.[5] Further, the research that does exist focuses mostly on liberalization and its sociological antecedents, such as level of individualization in society (e.g., Frank & McEneaney, 1999; Frank et al., 2010). Instead, here we examine institutional and legal evolution, and the political and economic variables that lead to changes in law and policy. Unlike work that examines legal trends such as contractions or expansions in the scope of legal regulation (e.g., Frank & McEneaney, 1999; Frank et al., 2010), we examine actual laws pertaining to the death penalty for sodomy, same-sex sex, and discrimination against sexual minorities. It is the renewed political power of religious denominations in recent decades that has preserved, if not reinstated, anti-sodomy laws in various regions of western Asia and Africa (Hinsch, 1990). Let us now examine each of those key influences—legal path dependence and the involvement of religion in the state—in more detail.

Path Dependence

Path dependence refers to the notion that social structures, human behavior, and various forms of human activity develop in ways that are dependent on earlier stages of their evolution; what happened earlier constrains the evolution in later stages and, in a real sense, it is dependent on the path previously paved. The evolution of technology is often path dependent. One such example is the qwerty keypad, which at a certain point in time was designed based on the needs and technological constraints of that period. Yet, switching between the qwerty design and any alternative offered thereafter has proven particularly tricky; not only are individuals and institutions used to the old design, but much of the technology they use is built to fit with the qwerty model. The same can be said for the Windows operating system. Without embroiling ourselves in the debates around the upsides and downsides of Windows, that this operating system has proven itself particularly impervious to replacement is not least due to the fact that it has been the infrastructure upon which much of the current technologies for various professions are founded. Thus, the notion of path dependence is theoretically powerful, as it helps us analyze current conditions based on the evolutionary path that has preceded them in the field of technology and otherwise.

Moving from the realm of technology to the context of political and social phenomena, path dependence refers to the "dynamics of self-reinforcing . . . processes in a political system" (Pierson & Skocpol, 2002, p. 699). This type of process is widespread in politics (Pierson, 2000). Once certain institutional rules are in place, alternatives forgone in earlier stages of the historical process cease to be available (Shepsle, 1986). Path dependence appears in the evolution of laws and legal systems (North, 1990) but also applies to a variety of other political phenomena (Collier & Collier, 1991; Ertman, 1997; Huber & Stephens, 2001; Kurth, 1979; Skowronek, 1993; Skocpol, 1979).

We argue that legal path dependence is a key to understanding the evolution of gay rights and, in particular, the decriminalization of homosexual intercourse cross nationally and over time. Of particular importance for the analysis of the legal treatment of same-sex sexual relations is the legal system put in place by the state. While this may be an external shock, its consequences are far reaching due to the dynamics of path dependence.

The pertinent case for sodomy laws is the export of the Common Law system that had criminalized buggery in Great Britain in 1533 and has proven particularly pernicious. Common Law adopted by other nations (or alternatively imposed on them) in conjunction with subsequent judicial decisions and statutes passed over the centuries, has led to criminalization of homosexual acts (Sanders, 2009). Conversely, the adoption and export of other legal systems, particularly French Civil Law (and its different derivatives in other European nations and colonial empires), did not have this effect, as sodomy was decriminalized immediately after the French Revolution. As a result, countries that were less influenced by British law were less likely to criminalize same-sex relations.

Two major self-enforcing mechanisms help entrench one legal system over alternative ones. The first is large setup (or fixed) costs. Setting up a new system of law entails costs, which short of a major event (such as a revolution or occupation by a foreign nation) are prohibitively high. These costs, therefore, considerably diminish the chances of putting in place a new system of law. The second mechanism involves adaptive expectations. Once a certain legal system is in place (e.g., after a territory is occupied and colonized), the belief that this system will persist is enhanced (North, 1990). The longer the system persists, the stronger becomes the belief. North (1990) contends that while there are multiple potential equilibria, which means that more than one legal system is possible and the final outcome is uncertain, an equilibrium, even one superior to the status quo (e.g., a superior legal system), may not win. This is due to the initial advantage of the existing system. Once established, an existing legal system is locked-in. Consequently, increasing returns and significant transaction costs due to imperfect markets shape institutional change. Once an equilibrium solution is locked-in, evolution takes a particular path, determined by legal and political institutions. This path dependence is a way "to narrow conceptually the choice and link decision making through time" (p. 98).

Although analysts have had difficulty in developing a clear definition of the meaning of path dependence (Mahoney, 2000), we refer specifically to the processes involving positive feedback, or increasing returns, that induce further movement in the same direction over time (North, 1990; Pierson, 2000, 2004; Smith, 2008). At the core of this definition of path dependence is the notion that, once out of the gate, institutions stay on a particular path because the costs involved in switching to a new one are prohibitively high (Kahn, 2006). The timing and sequence of events in such a theory matters a great deal because future outcomes are shaped by past decisions (Maioni, 1998; Pierson, 2004; Rose-Ackerman, 2010).

While past research indicates that the phenomenon of path dependence is widespread in politics (Ertman, 1997; Hacker, 1998; Huber & Stephens, 2001; Kurth, 1979; Pierson, 2000, 2004), relatively little has been said regarding the path-dependent nature of legal development (Asal et al., 2013; Sommer et al., 2013). We define *precedent* as previously defined legal rules (Segal & Spaeth, 2003). In a Common Law system, the principle of *stare decisis* dictates that precedent must be upheld and respected in future cases. As an important institutional norm, stare decisis produces the law's path-dependent character (Hathaway, 2003). Specifically, stare decisis compels lawmakers and judicial decision makers to respect the decisions of their predecessors. Once a precedent is set, lawmakers have limited ability to switch paths and induce change.[6] In sum, by explaining how the legal system has the capacity to lock in laws and thus generate stability over time, path dependence is critical for explaining the legal state of affairs.

The crucial aspect of legal path dependence, which is of particular interest for us, relates to laws passed in England in the 16th century (under the influence of religious-state ideology) and the laws repealed in late 18th-century France. While in Chapter 3 we delve into the historical details more fully, it makes sense here to canvass some of the historical evolution of sodomy laws. As discussed, we identify three key pillars that served the path-dependent nature of sodomy laws over the centuries. The first pillar is legal codification, which was a key element in the British colonial project and that served the transportation of laws from the motherland to the colonies. A quintessential example of such legal codification is the Indian Penal Code, which was implemented in India in 1862, but whose derivatives influenced legal reality in vast swaths of the British Empire and continued to do so for decades after. The second pillar supporting path dependent legal evolution is judicial rulings rendered by local courts. As courts play a key role in the system of Common Law and as case law is a central source for legal precedent in such systems, it was judicial rulings in the spirit of the laws of England that for decades and centuries helped perpetuate the same legal reality. The *Bowers* ruling in the United States, mentioned at the start of this chapter, is but one example of the role courts have played in sustaining the legal status quo concerning gay rights put in place in colonial eras. Lastly, the third pillar of path dependence is legislation passed by local legislators. In Chapter 4, we thoroughly examine legislative decisions concerning sodomy laws and their repeal. The legal and political status quo entails sunk costs; and once a certain path is paved due to an initial decision, switching paths becomes particularly tricky. This reality is clearly reflected in the type of legislation that was passed in many legislatures in British colonies and territories. This type of legislation, which largely preserved the principles of the legislation from the motherland, sustained legal development along the same path. The source of all those is the original anti-sodomy legislation passed in England centuries earlier, when King Henry VIII was in power.

We go into details of the historical background to the Buggery Act of 1533 in the next chapter. Yet, the effect of the act on the legal status of sodomy was far reaching, as legal prohibitions against sodomy became entrenched in English law (Dundes, 2002; Gilbert, 1976, 1981; Rayside, 1992). It was not until 1861 that the capital punishment prescribed by the law was irrevocably removed.[7] The Sexual Offences Act of 1967 provided limited decriminalization of homosexual acts.[8]

The Buggery Act is critical to our story, not just because of the extensive powers this legislation granted to the king of England nearly five centuries ago. Rather, it was the act and its legal derivatives—which were exported to British colonies around the world either in its original form or as a part of legal codes—that made this act particularly consequential. The legal codes included initiatives by the colonial authorities such as the Indian Penal Code (the Macaulay Code), the Fitzjames Stephen Code, the Griffith Code, and the Wright Penal Code. Interestingly, the push towards codification inside England was substantial, with the idea of legal codification warmly endorsed by Jeremy Bentham in *A Fragment on Government* (1776) and *An Introduction to the Principles of Morals and Legislation* (1789), as well as by his disciple John Stuart Mill. Yet, it was predominantly in the colonies, at least initially, that the notion of legal codification materialized. This process of legal codification, implemented in the colonies, became a key means by which legal path dependence took shape. The extensive codification in the colonies was a significant element in the legal infrastructure supporting the path-dependent legal evolution that eventually led to the morphing of the Buggery Act into the legal prohibitions of later years.

Conversely, in other colonial empires, such as France, same-sex sexual relations have been legal since 1791. The criminal code drafted by the National Constituent Assembly after the French Revolution rejected the definition of crimes based on the proscriptions of the Christian religion. Homosexual acts were thus not mentioned in the new penal code. The Napoleonic Code of 1804 and its subsequent Penal Code of 1810 did not undo the decriminalization of homosexual intercourse. French Civil Law was introduced in many countries under French occupation during the Napoleonic Wars. Due to path dependence, this has had extensive influence in Europe and, because of colonization, beyond the continent as well (e.g., in many Latin American countries, several of which adopted it voluntarily after the Spanish occupation was over).

The concept of path dependence applies to the case of the French code just as well. As provisions prohibiting homosexual acts were absent from the Napoleonic Code of 1804 and the Penal Code of 1810, there was no prohibition on same-sex sex entrenched in the legal system in nations that adopted Civil Law. Hence, law in Civil Law jurisdictions developed along a different path. The legal system was lacking a prohibition on sodomy in many Civil Law countries, and this was the equilibrium that was locked in. Any attempts to alter the status quo by proposing alternative equilibria, even if superior in certain ways, were unlikely to succeed because of the prohibitively high cost of change once path dependence was set in motion (North, 1990).

Whereas Great Britain was exporting a legal system that outlawed sodomy, French code (which in various forms was imposed by France, Spain, and the Netherlands on their colonies, or adopted voluntarily by many other states) did not contain such a provision. For centuries to come, its influence on the way legal and political institutions dealt with the issue of homosexual acts was, thus, fundamentally different. As for systems with origins in communist or socialist law, many of these states have gone through a process of democratization in the 1990s. As a part of this process, those states adopted a Civil Law system. While some of those states had previously had anti-sodomy laws in place, the process of democratization in many cases was followed by decriminalization of gay sexual activity.

State-Religion Relations and Prohibitions on Sodomy

A Common Law system is not the only factor that decreases the legal protections sexual-minority groups enjoy. Another key variable is the influence of religion on the state. Establishment of a state religion, or even more so, a legal code that stems from religious principles, increases the likelihood that legal proscriptions against homosexual acts would be codified. One example of this influence of religion comes from Egypt. On May 11, 2001, the police in the Egyptian capital of Cairo arrested 52 men. The group, which later became known as Cairo 52, was aboard the Queen Boat, a floating gay nightclub. While all 52 pleaded innocent, they stood trial, some of them more than once (Hawley, 2001). They were found guilty of charges ranging from "habitual debauchery" to "contempt for religion." Even in the face of international criticism, the courts carried on with the trials, in a nation where Islam was the state religion. As Ottoson (2009) indicates, there is no general prohibition on homosexual acts in the Egyptian Penal Code. Yet, the state would take advantage of statutory provisions concerning religion, morality, and debauchery, to prosecute homosexuals and bisexual individuals.

Based on the principles of the Qur'an, the central text of Islam, and Hadith, which are oral traditions determining the Muslim way of life, Islam proscribes homosexual acts. As with versions of Judaism and Christianity, from its beginning as a religion, Islam rejected homosexual intercourse. Different schools of thought within Islam have different legal prescriptions when it comes to sodomy, also termed *zina*, with some regarding it as unlawful sexual relations between individuals. Saifee (2003) provides a brief summary of some of the current perspectives on this matter within Islam:

> The majority of Sunni jurists regard heterosexual anal intercourse between a non-marital couple a *zina*. Such activity within marriage, although considered sinful, is not a crime of *zina*. Sunni schools of thought differ in their criminal classification of homosexual sodomy. The Shafi'i, Hanbali, and Maliki schools regard homosexual intercourse as *zina* and thus liable to *hadd* punishment, while the Hanafis consider homosexual sodomy a crime of *ta'azir*, or discretionary punishment. (p. 378)

Some nations with a Muslim majority but which are relatively secular in nature or multi-religious, (e.g., Indonesia) do not treat homosexual activity as a crime; as such, there are no prohibitions against it in their legal codes. In some cases (e.g., Turkey), a certain level of tolerance for homosexual sexual activity has been entrenched in the system for years (Murray & Roscoe, 1997). Yet, nations in which Islam is the state religion (e.g., Egypt), and in Islamic states where Sharia law and the Qur'an are the primary sources for legislation, there typically exists a codified prohibition of homosexual activity. Furthermore, in several of those states (e.g., Saudi Arabia, Somalia, and Mauritania), death is the prescribed punishment for engaging in such activity. In Chapter 2 and then again when we develop the Gay Rights Index in Chapter

6, we delve into the discussion of the effects of religion in this context from both theoretical and empirical perspectives.

This book examines sodomy laws and their repeal side by side with other aspects of the legal treatment of sexual minorities. We explore cases where sodomy leads to the death penalty, as well as very different cases where equality under the law is mandated by the state. We think of those as placed along a continuum of legal treatment of gays, from the most discriminatory on the one hand (capital punishment for same-sex relations), to the most equal on the other (legal prohibition on discrimination). Since sodomy provisions are the ones that were by far the most frequent (they existed the longest on the law books of many countries), the discussion of those provisions and their repeal also takes the lion's share of this manuscript. Before we discuss the methods used in this book and outline its chapters, let us briefly examine the explanations in the extant literature. This will not only situate our work in existing scholarship but also highlight the unique contribution that each of the chapters in this treatise makes.

Existing Accounts in the Literature

The contribution that this book is making to the literature on rights for minority groups, and in particular the rights of sexual-minority groups, or LGBT is twofold: we not only expand the limited literature on the effects of legal systems and delve into the intricacies of those systems and how they transported sodomy laws over the years, but we also underline the role of religion, religious law, religious authorities, and religious constituencies in this story. So far we provided a brief outline for these two contributions: legal path dependence and the effects of religion on sodomy provisions. In Chapter 3 we go into further detail in explaining those effects. Before doing that, however, we here discuss additional variables that appear in the existing literature (West & Green, 1997).

Democratic Conditions and Sodomy Laws

Based on the democratic understanding of consensual sexual activities between adults as a human right (Mertus, 2007), extant literature indicates that the spread of democracy influences rights of minority groups of various sorts

(Davenport, 1999; Gurr, 2000). Along the same lines, there is a great deal of empirical analysis to support the contention that established democracies are more likely to make greater legal provisions for historically marginalized populations (Davenport, 1999; Gurr, 2000; Wilensky, 2002). Thus, literature on this topic suggests that better democratic conditions lead to improved legal conditions for LGBT groups. Democracies are unlikely to prescribe the death penalty for sexual minorities; they are more likely to decriminalize sodomy, and it is more likely that their legal code prescribes equality for LGBT individuals.

Economic Development, Modernization, and Sodomy Laws

As economic conditions improve and the country modernizes, literature suggests that improvement in the legal conditions of sexual minorities would come about as well. Modernization has been shown to act as a causal variable in increasing levels of democracy generally (Doorenspleet, 2004; Huntington, 1991; Lipset, 1960; Przeworski et al., 2000; Ramirez et al., 1997), and specifically enhancing the rights of women (Inglehart & Norris, 2003) and minorities (Gurr, 2000). Political inclusion and political-opportunity structures are related to changes in the economic composition of a state. Economic development and modernization thus lead to political inclusion. In a variety of ways, such as through literacy, education, and cultural change, modernization can change the view of who should be accepted in society as equal, which would have consequences for the legal conditions for sexual-minority groups.

Globalization and Sodomy Laws

Conventional theories of sovereignty have emphasized the nation-state as the guarantor of rights and liberties (Anderson, 1983; Weber, 1994). Yet, some have argued that globalization erodes the nation-state and leads to porous national boundaries in terms of legal arrangements, capital flow, immigration, and in a variety of other ways (Grewal, 2005). Globalization reduces transaction costs across a range of human interactions, opening up new opportunities and exposing social systems to new ways of thinking (Hollingsworth, 1998).

Globalization has grown in scale, speed, and importance (Kinnvall, 2004). While some argue that globalization is not an unprecedented phenomenon

(Hirst & Thompson, 1999; Williamson, 1996), current levels of globalization are different from those in the past. People move more freely across the globe as tourists, immigrants, refugees, or international students and businesspersons (Appadurai, 2000). Globalization has also increased contacts between societies. There is heightened awareness of different political arrangements through mass media. Likewise, there is a major increase both in volume of trade and the financial flows involved, as well as in the intensity of these interactions and the key role of information and communication technologies (Giddens, 2002). This phenomenon has reduced transaction costs across a range of human interactions (Hollingsworth, 1998) with vast political implications. It permits the exchange not only of goods and services but also of ideas, values, beliefs, and political institutions (Hermans & Kempen, 1998).

Scholars contend that globalization leads to more rights and freedoms by diffusing the ideals of freedom and democracy (Fukuyama, 1992; Tsutsui & Wotipka, 2004) or by forcing states to adopt norms of rights and freedoms in response to increasing international pressures (Finnemore & Sikkink, 1998). Information about alternative legal arrangements should be more readily available in a globalized state. It becomes easier to identify alternative legal frameworks and the way civil rights and liberties in general, and gay rights in particular, are organized in other jurisdictions. In this sense, the strengthening of links between countries allows for the diffusion of new human rights and norms of tolerance (Tsutsui & Wotipka, 2004). Moreover, the world-culture and normative-diffusion literature argues that the strengthening of links between countries allows for the diffusion of new human rights and norms of tolerance (Boli & Thomas, 1997, 1999; Ramirez & McEneaney, 1997). In terms of legal elites, an increasing trend towards communication between members of the judiciaries across national borders also seems to exist. For instance, to support its 2003 decision in *Lawrence v. Texas* (as well as in more recent cases), the Supreme Court of the United States has cited a number of authorities beyond the Fourteenth Amendment, including *Dudgeon v. United Kingdom*, a decision by the European Court of Human Rights invalidating sodomy laws (Wells, 2004).[9] In a more formal context, the 1996 constitution of South Africa explicitly requires the consideration of foreign law by members of the Constitutional Court. In the case of the legal rights of sexual minorities (death penalty, sodomy laws, and legal equality), we argue that there is a norm diffusion that happens between countries. The effect of globalization is mediated via political globalization, elites (such as judges), cultural globalization, and economic ties. More highly globalized countries should thus be more likely to have legal provisions favorable of

LGBT individuals. We thus expect that with higher levels of globalization, the state would be less likely to have the death penalty on the books for those engaging in same-sex sex, would increase the likelihood of decriminalization, and would elevate the probability of statutory prohibitions on discrimination against sexual minorities.

Data and Methods for the Book

Quantitative data for the key dependent variables in this book are taken from the 2009 and 2013 reports on "State-sponsored Homophobia: A World Survey of Laws Prohibiting Same Sex Activity between Consenting Adults." This is the most comprehensive dataset that we were able to locate that related to the treatment of homosexuals by states. This report was created by the International Lesbian, Gay, Bisexual, Trans and Intersex Association, which claims to represent "over 700 groups in over 110 countries campaigning for lesbian, gay, bisexual, trans and intersex (LGBTI) rights" (International Lesbian, 2010). In addition, we make extensive use of the University of Gothenburg: Quality of Government Institute's June 2009 "The Quality of Government Dataset" (Teorell et al., 2009).[10] This constitutes our combined "Global Sexual Discrimination" dataset.

As Table 1.1 indicates, there are 89 countries where consensual homosexual intercourse has been outlawed throughout the nation's entire existence. Some of the 89 countries in which sodomy has been illegal have ceased to exist before the end of the period (e.g., East Germany). Indeed, by the year 2008, in only 80 nations and territories worldwide was sodomy illegal. Our second group depicts states that have decriminalized homosexual relations sometime within the last four decades, and indicates the year of legalization; there are 50 such nations in our data. Our third group lists the 61 nations in which consensual homosexual intercourse has been legal since at least 1970.

Many of the countries decriminalizing sodomy since 1970 did so in the 1990s. As Figure 1.2 demonstrates, between 1970 and 2008, the decade with the most cases of legalization was the 1990s. In the database, more than half of the countries that legalized homosexual acts during the time period studied accomplished this legal reform sometime during this decade. A considerable number of the countries legalizing homosexual relations during this period were republics from the former Soviet Union. For instance, in 1998, the year with the greatest number of cases of legalization, three of the six countries legalizing consensual homosexual intercourse were Tajikistan, Kyrgyzstan, and

Table 1.1. The Types of States in the Dataset (1970–2008)

Homosexual intercourse is illegal throughout country

Afghanistan	Guyana	Pakistan	Timor-Leste
Algeria	India	Palau	Togo
Andorra	Iran	Papua New Guinea	Tonga
Angola	Iraq	Qatar	Trinidad and
Antigua and	Jamaica	Samoa	Tobago
Barbuda	Kenya	Sao Tome and	Tunisia
Bangladesh	Kiribati	Principe	Turkmenistan
Barbados	Lebanon	Saudi Arabia	Tuvalu
Belize	Lesotho	Senegal	USSR
Bhutan	Liberia	Seychelles	Uganda
Botswana	Libya	Sierra Leone	United Arab
Brunei Darussalam	Malawi	Singapore	Emirates
Cameroon	Malaysia	Solomon Islands	Uzbekistan
Comoros	Maldives	Somalia	Vanuatu
Djibouti	Mauritania	Sri Lanka	Vietnam
Dominica	Mauritius	St Kitts and Nevis	Vietnam, South
Egypt[i]	Micronesia	St Lucia	Yemen
Eritrea	Morocco	St Vincent and the	Yemen, North
Ethiopia (-1992)	Mozambique	Grenadines	Yemen, South
Ethiopia (1993-)	Myanmar	Sudan	Zambia
Gambia	Namibia	Swaziland	Zanzibar
Ghana	Nauru	Syria	Zimbabwe
Grenada	Nigeria	Tanzania	
Guinea	Oman	Tibet	

Total = 89

Homosexual intercourse status (year of legal change) changes from illegal to legal

Albania (1995)	Ecuador (1997)	Nepal[v] (2007)
Armenia (2003)	Estonia (1992)	New Zealand (1986)
Australia (1994)	Fiji[iv] (2005)	Nicaragua (2008)
Austria (1971)	Finland (1971)	Norway (1972)
Azerbaijan (2000)	Georgia (2000)	Panama[vi] (2008)
Bahamas (1991)	Guinea-Bissau (1993)	Portugal (1983)
Bahrain (1976)	Ireland (1993)	Romania (1996)
Belarus (1993)	Israel (1988)	Russian Federation (1993)
Bosnia and Herzegovina[ii] (1998)	Kazakhstan (1998)	Serbia (1994)
	Kyrgyzstan (1998)	Slovenia (1977)
Cape Verde (2004)	Latvia (1992)	South Africa (1998)
Chile (1999)	Liechtenstein (1989)	Spain (1979)
China[iii] (1997)	Lithuania (1993)	Tajikistan (1998)
Colombia (1981)	Macedonia (1996)	Ukraine (1991)
Croatia (1977)	Malta (1973)	United Kingdom[vii] (1982)
Cuba (1979)	Marshall Islands (2005)	United States (2003)
Cyprus (1998)	Moldova (1995)	Yugoslavia (1994)

Total = 50

Table 1.1. (continued)

	Homosexual intercourse is legal throughout country		
Argentina	Cote d'Ivoire	Iceland	Paraguay
Belgium	Czech Republic	Indonesia	Peru
Benin	Czechoslovakia	Italy	Philippines
Bolivia	Denmark	Japan	Poland
Brazil	Dominican Republic	Jordan	Rwanda
Bulgaria		Korea, North	San Marino
Burkina Faso	El Salvador	Korea, South	Slovakia
Cambodia	Equatorial Guinea	Laos	Suriname
Canada	France	Luxembourg	Sweden
Central African Republic	Gabon	Madagascar	Switzerland
	Germany, West[viii]	Mali	Taiwan
Chad	Greece	Mexico	Thailand
Congo	Guatemala	Monaco	Turkey
Congo, Democratic Republic	Haiti	Mongolia	Uruguay
	Honduras	Netherlands[ix]	Venezuela
Costa Rica	Hungary	Niger	Vietnam, North
Total = 61			

Note. In 2008, only 80 of those original 89 nations still exist, and they persist in criminalizing sodomy.

i. There is no general prohibition on homosexual acts in the penal code. However, statutes on offences against the religion, morality, and debauchery are used to prosecute homosexual and bisexual men in particular.
ii. Republika Srpska in 2000.
iii. Homosexual acts are also legal in all Chinese associates, Hong Kong (1991), and Macau (1996).
iv. The sodomy statutes were declared unconstitutional and unenforceable by Supreme Court Justice Gerard Winter on 26 August 2005, but they are still on the books.
v. Sodomy was decriminalized by a Supreme Court decision on 21 December 2007.
vi. Decree No. 332, Official Gazette of 31 July 2008.
vii. England and Wales (1967), Northern Ireland (1982), Scotland (1981).
viii. East Germany (1968) and West Germany (1969).
ix. Homosexual acts are also legal in Aruba and the Netherlands Antilles.

Kazakhstan. Chapters 5 and 6, where we deal with legal equality and with the development of the Gay Rights Index, include extensive discussion of additional data sources for variables measuring legal equality.

Several types of regressions are estimated to test hypotheses. First is a multinomial logistic regression with year dummies (this type of regression model is estimated only in Chapter 3). Second is GEE time-series cross-sectional analysis. We estimate ordered logistic regression models to test our predictions concerning the Gay Rights Index in Chapter 6. We also estimate a Heckman Model for our analyses of capital punishment for same-sex sexual relations in Chapter 2. Since the time component in our data is important, as robustness tests we also estimated multilevel mixed-effects models similar

Figure 1.2 Number of Countries Legalizing Homosexual Relations

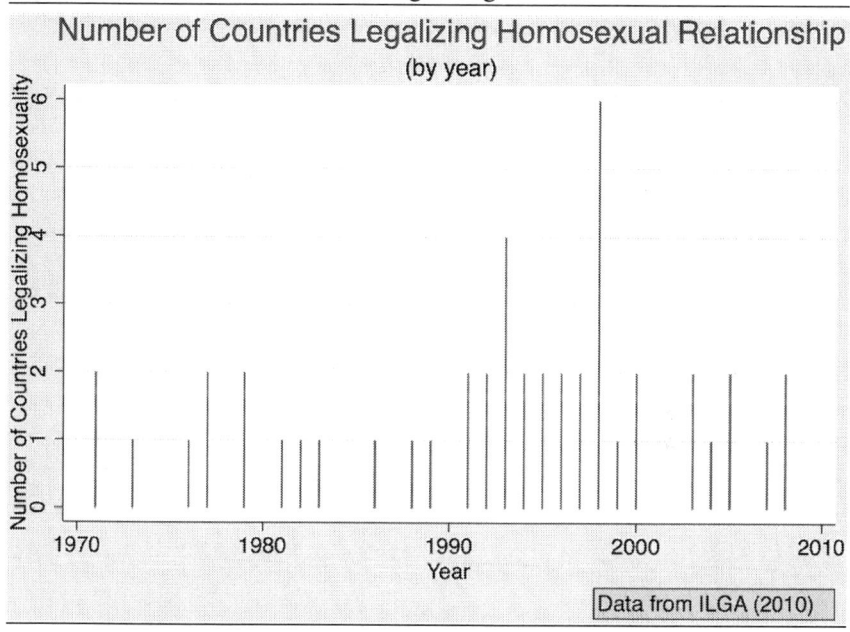

in specification to the models reported here. The findings were substantively indistinguishable.

As for our outcome variables, the dependent variable for the multinomial logit in Chapter 4, *Repeal Type*, has three levels—0 for no repeal; 1 for non-judicial repeal; and 2 for judicial repeal. For the GEE analyses, several dependent variables are coded. In Chapter 4, *Legal* indicates whether a country decriminalized sodomy (1 if sodomy is legal; 0 otherwise). In the same chapter, *Court Repeal* is coded 1 for countries where repeal happened in court in the three decades following 1972, and 0 otherwise. *Non-Judicial Repeal* is equal to 1 when non-judicial institutions repealed sodomy, and 0 otherwise. In Chapter 5, *Discrimination* is coded 1 for countries where the legal code prohibits discrimination based on sexual orientation in the workplace. This variable equals 0 otherwise. In Chapter 6 we develop the Gay Rights Index (GRI), and delve into the methodology of this index. The various models we estimate to test our hypotheses concerning the index use outcome variables derived from the GRI.

As for the predictors used as independent variables, we briefly discuss them in the later chapters, but let us also examine those variables right at the outset. *Common Law* is a dummy that equals 1 for countries whose legal origin is Common Law, and 0 otherwise. Based on the CIA fact book, *Percent Catholic* indicates Catholics as percentage of the population and *Percent Muslim* indicates Muslims as percentage of the population. *Percent Protestant* measures the percent of members of this faith in the population of the country at a certain point in time. To measure international connections, we use a measure of globalization—the KOF Indexes of Globalization (Dreher, 2006; Dreher et al., 2008). The indexes for the globalization variables are measured in line with the standard in comparative public law (Tsutsui & Wotipka, 2004; Frank & McEneaney, 1999) and range from 0–100. Higher values indicate higher levels of globalization. The *Globalization* predictor is a weighted average of social, political, and economic globalization. The measure for economic globalization is defined as the long-distance flow of services, goods, capital, information, and perceptions that accompany market exchanges. This index measures not only actual flows of trade and investments but also trade restrictions, such as tariff rates (Dreher, 2006; Dreher et al., 2008). The index of political globalization is measured by the number of embassies and high commissions in a country, the number of memberships the country has in international organizations, participation in UN peace-keeping missions, and the number of international treaties signed since 1945 (Dreher, 2006; Dreher et al., 2008). Lastly, the social globalization measure includes three categories of indicators: personal contacts (e.g., telephone traffic and tourism), information flows (e.g., number of Internet users), and cultural proximity (e.g., trade books and number of warehouses of Ikea per capita; Dreher 2006; Dreher et al., 2008). To measure *Democratic Conditions*, we utilize the POLITY score, which was imputed using Freedom House data where it was missing. The scale ranges from -10 (least democratic) to 10 (most democratic) (Hadenius & Teorell, 2005). GDP per capita in constant US dollars at base year 2000 was used (Gleditsch, 2002). Appendix A has the descriptive statistics for the different variables, and the correlation matrix between those variables is in Appendix B.

Outline of the Book

In this first chapter we provide an overview of the project and its theoretical framework. In addition, we outline some of the key methodological aspects of the research described in the book. Equality under the law is crucially important for the political inclusion, recognition, and empowerment of a minority group. In fact, some argue that basic rights are a stepping-stone for full equality under the law in all aspects of life. The theoretical framework initially developed in the introduction chapter adopts this understanding of legal progress. In our theory, the evolution from basic legal protections, such as the decriminalization of sodomy, is a necessary but not sufficient condition for the later stage of prohibition on discrimination against sexual minorities in various aspects of life. It is important to stress that as states may revert to criminalization (see in Chapter 3 for the expanded discussion of the case of India in 2009 and in 2013), the legal development analyzed is not necessarily a unidirectional process. Apart from introducing the topic and theory, this chapter also includes an overview of the legal conditions for sexual minorities in countries around the world, which is what we seek to explain. Additionally, figures, tables, and maps are presented to describe variables we use throughout the book as explanatory variables such as systems of law, religious constituencies, and democratic conditions.

In Chapter 2 we canvass the history of sodomy laws as it dates back to biblical times, as well as to the Middle Ages, and then the English Reformation in Europe. We then trace how those provisions translated into legal reality throughout the 20th and the 21st centuries in all corners of the world. We put particular emphasis on the legal systems of Common Law and Civil Law, and on the role of colonial heritage and its influence on the rights of sexual minorities as those are prescribed on the law books of different countries. This discussion leads us to the full development of our theory concerning legal path dependence and its influence on the evolution of sodomy laws. We develop our argument about the three pillars of path dependence—legal codification in the colonies, judicial rulings, and legislative decisions that have been critical to legal path dependence. We go into great detail in studying the Indian Penal Code and other codification efforts, their origins, and the way they help us explain and analyze the legal conditions of homosexuals around the world.

The second key component of our theory, the influence of religion on the state and its consequences for gay rights, is developed in the next chapter and then empirically tested. Chapter 3 examines the death penalty imposed on sodomy offences. Some countries not only punish same-sex relations as a criminal offence but also inflict state-sanctioned death in such cases. Chapter 3 explores the factors that make the death penalty for same-sex consensual sex between adults more likely. We argue that the key factor related to the death penalty for same-sex relations is the religious power of the state. This is so because of the need to fulfill normative attitudes towards homosexuality that are doctrinally imposing in many religions. We specifically discuss views on homosexuality in Christianity and Islam, as well as the historical behavior of states, from Victorian England to Saudi Arabia, where religious authorities were empowered by the state to dictate laws on a variety of issues. We then present a systematic analysis of the variables explaining the death penalty for homosexuals, where we find strong support for our theoretical framework. While we deem the death penalty for gays an important component of a comprehensive analysis of gay rights worldwide, the reality is that this kind of legal prescription is extremely rare and, indeed, has been for several decades.

The next chapter (Chapter 4) examines the question of decriminalization of sodomy provisions. We further develop the notion of legal path dependence as it pertains to Common Law and Civil Law jurisdictions, and we examine annulment of sodomy provisions in both legislative and judicial institutions. We first find unequivocal support in Chapter 4 for the effects of legal path dependence and religion on the likelihood of sodomy provisions being on the books. We then delve further into this examination with the study of the type of institution within which this repeal had taken place. The juxtaposition of judicial and non-judicial repeal helps us establish the causal mechanism we argue is in place; in the theoretical framework proposed, the path-dependent nature of law has a differential impact on courts and legislatures. Likewise, certain political institutions, including elections and political accountability, lead those bodies to introduce policy change under dissimilar circumstances. Global trends, however, affect both institutional paths equally. We find that the unique institutional position of courts of last resort allows them to be less constrained than legislatures either by legal status quo or political accountability when repealing sodomy provisions.

Chapter 5, "Equalization of Rights," examines a higher level of legal protection granted sexual minorities. Previous chapters focus on criminalization or decriminalization of same-sex activity. In this chapter, we examine the next stage in the legal evolution conceptualized in our theoretical framework; we study cases where the state chooses to equalize the legal status of sexual minorities. More specifically, we examine legal protections afforded against discrimination based on sexual orientation in the workplace. We first provide a history of the development globally. Next, we develop our argument that the key factors impacting such change have been the spillover of norms both globally and domestically. We examine the effects of regulation by supranational bodies and the impact of country-level treatment of minorities. In sum, therefore, in the theoretical framework a combination of domestic forces (past inclusion of minorities, culture, and democratic conditions) and global trends (regulation by supranational bodies and globalization) predict guarantees of rights and equality under the law for sexual-minority groups (Sommer & Asal, 2014). The empirical findings lend support mostly to the notion of domestic norm spillover.

Chapter 6 is the culmination of the theoretical and empirical work in this book. In this chapter we propose a theoretical framework and an empirical scale to comparatively examine different levels of legal protection granted to sexual minorities. We bring together our theoretical discussion and empirical analyses in earlier chapters to suggest that there is a need to look at gay rights as a continuum of rights and to examine how different factors impact progress on that continuum. The Gay Rights Index (GRI) is an original measure for the legal status of LGBT individuals in different countries and over time. We argue that the level of de jure legal protections afforded gay individuals can be measured on a scale with three levels. The highest level would be equality under the law (e.g., in employment). The second would be the lack of legal prohibitions on same-gender sexual activity, also due to decriminalization. Lastly, at the lowest level there would be countries with no legal protections and where same-sex relations are criminalized. We also deal with the mythological issues of potential overlap, in particular between the second and third levels. As mentioned above, capital punishment for homosexuality has been particularly rare in recent decades, which is why we do not include this condition in the index.

GRI has clear advantages both for explaining cross-sectional variance as well as for deciphering changes over time. In addition, we proceed to show a series of descriptive statistics in maps that lay out how and where these countries are located and how the level of protection along this index has changed over time. We discuss theoretically what should be driving this hierarchical normative change in the way the state treats sexual minorities. We analyze what factors make a country more likely to be at a certain level on the index. To test a theory that explains variance in GRI, we analyze data for the majority of the world's countries for nearly three decades since the mid-1970s. We find that the status of women (both in terms of political inclusion and under applicable international law), religious constraints on politics, democratic conditions, economic conditions, and the type of legal system, explain a good amount of the variance in the legal status of sexual minorities.

Chapter 7 concludes this book. In this chapter we compare our results across the different chapters and discuss what these findings mean theoretically. We examine more specifically the impact of different religions and the effects of different world regions on our findings. We then discuss where research on sexual minorities should be going next, as well as the import of our research to the broader challenge of understanding discrimination based on gender, race, or ethnicity. Our work is situated in the interface of law and politics in the context of gender and sexuality, and we examine its contribution to this body of knowledge. Thus, while the focus here is the rights of a minority defined by sexual orientation, this study also offers some important lessons about civil rights more generally (Haider-Markel & Meier, 1996; inter alia).

2

The History of Sodomy Laws and the Theory of Legal Path Dependence

When the second monarch of the Tudor dynasty, Henry VIII, became king of England in April 1509, the era that was about to transform England, the 16th century, was just beginning. This century irrevocably changed church and state relations with far-reaching legal and political ramifications. This disengagement of state from religion inscribed Common Law with a fundamental element of religious intolerance against homosexuals, which was transmitted to large areas of the world. Through legal path dependence, this system of law has influenced over the years a large share of the world's population.

While the processes leading to those monumental changes may be traced back historically to predate Henry VIII, changes that took place during his reign proved to be crucial. Stemming partly from the personal story of Henry himself and partly from the political circumstances of the time (in Europe generally as well as specifically in England), the reforms that this king oversaw concerning the role of religion in the English state had far-reaching implications. We delve here into the stories behind those reforms generally, but it is important to underscore at the outset that of particular interest to us for the discussion in this book is the aspects of those reforms that eventually influenced the legal conditions for homosexuals. These influences reached well beyond England and lasted for centuries. Accordingly, after examining the relations between state and religion in England and the ways those changed during the reign of Henry VIII, we delve into the act that proved to be by far the most consequential in the context of gay rights. This is the Buggery Act of 1533.

It is this act and its legal derivatives that later on were exported to British colonies around the world—either in their original form or as a part of legal codes such as the Indian Penal Code (the Macaulay Code), the Fitzjames Stephen Code, the Griffith Code, and the Wright Penal Code—that have had long-lasting implications for sexual-minority groups and the rights members of those groups can claim around the globe. Later transfigurations of the legal provision that dates back to the time of Henry VIII have influenced a surprisingly large number of territories in several continents. But first, let us return to the English royal court in the early days of the 16th century.

Henry was raised from an early age in the company of his mother and sisters. He was not expected to become king, as this privilege was to be bestowed upon his older brother, Arthur, who was to succeed their father, Henry VII. In 1501, as a part of the effort to further establish the relationship between the English and Spanish courts, Prince Arthur was married to Catherine of Aragon, daughter of Isabella, Queen of Castile and Leon, and King Ferdinand II of Aragon. The political clout, which her parents had amassed with the consolidation of the Iberian kingdoms, was key for English interests (Baker, 2002). Arthur's younger brother, Henry, was at the time known for his love for an adventurous life. This passion started during the early years that Henry spent with his mother and sisters, and his passion for hunting and dance can be traced back to those days.

However, when Prince Arthur died shortly after marrying Catherine, Henry's fate was to change dramatically, and with it, the kingdom's fortunes. Henry became king of England in 1509, a position he was to maintain for nearly four decades. He married his brother's widow, Catherine. While aiming to maintain the political alliance with the Spanish court, Henry wanted Catherine to give him a male heir. In Henry's eyes, a male successor was necessary for the Tudor dynasty to last.

His devotion to the dynasty, and first and foremost to his marriage, stemmed not least from his strong religious convictions. Apart from his diverse range of activities as a musician, hunter, and patron of the arts, Henry was also a devout member of the Roman Catholic Church. Indeed, the pope awarded him the title Defender of the Faith in 1521, owing at least partly to his book, *Defense of the Seven Sacraments*. Among other things, in this book Henry VIII attacked the reforms of Martin Luther (Bellomo, 1995). Published in more than 20 editions, the book endorsed the supremacy of the pope and thus naturally opposed the Protestant Reformation. Notably, *Assertio Septem Sacramentorum,* in its Latin title, sustained the sacramental nature of marriage. This focus on the unique privilege of the pope in the realm of marital affairs was to prove trying for the book's author, King Henry himself, less than a decade later (Llewellyn, 1960; Norton, 2005).

Much of the political and religious clout under Henry VIII was initially concentrated in the hands of one person. This man, Thomas Wolsey, epitomized the extent to which political affairs in England were closely related to the Roman Catholic Church. In his first few years in power, Henry was not troubled by economic issues principally due to the financial surplus left by his father. Relatedly, Henry remained largely uninvolved in political issues. Indeed, the king left much of the business of the state to Cardinal Wolsey, who became lord chancellor in 1515.

A Male Heir

As there had been no precedent in England for a woman monarch, Henry VIII believed that to solidify his family's hold on power he would have to have a male heir. It was only with a son that his dynasty was to survive and thrive. With the relatively recent memory of the Wars of the Roses in England a few decades earlier, Henry would not take the risk (Baker, 2002). Yet, Catherine of Aragon had no surviving sons. By 1525, it was Catherine's daughter with the king, the future Mary I of England, who was the sole heir to the throne. From this point on, state and religious authorities in England were inevitably heading on a collision course (Bellomo, 1995; Llewellyn, 1960).

Henry VIII, who by this point was in love with his mistress, Anne Boleyn, petitioned the pope to annul his marriage to Catherine of Aragon (Harvey, 1978). The King provided a rationale for the annulment that had basis in religious law; due to her marriage to his brother, their marriage was in violation of biblical prescriptions. Furthermore, his own marriage to Catherine followed papal dispensation that had been based on the wrong assumption that she had been a virgin. Yet, the pope refused to annul King Henry's marriage (Bellomo, 1995).

As mentioned, Thomas Wolsey, a cardinal in the Roman Catholic Church, played a key role in the court at the time, being the chancellor and thus the epitome of the deep ties connecting the English state with the Roman Catholic Church. The actions of Wolsey, both those that brought him to power as well as those that led to his demise, offer an interesting angle on the anti-Catholic campaign that Henry was about to pursue. Accordingly, in the next few paragraphs we discuss the process of the monarchy breaking away from the Roman Catholic Church, while we follow Wolsey's role, as it clarifies the important aspects of this sea change in English political history and in the history of the religious state (Norton, 2005).

A short five years after he became the king's almoner in 1509, Wolsey was the most powerful figure in both matters of state and church. As the chief adviser to the king, Wolsey, who was also called *alter rex* (other king), was an extremely powerful lord chancellor. Wolsey quickly gained political prominence in the court by working closely with the king and adapting to his will (for instance, he won precedence over his seniors in the case of the French War, when he supported the invasion of France, played a key role in the invasion, and negotiated the Anglo-French treaty of 1514). Indeed, his eminence in foreign affairs was not limited to the French campaign and extended to later playing a leadership role in the Treaty of London. Wolsey's rise to power among the king's people was matched only by his increasing powers within religious institutions. Wolsey had won several distinctions from the church, including *S. Caecilliae trans Tiberim* from Pope Leo X himself (Baker, 2002).

It is not surprising then that Wolsey played such an important role when Henry VIII petitioned the pope to annul his marriage to Catherine of Aragon. With Henry pressuring the pope to terminate the marriage on the one hand, and Charles V, Catherine's brother, pushing the other way, the decision by Pope Clement VII became a matter of international diplomacy. Accordingly, it was Wolsey who was made to serve appeals to the pope. Beyond the aforementioned objections to the validity of the marriage on biblical legal grounds, Wolsey appealed to the papacy to delegate the power of final resolution in this matter to papal legates in England. Whereas the pope acceded, Cardinal Campeggio used delay tactics that ultimately blocked Wolsey from annulling the marriage. Indeed, it was this failure that led to Wolsey's downfall (Llewellyn, 1960).

Wolsey's power stemmed first and foremost from his close relations with the king. However, when he failed to deliver for Henry in the critical matter of the dissolution of the his marriage to Catherine (the pope eventually decided that the ultimate decision on the annulment would be made in Rome), Wolsey's accomplishments both at home and abroad did not secure his position anymore. He died in 1530 after being persecuted and stripped of his property and his government offices. His demise personifies the end of the close association of the English court with Rome.

Breaking Away with Rome

King Henry VIII did not stop with banishing his most trusted adviser. His disenchantment with the church grew ever stronger. Wolsey's successor in office, one of Henry's most trusted advisers, Thomas Cromwell, who was chief adviser to the king from 1532 to 1540, epitomizes the break away from the Roman Catholic Church. Just as Wolsey signifies the proximity Henry's kingdom had with the pope initially, it is Cromwell who symbolizes the anti-Catholic sentiment that spread through and eventually dominated the court in later years (Van Caenegem, 1988).

Cromwell's distaste for the clerical establishment made him one of the chief advocates of the English Reformation. He was able to succeed where his predecessor failed, and annulled Henry's marriage to Catherine, opening the way to the king's marriage with Anne Boleyn. His influence, however, was not limited to the scope of marital issues, and extended to overseeing the establishment of a splinter Church of England. Royal supremacy over the church was a leading principle in the Reformation. It was in May 1532 that Cromwell was able to secure a resolution in parliament, over objections from the clergy, to position King Henry VIII as the head of the church. Henry married Anne Boleyn the following year, by which time she was already carrying his child.

Ties to Rome were severed, and the superiority of Rome in any religious or legal manner in England was irrevocably diminished. Cromwell oversaw the passage of legislation in parliament that restricted the right to appeal to Rome. The combination of the declaration of the king's marriage to Catherine unlawful (and thus, its subsequent annulment), and curtailing the link to Rome as a superior religious authority, irreversibly reformed the relations of state and church in England. The Ecclesiastical Appeals Act 1532 (also called the Statute in Restraint of Appeals) was the legislative cornerstone for the English Reformation. Pursuant to the Act, the king became the final legal authority in religious and other matters, replacing the papacy in Rome. A string of acts altered the previous constitutional arrangement, revoking papal authority over church, faith, or other matters (Baker, 2002).

The Act of Supremacy in 1534 etched into law the principle of royal supremacy. As a result of this act, Henry became the head of the Church of

England, establishing the position of civil laws as superior over the laws of the church and any ecclesiastical law in England. The Treasons Act provided that disobeying the Act of Supremacy amounted to treason (Van Caenegem, 1988). From then on, all offences that had been tried by ecclesial courts in England were to become offences under the king's law and be tried as such. It is in this political context and in that legal landscape that the Buggery Act of 1533 was passed. This was the act that, due to legal path dependence, had far-reaching implications for gay rights for centuries to come on the British Isles as well as far beyond them. Yet, before we deal with this act in depth, let us examine some earlier sources of sodomy laws.

Medieval Bases of Modern Sodomy Laws and the Sodomy Laws in England in the Middle Ages

While the United Kingdom moved away from Catholic practice, it continued to embrace Catholic perspectives on homosexuality that were entrenched in the Middle Ages. Thomas Aquinas's *Summa Theologica* served as the intellectual basis for much of the anti-homosexual sentiments in the church. In particular, his definition of the sin of lust, *peccata contra naturam,* and the distinction he drew between intercourse for the purpose of procreation and intercourse intended for pleasure, were of foundational importance in this respect. Likewise, popular authors such as Dante wrote about homosexuality as a vice. Dante used homosexuality in a defamatory fashion in his *Inferno*. Laws against homosexuality were prevalent at various levels, and in much of Europe (Florence, Pisa, Sienna, Touraine-Angou, *inter alia*) (Stein, 1999). Provisions for the persecution of homosexuals ranged from investigation and denunciation of sodomy, to fines and burning (of those who committed the crime as well as their property or the location of the crime itself). Likewise, the persecution of homosexuals was one of a repertoire of repressive elements—for instance in the case of the Inquisition (Goodish, 1976).

As for England specifically, the sources of anti-sodomy laws can be traced back to the 10th and 11th centuries with the moral reform of the church, led by St. Dunstan, Archbishop of Canterbury, and the actions of King Henry I, who set out to clean up the court of his predecessor, where homosexuality was prevalent. Yet, even when the Good Parliament petitioned Edward III in 1376, the reference to civil law against homosexuality was unsuccessful, and it was not for nearly 150 years, in the Buggery Act of 1533, that a statutory provision against homosexuality was passed.

The Buggery Act of 1533

The Buggery Act of 1533 was the first case of a civil-legal provision prohibiting sodomy. The word *buggery* is derived from *bougre* in French, whose source is probably the Latin word *bulgarus*, used in a disparaging fashion to refer to heretics from Bulgaria in the late Middle Ages. The prosecution of matters such as buggery had traditionally been the province of ecclesiastical courts. King Henry VIII's buggery statute was reenacted several times, even within his own lifetime (in 1536, 1539, and 1541). While the first parliament of Edward VI repealed the act, it was reenacted in 1548. Repeal happened again under Mary in 1553, only to be revived by Queen Elizabeth in 1563. The latter, as a part of her attempt to appear as a direct heir to Henry VIII, reenacted the Buggery Act in its original 1533 form, nullifying the amendments entered in 1548. Cromwell's words in parliament concerning the act highlight the collision with the church both in terms of the power to determine moral principles and in terms of etching said principles into law:

> Forasmuch as there is not yet sufficient and condign punishment appointed and limited by the due course of the Laws of this Realm for the detestable and abominable Vice of Buggery committed with mankind or beast: It may therefore please the King's Highness with the assent of the Lords Spiritual and the Commons of this present parliament assembled, that it may be enacted by the authority of the same, that the same offence be from henceforth adjudged Felony and that such an order and form of process therein to be used against the offenders as in cases of felony at the Common law. And that the offenders being hereof convict by verdict confession or outlawry shall suffer such pains of death and losses and penalties of their good chattels debts lands tenements and hereditaments as felons do according to the Common Laws of this realm. And that no person offending in any such offence shall be admitted to his Clergy, And that Justices of the Peace shall have power and authority within the limits of their commissions and Jurisdictions to hear and determine the said offence, as they do in the cases of other felonies. This Act to endure till the last day of the next Parliament. (Boris, 2004, p. 82)

Cromwell not only highlights the role of the king in consolidating moral principles, he also outlines the institutional path that would lead to the dominance of the state. It is the common laws of the realm, as adjudicated in common law courts that would set normative standards. What is more, the act granted the king enforcement powers, predominantly through the ability to take and confiscate property, of the type that would make it particularly useful for him when dealing with the church (Harvey, 1978). Pursuing key elements of the church establishment, such as monks, led to the reaffirmation of the powers of the king. Henry's moves against the church, and the use of the confiscation of property, were similar to earlier cases elsewhere. Indeed, Henry's actions in England echo the actions of King Philip IV of France, in the case of the Knights Templar (Van Caenegem, 1988).

The Order of the Temple was an important precedent where a conflict unfolded between a monarch and a powerful religious institution. This precedent is of particular interest for our discussion since while the king was vying over power with a religious institution with considerable political and economic clout, it was the king who ended up with the upper hand. The Order of the Temple was not only prominent for the bravery of its fighting units in the crusades but also for its financial and economic infrastructure. For instance, knights who went on a crusade would often entrust their assets with the Templars, who in some cases would issue a document that would allow a knight to retrieve his funds elsewhere (e.g., when arriving in the Holy Land). The result was financial networks throughout Christendom that were controlled by the Order of the Temple. Its innovative financial techniques and overall economic clout made the order powerful as far away as in the Holy Land, where its members erected several fortifications.

Even within Europe, the order was not subject to local government. Yet, it was this very economic might that put the Templars under pressure from the King Philip IV of France. The king, who was heavily indebted to the order, used large-scale arrests and torture, in addition to pressuring the pope in 1307 to disband the order. King Philip used the threat of using military power to force the pope to eventually move forward with dissolving the order. The struggle over power between Philip and the Templars in the early 1300s was in certain ways a precursor of Henry's challenging times with the church two centuries later. While there is a litany of legislative measures that came out of this conflict between church and state—some of which are discussed above—it is the Buggery Act of 1533 that is of greatest importance for our purposes.

For centuries after the Buggery Act, prominent writers of English law deemed sodomy an abominable offence. Edward Coke, for instance, states, "Buggery is a detestable, and abominable sin, amongst Christians not to be named. . . . [It is] committed by carnal knowledge against the ordinance of the Creator and order of nature, by mankind with mankind, or with brute beast, or by womankind with brute beast" (1797, 3rd part, p. 58). Most consequential in this context is the fact that the prohibition on sodomy remained in Blackstone's Commentaries (see Appendix F). Subsequently, when the system of Common Law was transported worldwide with British colonialism, the sodomy provision travelled alongside that corpus. In sum, it was a combination of common law, statutory law, and judicial and legal scholarship that together helped criminalize sodomy throughout the expanding British Empire. This point is further elaborated in the next sections, where we fully develop the notion of path dependence.

Path Dependence and Its Three Pillars in Common Law Systems

Path dependence applies to the evolution of law in a variety of ways, and Common Law is a prominent example of such institutional development (North, 1990). Largely speaking, path dependence is an impediment for major and dramatic changes in the evolution of law. For instance, one reason why legal systems are hard to change is the interdependence between legal education, case law, judicial selection, and the existence of juries and other legal and paralegal institutions. Thus, it would be difficult to change from a system based primarily on codes, to one based on cases. Doing so would require fundamental changes, such as reforming legal education and the retraining of magistrates, judges, and justices. Along the same lines, the adoption of a jury system in systems with no juries would require, among other changes, a distinction between law and fact, trials which occur on consecutive days, and judges and lawyers trained to deal with juries. Granted, certain laws are not locked-in. Speed limits, for example, are not entrenched in the system. In most countries, those limits may be changed. However, by its nature, the legal framework of Common Law has the capacity to lock in laws, particularly if different players have vested interests in those laws. Those vested interests may be economic, moral, religious, or sociopolitical in nature.

The legal framework in Common Law consists of constitutional provisions, acts of the legislature, and judicial decisions. It is a precedent-based system in which past decisions are integrated into the law; as such, in keeping with stare decisis, each case sets a legal precedent. Therefore, the law changes marginally as new cases are decided, and a new legal precedent is set, thus becoming part of the legal structure. Judicial decisions "reflect the subjective processing of information in the context of the historical construction of the legal framework" (North, 1990, p. 97). The Northwest Ordinance, for instance, passed in 1787 by the Continental Congress, illustrates path dependence and the historically derived continuity it implies. This ordinance is an example for how following the initial adoption of a certain legal framework decreases the likelihood of change in the law. Further, when there is change, it is gradual rather than abrupt. The Northwest Ordinance stemmed from preexisting English and colonial provisions, and concerned governance and settlement of the West and its integration into the new nation. Due to the vested economic and political interests of various parties, for decades after, the political and economic structure in the territories was derived from the framework dictated by the ordinance. Along the same lines, for political, moral, religious, and, in some cases, economic reasons, the legal status of gay marriage or abortion law in the United States is difficult to change. Before we delve into the intricacies of the codes and institutions that allowed for sodomy provisions to persevere for so long in Common Law systems—the United States being one of those situations—let us first examine the general characteristics of this type of legal system (Bellomo, 1995).

Echoing the centrality of legislators in systems of Civil Law, it is judges that figure as key players in a system of Common Law. Thus, the intellectual basis for Common Law is decisional law that is largely based on judicial rulings. Prior rulings by courts are given precedential authority, at least partly due to the unfairness inherent to treating cases with similar facts differently. Thus, as opposed to the system of Civil Law, Common Law is uncodified. There is no code that constitutes a comprehensive compilation of statutes and rules of law. The body of judicial decisions replaces the code as a key source. Those decisions are recorded as precedent (stare decisis). Thus, Common Law relies heavily on judicial precedent that applies in new cases with the manner of application being decided by the presiding judge. This is the source of major influence judges have had in this tradition (Van Caenegem, 1988).

Attorneys representing the parties to the case present their case before the court in an adversarial process. This adversarial procedure is a cornerstone of the Common Law system. In countries where the jury system is in place, it is the jury of the defendant's peers that determines the verdict. It is then left to the discretion of the judge to set the sentence, usually according to statutory standards and within statutorily mandated limits. Courts are so prominent in this system of law, to a large extent due to the principle of stare decisis. A judge is expected to refer to similar cases decided in the past in order to make a judgment about the case at hand. Only in cases where legal precedent and the body of case law do not provide satisfactory guides for how to decide the case would a judge make a decision that has precedential value within the appropriate jurisdiction. Thus, in the Common Law system, judges revise the law and reinterpret it even in the absence of intervention on the part of the legislature.

The Common Law system provides continuity and a level of predictability since precedent holds. This stability within the system, and over time, stems from the position of courts. This continuity is central to the nature of Common Law systems. When change happens, it usually happens gradually and as a result of an inductive process. This is an incremental change where, according to the American Supreme Court Associate Justice Oliver Wendell Holmes, "the proper derivation of general principles . . . arise[s] gradually, in the emergence of a consensus from a multitude of particularized prior decisions." Thus, the changes in Common Law systems often stem from judicial rulings. Accordingly, the decisions on the merits are often accompanied by opinions of the court that provide the legal rationale. These opinions are then compiled to form the body of case law and legal precedent. Indeed, to apply the law in a particular case, one could not focus solely on statutory or constitutional provisions, but rather would have to consult the leading precedents on that matter (Milsom, 1981).

Legislatures in jurisdictions of Common Law operate under the assumption that pieces of legislation will be interpreted by courts in light of existing case law. This detailed, elaborate, and rigorous nature of law in Common Law systems influences economic and political reality. One prominent example is higher levels of economic efficiency. With the ease in forming contractual obligations, and the clarity and predictability of judicial decisions, economic activity is enhanced (Bellomo, 1995). The same holds, however, for other types of entities, such as religious groups, political parties, and newspapers.

The emergence of this system of Common Law can be traced back to the 11th century, and the centralizing powers of the English king in the Middle Ages. In an attempt to unify his kingdom under one system of law that would replace disparate systems at the time, Henry II of England, for instance, established a series of courts whose judges followed each other's decisions to establish a coherent system of national law. This judiciary also had a system of writs (of which the writ of habeas corpus, which lends protection to detainees, is a remnant until the present day) and an appeals procedure. While writs were originally orders originating from the court of the king, with time, judicial and administrative authorities were granted the power to issue such writs in order to direct certain actions (Van Caenegem, 1988). This era in British history also produced the Magna Carta. One of the results of the charter was another quintessential component of Common Law—the right to a trial by jury.

For much of the following centuries, Common Law coexisted in Britain side by side with other systems of law. In fact, it was not until the 17th century, when the House of Commons was gaining considerable political power allowing the commoners to check the king, that parliament declared Common Law a national legal system and all other sources of law secondary. Thus, canon law (the body of law produced by the Catholic Church, and governing its actions consisting of rules and decrees by the pope and ecclesiastical councils) and Civil Law (the continental system of law where laws were compiled and systematized into a legal code) were declared subsidiary to Common Law by the legislature. Echoing processes of legal codification in continental Europe, in this period the British consolidated a legal system that was established largely on unique British legal institutions. The cornerstone of this legal edifice was William Blackstone's work, *Commentaries on the Laws of England*. Blackstone's work was of such monumental significance that until the present day, the understanding in the United States, for instance, of Common Law prior to the existence of the United States itself, is tantamount to the *Commentaries*. His work is prominent as the key source in the United States of pre-American legal precedent (Epstein &Walker, 2014).

The following passage from Woodfin's chapter in Dainow's (1974) edited volume provides a sense of the process under a Common Law system:

> The common law lawyer, by and large, simply doesn't care whether such a system exists or not. He is busy deciding cases, with the aid of judicial precedent and with or without the aid of statutory enactment of rules in particular cases. If from this process scholars can begin to see bits and pieces of a system emerging, he is interested in it as a potentially useful tool; but he does not regard the discovery or the development of such a complete and logical system as essential or even important in his continuing task of achieving justice in an infinite number and variety of individual cases. (p. 315)

Now that the system of Common Law is more clearly expounded, let us examine how legal path dependence in this system accounts for the longevity of sodomy provisions and their transportation from the English motherland to the British Empire. The following sections examine the legal and political institutional infrastructure that supported this phenomenon.

The First Pillar of Legal Path Dependence: Colonial Codification

The system of Common Law that due to legal path dependence is hard to adjust, if not utterly impervious to change in certain respects, incorporated sodomy prohibitions, which originated in the Buggery Act, into key texts such as Blackstone's *Commentaries*. With the characteristics of Common Law, as described in the previous sections, the legal status quo in England consistently tilted in that direction for centuries. Yet, our argument concerning legal path dependence goes well beyond the British Isle. The question remains: What sustained sodomy provisions elsewhere? Our analysis suggests that it was codification that was critical to the legal path dependence that helped sodomy provisions travel overseas.

In *An Introduction to the Principles of Morals and Legislation* (1789) and in *A Fragment on Government* (1776), Jeremy Bentham endorsed the idea of legal codification, also adopted by his disciple John Stuart Mill. Those ideas were very influential in England. Yet, while codification efforts were considerably less successful in the motherland, it was predominantly in the colonies that this notion materialized. The process of legal codification implemented in the colonies became a key means by which legal path dependence took shape. The legal codes included initiatives by the colonial authorities such as the Indian Penal Code (the Macaulay Code), the Fitzjames Stephen Code, the Griffith Code, and the Wright Penal Code. In this section we examine each of those legal provisions, which we deem crucially important for the colonial transportation and imposition of British legal standards and morals to large parts of Asia and Africa.

(1) *The Elphinstone Code of 1827 for the Presidency of Bombay in India*

A noted administrator in the government of British India, Mountstuart Elphinstone, the governor of Bombay, has been recognized for his reform of the services given to indigenous Indians, and in particular for his contributions to the systems of public education. In addition, however, he served as governor during the expansion of the Bombay presidency. After assuming office, Elphinstone observed how the legal system in the area under his rule—and the criminal system in particular—was "in the last state of disorder and corruption" (*Background to Indian Law*, p. 195). Elphinstone identified the need for a consistent system of civil and criminal law. Improving upon the Cornwallis

Code of 1793, Elphinstone was influenced (as were many of his compatriots at the time) by the ideas of Jeremy Bentham, and he helped initiate British rule in the Deccan with the Elphinstone Code, published in 1827. This code was the first systematic legal system in British India. It was "a great advance upon anything previously attempted in India, and served to prove, by thirty years' experience of its working, that there was no difficulty in applying a general code, founded upon European principles, to the mixed populations of India" (Sir Alexander Arbuthnot, cited in *Background to Indian Law*, p. 197).

(2) The Indian Penal Code of 1860—The Macaulay Code

With considerably broader intended scope than the Elphinstone Code, the Indian Penal Code was designed to cover all aspect of criminal law in the British colony of India. This code had far-reaching influence inasmuch as it was adopted over the years in various forms in many of the neighboring British colonies, including Pakistan, Bangladesh, Burma, Ceylon, Malaysia, Singapore, and Brunei. As the discussion of the Elphinstone Code suggests, English criminal law had certain influence in limited parts of India. This was true in particular in the presidency towns of Bombay, Calcutta, and Madras. The code is also dubbed the Macaulay Code after Thomas Babington Macaulay, who chaired the First Law Commission that drafted it. The Indian Rebellion of 1857 gave impetus to the adoption of the penal code, which was passed into law in late 1860 and came into operation on the first day of 1862. The goal of the Macaulay Code was to provide a general penal code for India, which in reality did not cover all offences, and thus did not overrule other penal codes of the time. This comprehensive code, which realized many of Bentham's utilitarian ideals, was described by Macaulay himself as something that would "make old Bentham jump [for joy] in his grave" (Macaulay, cited in Wright, 2006).

The different sections of the code cover a range of topics including criminal conspiracy, offences against the state, offences relating to elections, and offences against public justice. Yet, of particular importance to the current discussion is Chapter XVI of the code, which pertains to offences affecting the human body. This chapter contains Sections 299–377, and it is in the very last section of this chapter that the code considers "unnatural offences." Section 377 has had immense consequences in the context of homosexual rights under British colonial rule in India and far beyond the subcontinent.

The 377 provision reads: "Unnatural Offences—Whoever voluntarily has carnal intercourse against the order of nature with any man, women or animal, shall be punished with imprisonment for life, or with imprisonment of either description for a term which may extend to 10 years and shall also be liable to fine."

The section or derivatives thereof were imported to or emulated in many countries in Oceania (e.g., Fiji), Africa (e.g., Zambia), and Asia (e.g., Singapore). Indeed, it was Section 377 that was the key legal provision under consideration by Indian courts in two recent highly visible rulings (Gupta 2002, 2006). In the first case, the Delhi High Court in 2009 interpreted the provision in a liberal fashion; the section could not be used to punish same-sex sexual relations between two consenting adults. The petitioner in the case, the Naz Foundation Trust, was an NGO that had filed the lawsuit in the Delhi court eight years earlier, seeking legal change. Initially the Delhi court rejected the petition (Joshi, 2010; Narrain, 2009). The rationale was that the foundation had no legal standing to bring the case before the court. Upon appeal to the Indian Supreme Court, however, the case was remanded to the Delhi court so it could decide the matter on the merits. A broad coalition of activists, groups, and pro-gay rights organizations coalesced (e.g., "Voices Against 377"), joining the movement to repeal the section. One of the arguments raised was that having the act on the books stood in the way of effective prevention of AIDS.

According to the ruling of the court, prohibitions of the sort of Section 377 violated basic fundamental rights protected under the Indian constitution. In particular, the court focused on Article 21 of the Fundamental Right to Freedom Charter as being violated. In addition, Article 14 under the Fundamental Right to Equality Charter was another provision mentioned by the court as contradictory in its spirit to the prohibitions in Section 377. Article 15, which protected against discrimination on the basis of sex, according to the court also protected against provisions targeting certain sexual orientations. Likewise, the section was in violation of the right to health, which was also constitutionally protected, as Section 377 hindered proper treatment and prevention of HIV.

As this was a judicial ruling interpreting a legal provision, it did not amount to repeal of the section, which still remained on the books. The fact that the Naz Foundation Trust court did not repeal the section but rather limited its own ruling to consensual sex between consenting male adults, meant that other provisions of the section remained intact. One example is the provisions pertaining to intercourse with minors. The decision in *Naz Foundation v. Government of NCT of Delhi* was perceived as a triumph in the eyes of advocates of gay rights in India. Some commentators likened the Naz Foundation ruling to the decision in *Roe v. Wade* by the Supreme Court of the United States; and news about the decision spread quickly from the courtroom, where it was read to a limited audience by Chief Justice Ajit Prakash Shah, and then to the entire country and overseas.

For several years following the ruling in the Naz Foundation in 2009, the Supreme Court of India was unwilling to accept appeals of the decision of the Delhi court, nor would the Supreme Court accept requests for an interim stay of the judgment. Some of those requests were filed shortly after the ruling, but as a July 20, 2009, a report in the *Indian Express* suggests, the Court stated that "we are not for stay as there is no threat of any consequences" and declared that it would wait to hear the position of the government in that matter before it renders its own ruling. The tendency to leave the Delhi court ruling standing was not limited to the Indian Supreme Court; the attorney general, G. E. Vahanvati, indicated that since there were three government ministries involved, consideration of the matter would take time and thus he was not in favor of a stay in the meanwhile. Opposition to the ruling from Delhi also attempted to block further progress in a liberal direction and petitioned the Supreme Court to declare gay marriage illegitimate.

The court, however, refrained from making any observation and reiterated in July 2009, days after the decision in *Naz,* that "cases under Section 377 are registered only with regard to pedophiles. People are being convicted but it has nothing to do with gay marriages." Even as late as March 2012, the Supreme Court stood firm in its opposition to accepting appeals of *Naz.* According to a report in *The Hindu* on March 27, 2012, this position won support from Attorney General Vahanvati who said of the Indian Penal Code that "insofar as it criminalizes consensual sexual acts of adults in private [before the provision was struck down by the High Court, it] was imposed upon Indian society due to the moral views of the British rulers." The attorney general here links the contemporaneous debate to the colonial roots of the provision in question, and he draws a clear causal relation between British colonialism and the present-day consequences of Section 377 of the Indian Penal Code.

Yet, the Supreme Court changed its mind. It was not more than four short years after the ruling in *Naz Foundation,* that the Supreme Court of India overruled the judgment of the Delhi High Court. The Supreme Court upheld the previous, more conservative interpretation of Section 377. According to the 2013 ruling, same-sex sexual relations, even between two consenting adult males, is against the order of nature. The Supreme Court deemed such acts criminal and thus punishable by law. The Supreme Court reversed the decision of the Delhi court and upheld Section 377 of the Indian Penal Code. While the Supreme Court initially resisted the petitions by political and religious groups in the wake of the decision in *Naz*, in December of 2013, it effectively reinstated the law.

While the provision had not been used very often for actual prosecution, the police in India used it to harass members of the LGBT community, as we discuss in the introduction to this book. The bench in the decision consisted of two judges. In its ruling, the court considered the aforementioned position voiced by the attorney general. Yet, the court also said that it was up to the legislature, not the courts, to legislate. With elections looming on the horizon, a swift action by the political branches to change the law was unlikely. Both local groups and international NGOs that were a part of the coalition behind the push that led to the *Naz* ruling expressed disappointment with what they deemed a regressive move on the part of the court. That said, religious groups such as Christian and Muslim groups who had opposed the 2009 decision welcomed the new ruling.

This court ruling restored Section 377 of the Indian Penal Code in its entirety and thus put the sodomy provisions it included back into force. The Indian Penal Code—which had been a codification of legal principles and morals that find their origins in the Buggery Act of 1533, and that had been codified over a century before the Supreme Court overruled the *Naz* decision—has a direct impact on gay rights in India at the time this book is going to press in late 2015. Yet, the Indian Penal Code and its Section 377 are just a part of an intricate web of institutions supporting the path-dependent nature of law as far as sodomy provisions are concerned, as the continuing discussion below suggests.

(3) *The Fitzjames Stephen Code*

The process of codification, which accounts for the transfer of buggery prohibitions overseas to British colonies and beyond, influenced domestic legal reality in England. The shift towards codification of some aspects of law took place in that country as well. When Sir James Fitzjames Stephen returned from India in 1872, he had considerable experience with the implementation of the Indian Penal Code there. As Stephen had codified certain aspects of the law (criminal procedure, inter alia), he was experienced in the process of codification, which was a major enterprise in Common Law England at the time. The advantages of codification were in its practicality; yet the British desired a system that would still preserve a certain level of flexibility, typical of the Common Law system, as discussed previously. Stephen's book *Digest of Criminal Law* landed him the assignment of writing a criminal code for England. When Attorney General Jack Holker introduced in parliament the bill drafted by Stephen, he mentioned codification in other dominions of her majesty, including India, where the code, he stated, was successful. Holker contended, "The success of this penal code was, to a great extent, due to the labours of a very learned jurist and sound practical lawyer, who was formerly the legal member of the Council of India. I allude to Sir James Stephen" (United Kingdom. House of Commons (Hansard). 14 May 1878. Vol. 239. 1937).

As for the proposed provision, in Holker's eyes it was "an experiment to a considerable degree." Yet, codification of that sort meant "condensation, simplification, explanation, and amendment of the criminal law rather than any other branch; because the criminal law is necessarily so largely resorted to, it is, moreover, so largely administered by persons who are not trained lawyers, and who require some plain statement of the law for their guidance" (United Kingdom. House of Commons (Hansard). 14 May 1878. Vol. 239. 1937.9). As such, the code would benefit those involved in the administration of justice, more than the lawyers. Yet, this bill failed to pass parliament, even in later drafts that had been prepared by a royal commission and endorsed by the lord chief judge.

Yet, the Stephen Code was important since it had far-reaching influence on the codification of criminal law elsewhere, outside of England. One such example is Canada. As a part of the project of unifying the nation under one system of law, Sir John A. MacDonald, the first Canadian prime minister, used an augmented—yet structurally similar—version of the Stephen Code passed in 1892 as a part of a broader reform to the Canadian criminal code. The codification of such national law was a part of the consolidation of a national identity in the dominion. That said, the purpose was not to create a code distinct from the English one. Indeed, as the debates in the House of Commons indicate, the intent was to preserve and even enhance English influence:

in . . . criminal Bills, the language was as nearly as possible the language of the criminal law of England. The language used in such measures in the Lower Provinces might be shorter and more concise, but he had chosen rather to adhere to that before the House, because it was of the greatest importance—and the members of the legal profession would fully appreciate this—that the body of the Criminal Law should be such that the Judges in the Superior Courts should have an opportunity of adjudicating upon it as on English law. It would be of incalculable advantage that every decision of the Imperial Courts at Westminster should be law in the Dominion. On every principle of convenience and conformity of decision with that of England, he thought it well to retain the English phraseology. (Canada. Debates of the House of Commons (Hansard). 27 April 1869, p. 89)

Thus the criminalization of certain types of conduct, inherited from English law, were a reflection of the values of the Canadian national identity. While Canada had had earlier prohibitions on sodomy, the one inherited with the Stephen Code was more comprehensive and encompassed all same-sex sexual activity. This had lasting implications for sexual-minority rights in this territory.

(4) The Griffith Code

The Queensland Criminal Code Act of 1899, drafted by Sir Samuel Walker Griffith, was another key component of the codification effort in British colonies. The code, influenced by such earlier codes as the Italian Penal Code and the New York Penal Code, not only had considerable influence on criminal law in all of Australia (Western Australia, Tasmania, and the Northern Territory) but was also exported to several of the Commonwealth of Nations and beyond, including but not limited to: Nauru, Nigeria, Kenya, Tanzania, Papua New Guinea, Israel, Zanzibar, and Uganda (Gibbs, 2002; MacKenzie, 2002). To the present day, Uganda is contentious grounds in the struggle over LGBT rights, as discussed extensively in other chapters of this book. With respect to sodomy and echoing much of the language in the codes described above, the Griffith Code states in Section 208 on page 6911 that:

Any person who—
   (a) Has carnal knowledge of any person against the order of nature; or
   (b) Has carnal knowledge of an animal; or
   (c) Permits a male person to have carnal knowledge of him or her against the order of nature
Is guilty of a crime, and is liable to imprisonment with hard labour for fourteen years.

Section 208 appears under Chapter XXII Offences Against Morality, and the title for the section is "Unnatural Offences." Later in this section, the Griffith Code covers the crimes of attempting to commit unnatural offences (Section 209), indecently treating boys under fourteen (Section 210), and more generally the issue of indecent practices between males (Section 211). The last, for instance, is considered a misdemeanor and the one convicted is "liable to imprisonment with hard Labour for three years" (p. 6912). The remainder of this chapter pertains to other types of behavior, deemed offences against morality, such as abuse of women in different ages (e.g., under twelve years of age) incest, abortions, and such (Wright, 2006).

(5) The Wright Penal Code

This last code on our list was drafted by Mr. R. S. Wright (later Justice Wright). While originally drafted for different purposes (for implementation in Jamaica), this code came into effect in Honduras, Tobago, St. Lucia, and the Gold Coast (Ghana). It was probably the liberal leaning of the code, influenced by the ideological persuasion of its author, which led to its failure in England.

The mutual influences among those different codes are an indication of the common path of legal development they conjointly paved. Not only do those codes stem from a common legal source in British law, but at some levels their drafters effectively competed over whose code would have the most sway. Indeed, competition between those codes persisted for years and decades after they were sealed; for instance, colonial administrators in Nigeria battled over whether the Griffith Code or the Indian Penal Code should be adopted (Adewoye, 1977; Morris, 1970). What is more, as they were solicited by different institutional branches of the British government (e.g., Lord

Chancellor's Office (the Stephen Code), as opposed to the Colonial Office (Wright's Code)), their influences were channeled via certain existing legal and political institutions. Likewise, there were influences between the different codes; for instance, although he never makes mention of it, Griffith had probably seen the Wright code before completing his own (MacKenzie, 2002).

Codification of the different types described was one legal infrastructure that served as the first pillar supporting the path-dependent nature of legal evolution preserving the prohibitions of the Buggery Act and its progeny on the books in British colonies. Indeed, the evidence for path dependence goes beyond the codes themselves, and it also pertains to the fact that British officials were deeply involved in their compilation. While there are many examples of how closely British officials followed this legal offshoot of the legal system in their motherland, let us examine one illustration here. This is a letter dated 12 June, 1879, from the lord chief justice of England. This first letter concerning the criminal code (to be followed by others)—in which the chief justice makes comments and suggestions concerning the bill—opens as follows:

> Dear Mr. Attorney General,
> Having carefully considered the Bill now before Parliament for "establishing a code of indictable offences, and the procedure relating thereto," a measure in which I cannot but take a lively interest, and having arrived at the conviction that the Bill ought not to pass without very many corrections and amendments, I am induced to trouble you-the conduct of the Bill having been most properly committed to your charge-with such observations as occur to me upon it.

In an illustration of how closely connected the new codes were to English law, over the next 19 pages of his letter, Justice A. E. Cockburn outlines extensive suggested revisions and changes to the bill's different provisions, indicating that to some he "must strenuously object" (p. 19). Furthermore, other institutions, such as royal commissions, were used to exercise oversight over the compilation of the criminal codes. In sum, these various codes discussed in this chapter and the institutional framework that enveloped their compilation and drafting process, were the key pillar securing the transportation of English law into the colonies. With no notable exceptions, this transportation of legal rules and standards from the motherland to the colonies and territories, due to codification, carried the sodomy provisions with it.

The Second Pillar of Legal Path Dependence: Legislative Decisions

The second means that led to legal path dependence of sodomy provisions was legislation passed by local legislatures. Those often preserved such legal provisions, in substance if not in language. Legal acts by local legislatures often preserved the spirit of the British provisions that had preceded them. Take for example the Crimes Act, passed by the parliament of New South Wales in the year 1900. Under the title "Offences Against the Person," Part III of the act also treats unnatural offences, which uses terms that heavily resemble the language in similar provisions mentioned above. Section 79 reads, "*Buggery and Bestiality.* Whosoever commits the abominable crime of buggery, or bestiality, with mankind, or with any animal, shall be liable to penal servitude for 14 years." The following sections of the act pertain to attempts to commit bestiality and indecent assaults. The New South Wales provision is but one example for a large body of legislation in various territories, colonies, and states where the spirit of the original English prohibitions on sodomy was preserved, such as in Section 347 of the Israeli Penal Code (repealed in 1988).

The Third Pillar of Legal Path Dependence: Judicial Rulings

The third means that served as the legal infrastructure that sustained the path-dependent evolution of sodomy laws pertains to another government institution in charge of legal continuity; courts in many jurisdictions were the institutional location where the legal path was sustained and preserved. In *Bowers v. Hardwick* (478 U.S. 186), the Supreme Court of the United States in 1986 preserved sodomy laws that were on the books of all the 50 states until the 1950s, and at the time the opinion was delivered were on the books of 24 states and the District of Columbia. In Australia, as Kirby (2013) suggests, series of court decisions sustained and further developed the legal prohibition on sodomy. Those pertained to issues such as the fact that adulthood and consent were improper defense (*R v. McDonald,* 1878), availability of propensity evidence (*O'Leary v. the King,* 1947), and penalties imposed upon conviction (*Veslar v. the Queen,* 1955). The decision of the Supreme Court of India from December of 2013, overruling the landmark *Naz* ruling is but another example for how, under certain circumstances, courts would serve as the institution where path dependence is sustained.

In sum, we have identified three pillars in the legal path dependent nature of sodomy provisions in systems of Common Law. The first is legal codification initiatives that transported key provisions from the English legal system into the legal system of the respective colonies and territories. Whereas the push for legal codification in England, inspired by the ideas of Bentham and Mill, failed to materialize in the motherland (Wright, 2006), it did take shape overseas. The criminal provisions that transported to the colonies and territories encompassed the buggery clause in various versions. This clause was thus inserted into local codes. Along these lines, the second pillar supporting legal path dependence is statutory provisions by national legislatures. It was not uncommon for legislatures in the colonies to preserve the spirit of British law. In the context of sodomy laws, that meant passing legal provisions prohibiting same-sex sexual relations of different forms. Lastly, the third pillar of path dependence is national courts, which often sustained the sodomy legacy in series of cases that interpreted it and developed it in various ways. Yet, this story is true for British colonial heritage and is limited for systems of Common Law. As the next sections clearly show, the evolution of legal provisions pertaining to sodomy was remarkably different in the French colonial sphere and in the systems of Civil Law that it yielded.

Legal Path Dependence in Civil Law and the Repeal of Sodomy Laws in Revolutionary France

While it would take sodomy centuries to disappear from English Common Law—and in some cases it is still on the books in former British colonies—it was shortly after the Revolution in late 18th-century France that such provisions were repealed from the French code. We delve into the distinctions between English Common Law and French (and other) Civil Law later, but first let us examine sodomy provisions and their repeal in France during the revolutionary period (Monter, 1974).

In pre-Revolution France, sodomy was a serious crime punishable by death. Yet, largely due to the religious origins of the prohibitions on sodomy and the complete distaste for anything religious, the Penal Code of 1791 was lacking any mention of same-sex relations or prohibitions against such relations. As important as the repeal of 1791 was, it was the codification in the French Penal Code of 1810 that proved particularly consequential in this respect. Side by side with the Napoleonic Code of 1804, the Penal Code was adopted either to the letter or as derivative codes all over continental Europe (Bellomo, 1995).

A key figure in the codification of the new legal reality that meant a complete revision of the criminal laws of royal France was a statesman and legal expert by the name of Jean-Jacques-Régis de Cambacérès. The first duke of Cambacérès was Napoleon's principal adviser in judicial matters and was thus instrumental in the formulation of the two key codes of the early 19th century: the Napoleonic Code (Code civil des Français or Code Napoléon), and the Penal Code six years later. The project was commissioned by the emperor from Cambacérès and four other lawyers, and it took four years to complete.

Winning the position of second consul under Bonaparte, Cambacérès attempted to take a moderating role with the emperor, and he largely focused on legal, judicial, and legislative realms, and less on the political. Cambacérès's work had a far-reaching impact throughout the world in general, and in particular with respect to the rights of homosexuals. The legal doctrine that he drafted concerning same-sex sexual relations under French Civil Law (and subsequently under Spanish, Portuguese, Italian, Polish, and many other legal systems) did away with the prohibitions. While this book does not focus on the gaps between de jure law and legal reality on the ground, it is worthwhile to mention parenthetically that as Sibalis (1996) indicates, the work of Cambacérès did not put an end to the prosecution of homosexuals, which continued under Bonaparte.

Yet, the fact that no legal provisions in the French code prohibited homosexuality meant that when this penal code spread to numerous countries through derivative codes and through the Napoleonic conquests, its influence increased exponentially. Considering the fact that this code then spread even farther into the colonies and dependencies of European countries where French law was adopted in whole or in part, its effects have indeed been considerable.

The repeal of sodomy in early 19th-century France quickly travelled to large parts of the world. It was as a result of occupation, legal emulation, or persuasion that the absence of sodomy provisions travelled to Scandinavian countries, Spain, the Netherlands, Portugal, Belgium, Japan, and their colonies and territories (McLelland, 2000; Wawrytko, 1993). This is not to say that Civil Law jurisdictions never had—or do not have today—sodomy provisions on the books. Those, however, are exceptions to the rule. Such cases include Germany, which had adopted parts of the French Penal Code, which remained on the books through the Third Reich, and into the first decade of the German Democratic Republic, and into the second decade of the Federal German Republic. The same holds for former French colonies such as Senegal and Cameroon (Kirby, 2013). Let us now examine the system of Civil Law. We argue that this system has been critically important, since with its spread to various territories beyond France and beyond continental Europe, it did not carry any provisions prohibiting sodomy and same-sex relations.

Civil Law

Civil Law is currently the most common system of law worldwide, this owing much to the colonial era, when this system of law expanded to dozens of countries and territories beyond Europe, including in Asia, Latin America, and Africa. Most Latin American countries have Civil Law systems and so do Asian countries such as Japan and Indonesia and many of the French colonies in Africa. The key institution in a system of Civil Law is the codification of legislation; the primary source of law is a system of referable rules and principles that apply to matters to be brought before a judge, the procedure, and the punishment applicable for each offence. This is a comprehensive set of rules that is accessible to citizens and jurists alike.

Civil Law (also interchangeably used with Continental law or Romano-Germanic law) encompasses a code that exhaustively covers the various types of legal terrains and issues. The corpus of law, compiled pursuant to the order of Justinian I, the Roman emperor (527–565), is a key source of Civil Law—first at the conceptual level but also in terms of legal content. This corpus consisted of imperial enactments, writings of Roman jurists, introduction to the code, and additional law. It was designed to be a sole source of law, replacing even the sources from which some elements of the code had been adopted. Accordingly, the model of law not only established a strong monarchical constitutional system, but it also covered issues running the gamut from wills and family law to contracts and procedural matters. This concept of a single source of law persisted through the ages and transfigured into the system of Civil Law.

The Code of Justinian (and in its Latin name, *Corpus Juris Civilis*), lost to the West a few decades after its compilation, was rediscovered and gained prominence after the Early Middle Ages. The revival happened mostly in northern Italy, where a jurist class, largely comparable to its Roman predecessor, developed and became known as the Glossators of Bologna (Dawson,

1959). At this time, both secular and church authorities increasingly used it, and the work of jurists was undertaken not exclusively by the nobility (as in Ancient Rome), but by teachers in university law faculties, drawn from the general public.

While there are some recorded influences of the Corpus on Common Law systems—particularly through church law and the Norman law—it was in Civil Law that the Roman law was particularly dominant. The notion of high levels of codification and a referable system was key to the system of Roman law; a sole source of law, which outlines the requirements for all citizens and the standards by which judges are to decide cases, was inherited by Civil Law (Merryman & Perez-Perdomo, 2007). Indeed, this was the source of the term *civil law*; that is, *jus civile*, the law that binds the civilians of the empire as opposed to *jus gentium*, which was the law governing the conquered peoples. The legal tradition of northern Italy penetrated much of Europe, including Spain, Germany, and the Netherlands, as law students trained in Italian universities and carried this tradition back to their home countries (Zweigert et al., 1998).

By the late Middle Ages, civil and canon law were the central systems of law taught throughout Europe. Beyond Roman law, the system of Civil Law was also influenced by Germanic and feudal traditions and by broader legal doctrines such as natural law. With the growth of several European states that sought to unify different jurisdictions and systems of law under their control, in the early modern period Civil Law became even more prevalent. Several attempts were made to codify Roman law and local customary law, with notable ones including the work of the Dutch jurist Hugo Grotius, *Introduction to Dutch Jurisprudence*, published in 1631; the *Code of Joseph II* in 1786 in Austria; the *Complete Territorial Code of 1794* in Prussia; and the *Civil Code* of France, also known as the *Napoleonic Code* in 1804.

The Napoleonic Code was the central piece of the codification of private and criminal law of France, and over the years it proved to be the most influential of all. We return to the Napoleonic Code at a later point, as it had far-reaching implications for the legal conditions for gay individuals in French, Spanish, and Portuguese colonies. We should mention here, though, that even within Europe, the code was of immense influence (Merryman & Perez-Perdomo, 2007). In Belgium and Luxemburg, for instance, it was incorporated wholesale.

Thus the French arrangements, rules, techniques, and legal training were fully adopted when those countries were incorporated into France under

Napoleon. Furthermore, other nations within continental Europe, even those that had not been incorporated into France, adopted not only the idea of a single code but also much of the substance and techniques of the Napoleonic Code. This was true for countries that were to become, if they were not already, colonial empires (the Netherlands, Italy, Spain, and Portugal). Legal arrangements, jurists, and judicial institutions in those countries were under considerable influence of French legal traditions and doctrinal developments.

The code provided a comprehensive set of principles, organizing key topics such as marriage and divorce, succession, property, contracts, and torts. In places such as Italy, this code influenced not only the law of different Italian states but also the law of 1865 when the states were politically unified. The emperor himself recognized the importance of the legal code, and in his later days even considered it of greater importance than his military conquests: "My true glory is not that I have won forty battles. Waterloo will blow away the memory of these victories. What nothing can blow away and will live eternally is my Civil Code" (Bergel, 1988, pp. 1078–1079).

In Civil Law systems, the legislature sets the legal standards both substantively and procedurally (Chu, 2009). Thus statutory law takes precedence in this system over case law. The body of law is organized according to issue areas, with new legislative enactments adding on to existing law with new statutes. This is a system of codified law. Substantive law, defined legislatively, codifies which acts are criminal and which fall under civil prosecution. Procedural law, equally determined by the legislature, codifies the process by which it is determined whether a certain act is criminal. The appropriate punishment, finally, is codified in penal law. Thus, whereas judges apply the law, their role is limited (Bellomo, 1995).

This is true in particular in comparison with systems of Common Law. Judicial decision-makers work within the framework established by the codified law. Consequently, their role involves questioning, bringing formal charges, and investigating. Yet, ultimately their influence in Civil Law systems is less than in Common Law, particularly in comparison with legislators or legal scholars. Indeed, judges are typically expected not to develop general principles of law in their decisions. This limited role of judges dates back to Roman times, where the Roman judiciary had a short-term and nonprofessional character.

Jurists in ancient Rome discussed specific questions in a document called *responsa*, in which specific statutory phrases provided the rationale for an opinion. This legal device was called *interpretario*. Even the positions of the praetor or the judex were limited in their appointment (one-year or one-case appointments, respectively) and in the scope of the decision, which was limited to the specific case at hand. Thus, by institutional design, there was no continuity between cases and over time in judicial decisions (Dawson, 1959). With that in mind, the fact that judges in Civil Law systems are not bound by case law but, rather, are expected to rule based on codified law, also means that their decisions may often be less predictable.

The system of Civil Law has expanded to countries around the world largely due to colonialism. The codification process in Chile, for instance, was led by Andres Bello and was based on the Spanish code—predominantly on the *Nueva Recopilación*, which was the consolidation of Spanish law in 1803—as well as Roman code and French and Prussian legal corpuses (Bosch, 1942). This new code was consequential throughout Latin America with complete adoption in countries such as Colombia and Ecuador, and it was used as a model in Argentina, Paraguay, Venezuela, El Salvador, and Nicaragua. Other Civil Law traditions in Europe were also transported overseas due to colonialism. A quintessential example here is the Brazilian code, where both Portuguese and German legal traditions had a major influence.

While there is variance in the scope of activity of courts in different systems of Civil Law, the judicial institutions' role is comparatively limited. In some high courts, such as those in French-speaking countries, the opinions of the court are given with limited legal rationale, particularly in comparison with the verbose opinions of Common Law supreme courts. Conversely, in Germanic Civil Law jurisdictions, it is more common for the court to produce opinions with more detailed legal reasoning.

The character of a Civil Law legal system is reflected in the quotation from Merryman and Clark's volume on comparative law. In systems of Civil Law,

> law is a science, and [. . .] the task of the legal scientist is to analyze and elaborate principles which can be derived from a careful study of positive legislation into a harmonious systematic structure. The components of this system are believed to be purely legal, a set of ultimate truths by rigorous deductive logic. Hence, the legal scientist's inquiry is almost exclusively directed towards the legal norm. Though lip service may be paid towards the relevance or utility of facts derived from non-legal disciplines, such as anthropology, sociology, political science, or economics, it is hard for the legal scientist to escape the feeling that consideration of non-legal facts detracts

from his search for absolute principles and the true nature of legal institutions. (p. 389)

The Napoleonic Code and Sodomy Provisions

As clear from our discussion, the paradigmatic example of codes in a system of Civil Law is the Napoleonic Code. This code is composed of the law of persons, commercial law, and property-law provisions. While certain codifications in Europe preceded the Napoleonic Code (e.g., Denmark in 1687 and Prussia in 1794), it is this code that proved the most consequential for legal systems worldwide. The conquests of the emperor—including, in particular, Spain, Portugal, and Italy—led to the adoption with certain modifications of the code in many of the European nations that were to become imperial powers themselves. The code was later imported into many of the French colonies, as well as (with some modifications) into the Spanish and Portuguese colonial empires. Whereas it was the French code that had by far the most influence overseas, the Germanic code was also influential in places where the motivation for matching Western standards led to the adoption of Western constitutional principles and structures. One such example is Japan.

Most important for our discussion is the fact that the Napoleonic Code did not include sodomy provisions. Those were rescinded following the Revolution, never to return to French Civil Law or its derivatives. Thus, the flip side of the legal path dependence story here is the story of the absence of such provisions in Civil Law systems. With the centrality of codified law in this type of system, the lack of such provision influenced the reality of LGBT throughout the world within Civil Law jurisdictions (Bellomo, 1995).

This chapter outlines the historical background, institutional framework, and organizational web that explains why we deem colonial legacy, and legal systems within it, to be so critically important for the analyses of variance in gay rights in general, and as those pertain to sodomy provisions in particular. The key prediction is that (holding everything else constant) having a Common Law system significantly increases the likelihood of having sodomy provisions on the books. In the next chapter we delve into the other main influence on sodomy provisions we identify in our theoretical framework—the role of religion. Then, in Chapter 4, we further develop the importance of legal path dependence and how it interacts with legal and political institutions of various kinds. In particular, beyond the empirical tests for how legal systems (Common Law vs. Civil Law) influence gay rights, we also offer the juxtaposition of judicial and non-judicial institutions to examine how legal path dependence leads to the treatment of sexual minorities. Chapter 4 provides comprehensive empirical analyses of the extent to which the theoretical framework proposed here and further developed later, is valid in large-N analyses employed on various sets of data.

3

THE RELIGIOUS STATE AND DEATH PENALTY FOR SODOMY

Although—as discussed in the introductory chapter of this book—homosexuality is becoming legally and socially acceptable in many parts of the world, there are still countries where the legal punishment for homosexuality is death. This chapter emphasizes the critical influence of religion on the rights of sexual minorities. More specifically, we analyze the influence of religion on the state in the context of the likelihood of death penalty being prescribed for same-sex sexual relations. To that end, we compare the death penalty in general, which is considerably more common in various countries in the world, with the death penalty prescribed for gay sexual activity, which is on the books in only a handful of countries. We contend that democratic conditions and a Common Law system influence the likelihood of the death penalty in general, as well as the death penalty for gays specifically. Conversely, religious governance is critical for the prescription of capital punishment for same-sex sexual relations. Of the states that have the death penalty on the books, it is those that also have religion closely entangled with government that prescribe this punishment for homosexuality. One state where this is true is Iran.

The president of Iran declared in his speech at the UN General Assembly in 2007 that unlike in the United States, there were no homosexuals in Iran. The claims by Mr. Ahmadinejad notwithstanding, LGBT individuals are part of the population in Iran (Reuters, 2007) as they are in every other country.

The difference between homosexuals in the United States and Iran, however, is not, as one of the president's advisors quickly scrambled to explain, that there were fewer of them in Iran. Rather, it is that engaging in same-sex sex in Iran is considerably more hazardous than it is in the United States; engaging in homosexual relations in Iran is done at one's own peril as by law this kind of sexual activity may carry with it the death penalty. This legal constriction has a real impact on how Iranian LGBT individuals interact among themselves as well as with the rest of society (Reuters, 2007).

While it is often hard to obtain accurate information concerning the exact reasons for which people are executed in the Islamic Republic of Iran, there is evidence that in 2005 and 2006, several people were hanged for homosexual behavior. In some cases, this type of behavior was defined as rape:

> Two men were publicly hanged in the northern town of Gorgan for homosexual acts in November 2005. In July 2006, two youths were hanged for homosexuality in northeastern Iran. In the most controversial case, in December a 20-year-old Kurdish Iranian, Makwan Mouladzadeh, was hanged for allegedly raping three boys when he was 13, despite a judicial review having been ordered and, according to Human Rights Watch, his accusers withdrawing their statements. (Penketh, 2008, p. 2)[1]

It might have been possible to dismiss these as executions motivated by punishment for rape and not for homosexual activity as such, if it were not for the Iranian legal code that suggests otherwise. The Islamic Penal Code of 1991 states that the death penalty for homosexuality should be applied if "both the active and passive persons are mature, of sound mind and have free will" (Ottoson, 2008, p. 24). Indeed, part of the reordering of Iranian society following the Islamic Revolution of 1979 included "the execution of hundreds of political opponents on the grounds of homosexuality" (Kligerman, 2007, p. 61). Noting that it is difficult to know the full scope of persecution and the accurate number of people executed in Iran for homosexual behavior because trials on moral charges in Iran are usually held *in camera* and the government stifles press coverage, Human Rights Watch (2005) still finds that cases documented in the Iranian media keep emerging. Statements such as those made by the Iranian president also support the data collected by international NGOs and think tanks, suggesting that the Iranian state executes individuals on grounds of their sexual orientation.

The death penalty for homosexual acts, however, is not unique to Iran. In 1980, six countries mandated death for those convicted of homosexuality, and the number of countries that had such laws rose to a high of eleven before it fell back to seven since. In 2008, for instance, the countries that prescribed the death penalty for homosexuality, in addition to Iran, were Mauritania, Nigeria, Saudi Arabia, Sudan, the United Arab Emirates, and Yemen (Ottoson, 2008, p. 46). Furthermore, there is evidence to suggest that those legal prescriptions were not merely de jure legislation; for example, five of these countries actually executed someone in 2007 for homosexuality (Ottoson, 2008, p. 4). Additionally, there are nations such as Uganda that, as mentioned in the introductory chapter of this book, have recently seen efforts to pass new legislation that would make same-sex sex punishable by death (Dixon, 2010).

As a first step in our examination in this book of the different levels of legal protections for LGBT, we delve in this chapter into the issue of the death penalty for gays. Apart from the descriptions and a limited number of illustrations, we are most interested in examining cross nationally, those factors that systematically make it more or less likely that a country would make sodomy a crime punishable by death. The prescription of the death penalty for a variety of heinous crimes such as murder is a controversial issue that generates debates in countries where the death penalty is still on the books, as well as in those where this type of penalty has been abolished (Bedau & Cassell, 2004; Radelet & Borg, 2000).

Unlike the application of the death penalty for murder and rape, which is still a contentious issue in many countries of the world, the idea that two adults should be executed for consensual sexual activity is largely in the distant past in the vast majority of nations. The norms of the international community as well are far from supportive of any such notion. The last execution for homosexuality in Great Britain, for example, took place in 1835 (Bates, 2004, p. 70). This makes the question about the variables that systematically predict which countries still have such a penalty on the books particularly fascinating. Yet, the literature on this topic is either descriptive or normative in nature (Clemens, 2005; Marks, 2006; Murray & Viljoen, 2007).

As identified in the Introduction, a key predictive variable in our theoretical framework is religion and the degree to which it influences state matters. Our key argument in this chapter is that due to the religious origins of state-imposed proscriptions on sodomy, government practices towards religion have a crucially important role in predicting whether the death penalty is prescribed for same-sex sexual relations. Within the context of using the death penalty to punish homosexuals, states that impose religious fiats—that is, states that restrict religious practices—should be the ones more likely to apply the death penalty for sodomy. The way we go about testing this contention is by focusing on countries that have capital punishment on the books and juxtaposing the subgroup that prescribes this penalty for homosexuality with those countries that do not.

Death Penalty for Same-Sex Relations and Limitations on Religious Freedom

The comparative literature on the death penalty is limited in scope and analytic leverage, and it becomes even more limited when we focus on the death penalty for homosexual acts. Much of the extant scholarship focuses on the United States (Bedau & Cassell, 2004). Furthermore, with much of the literature on this topic making normative claims (Hood, 2002), positivist analysis of this political phenomenon is hard to come by. The case studies of the death penalty, which dominate the literature on this topic, provide a wealth of information (Bates, 2004, inter alia). Yet, there are very few quantitative cross-national studies of the death penalty (Rosenfeld, 2010) that allow us to pinpoint those predictors that systematically explain this form of punishment.

This scholarship on the death penalty identifies a range of explanatory variables. One strand of the literature identifies religious-cultural norms as being key to the continued use. A number of authors have argued that the more religious a country's government becomes (Sullivan, 2001) or the more its legal codes specifically reflect a religious character (Peters, 1994), the more likely this country is to employ capital punishment. Culture has been noted as having an important impact on the likelihood that a country has capital punishment on the books.

The rules for punishment in different countries are tied to cultural values (Young & Brown, 1993). Furthermore, cultural norms influence how the death penalty is seen (Sarat & Boulanger, 2005). Similarly, Neapolitan (2001) found that historical and cultural factors related to religion were important for variation in the degree of punitive punishment for crimes; certain religious views make support for the death penalty much stronger in some countries than in others. Hence, religiosity is likely to influence the likelihood of having death penalty on the books.

The argument advanced here is that when comparing the death penalty in general to the death penalty for homosexuality, it is countries where the state is involved in prescribing religious practice that will be more likely to have the death penalty specifically for homosexual practices. As there are a variety of sources for the prescription of death penalty in general (see more details below), we do not expect limitations on religious freedom to predict the likelihood of capital punishment in general, when both types of punishment are specified in the same model. When including specification for both death penalty in general and death penalty for gays in the explanatory model, only the latter should have a significant connection to limitations on religious freedom.

Whereas murder or any other type of violent crime can be equally viewed as heinous through either religious lenses or secular ones, the condemnation of same-sex relations is tied to religious perspectives. In Judeo-Christian traditions, and later on in Islam, the death penalty is divinely prescribed by either holy texts or by those who interpreted them. Indeed, in response to the Human Rights Council of the United Nations, Nigeria defended capital punishment for same-sex relations using religious justifications. Nigeria contended that it was a "just" penalty (Strasser, 2010).

States that limit religious freedom are more likely to frame sodomy as a sin and to take religious texts as guides on how to punish such acts. As mentioned in Chapter 1, the scripture of Judaism, Islam, and Christianity all have clear prohibitions against sodomy, which also influences non-Abrahamic faiths (Bacchetta, 1999; Crompton, 2006; Dynes, 1992). We go into some detail concerning the proscriptions of the different religions; however, at this point, let us stress that while the link between religion and the view of sodomy as a sin is not true everywhere, for every religion or every religious authority within different religions, it is this connection, we believe, that is the driver pushing those governments that tend to limit the extent of religious freedom to also punish homosexuality with death.

This appeal of the death penalty, motivated by certain religious ideologies, is still present in various world nations. It is worth quoting the view of the archbishop of the Anglican Church in Nigeria, for he clearly lays out a religious view of same-sex sexual relations that sees this behavior as evil and worthy of extreme punishment. Archbishop Akinola contends:

> In recent times, we have been told that the issue of homosexuality is relative. We believe it is not a relative matter. In the context of

our part of the Church and society, we see it as a behavior that is expressly forbidden and roundly condemned in scripture [. . .] The issue is such a defining one because two cannot go together except if they agree. To overlook this fundamental departure from scripture is not safe for faith or conscience; it means "walking in the counsel of the ungodly." The consequence is to risk the displeasure of God. (Blackelectorate.com)

The same can be said of certain views of Islamic law. Islamic law identifies the punishment of sodomy as one of the top "Five or Six Sharia Interests" (Rahami, 2005, p. 588). This system of law prescribes punishment for this practice because it is a "crime against family values" (Rahami, 2005, p. 588). The Qur'an is explicit in its condemnation of what it calls *qaum Lut* (Lot's people) referring to the prophet Lot who preached against homosexuality in the cities of Sodom and Gomorrah. Mohammad singles out sodomy—either with a woman, a man, or a boy—as leading directly to hell (Kligerman, 2007). Most schools of Islamic legislative thought prescribe death in such cases. Some suggest stoning, others execution with a sword, and others still leave the method of execution of the offender to the court (Abiad, 2008, pp. 24–25). In many Muslim countries, particularly since the 1970s, we have seen a growth in states mandating religious behavior—and mandating the death penalty for homosexuality (Greenberg & West, 2008; Hajjar, 2004; Mortensen, 2008). A number of nations are going through the process of adding Sharia law to the existing legal codes. This process often includes the view of homosexuality as a crime, which in accordance with religious principles, should be punishable by death (Peters, 1994).

In sum, we propose that states that embrace religious mandates are more likely to have capital punishment for homosexuality. The operationalization we use for this variable is limitations on religious freedoms. We hypothesize that countries where religious freedom is limited by the state are more likely to have death penalty prescribed for individuals engaging in same-sex sexual relations. Furthermore, limitations on religious freedom are not likely to influence the likelihood of having death penalty in general on the books.

Common Law and Capital Punishment for Sodomy

As mentioned in the previous chapter, the prohibition on sodomy in 16th-century England, the Buggery Act of 1533, included in some of its incarnations death as a penalty. Indeed, in the English motherland, it was not until well into the 19th century that the death penalty component was abolished in the sodomy provisions. Thus, when this law travelled to British colonies around the world oftentimes it carried with it this type of penalty. In Chapter 2, we go into the details of the codification process that served as the institutional mechanism by which this type of legal transference took place within the colonial hierarchy.

Holding everything else constant, it is clear that Common Law origins increased the likelihood of the death penalty for sodomy (Dundes, 2002). Citing the destruction of Sodom, William Blackstone, the prominent English jurist, supported the punishment of sodomy with death (Crompton, 1976). The death penalty was not removed as a punishment for sodomy in the United Kingdom until 1861, when the punishment was reduced to "10 years and life imprisonment" (Weeks, 1996, p. 46). Over centuries of colonialism, the British Empire spread its system of law throughout its colonies around the world, either via imposition or simple adoption. Many have credited British colonization with the spread of wealth and democracy (Ashkanasy et al., 2002; Bollen & Jackman, 1985; Wejnert, 2005). The British Empire should also be credited with spreading the criminalization of homosexuality around the world.

Indeed, for a long time after achieving independence from the British crown, numerous countries held on to not only the criminalization of sodomy but also its punishment by death (Crompton, 1976, p. 287). Even beyond death penalty that is prescribed specifically for homosexuality, we find support in the literature for the type of legal system having an impact on the use of capital punishment in general (Mortensen, 2008). Greenberg and West (2008) found that a Common Law system was positively correlated with having the death penalty, and it had a stronger correlation to the death penalty than either Civil Law or Islamic law (see also Neumayer, 2008b).

On the other hand, in 1791 "buoyed by Enlightenment ideals of individuality, rationality, privacy and secularism, the French National Assembly abolished the country's old sodomy prohibition on the ground that 'liberty consists in the freedom to do everything which injured no one else' (Declaration of the Rights of Man, 1789)" (Frank et al., 2010, p. 136). As discussed extensively in Chapter 2, as it spread around large parts of the world, Civil Law did not carry with it the 'baggage' of anti-sodomy provisions. The system of Civil Law, therefore, whether imposed or adopted freely, did not include these types of measures. This decreased the likelihood that sodomy would be punished criminally, let alone punished through capital punishment, in countries that have a Civil Law legal system (for a more extensive discussion see Chapter 2).

There should be no difference in terms of the effects of having a Common Law legal system between death penalty in general and death penalty for homosexuality. Thus, we hypothesize that Common Law countries are more likely than Civil Law countries to have the death penalty on the books. In addition, Common Law countries are more likely to have the death penalty prescribed for individuals engaging in same-sex sexual relations.

In addition to limitations on religious freedom and having a Common Law legal system, other factors have been identified as key for the presence or absence of the death penalty cross nationally. Miethe et al. (2005) find evidence that economic development, regime components, and stability are associated with the continued use of capital punishment. Undeveloped countries, for instance, are more likely to retain capital punishment (Ruddell, 2005). Miethe et al. point out that this relationship is probabilistic. Indeed, there are certain very important exceptions such as the United States and Japan. Yet, as economic development is unrelated to religion, we do not expect this variable to influence the likelihood of death penalty prescribed for same-sex sexual relations.

Democracy is another predictor that has been found to influence the probability of the abolition of the death penalty. In two important pieces, Neumayer (2008a, 2008b) explored various aspects of capital punishment as a part of national policies. When examining a wide range of countries over a period of over 50 years, he found that, *ceteris paribus*, the more democratic a country, the more likely it is to have abolished the death penalty. Furthermore, as democratic conditions in the nation improve, it is not only more likely to abolish the death penalty but also to support international protocols, specifically the Second Optional Protocol to the International Covenant on Civil and Political Rights (Neumayer, 2008a). Ruddell and Urbina (2004) and Neapolitan (2001) have identified similar relationships between democracy and freedom on the one hand, and the abolition of the death penalty on the other.[2]

We should also note that this argument about democracy and freedom fits well into the larger world-culture literature (Boli & Thomas, 1997, 1999). Here too, the relationship is not deterministic in the sense that higher levels of democracy would not necessarily lead to the abolition of capital punishment. As we are well aware, high levels of democracy in places such as the United States or Japan have yet to lead to the abolition of the death penalty there. Indeed, many of the normative discussions in the literature around this punishment, mentioned above, develop exactly in those places. Yet, the very fact that these normative debates develop especially in those countries (and to a lesser degree in countries that are not developed democracies and death penalty is on the books such as China or Russia) is another indication to the *prima facie* contradiction between democracy as a form of government and the prescription of such punishments. In other words, it is the fact that the legal systems in those established democracies actively engage in sentencing people to death that is the key motivator for those debates, as democracy and the death penalty seemingly negate each other.

Ethnic and religious diversity may also influence the likelihood of death penalty. The evidence in the literature, however, is mixed. While Greenberg and West (2008) did not find ethnic fractionalization as being statistically significant in relation to the use of the death penalty, Kent (2010) suggests that having large ethnic minorities in the nation is related to the use of the death penalty. Kent draws from the criminological theories of conflict to argue that ethnic divisions increase the likelihood that a country will retain the death penalty because it serves "as a mechanism to deal with those groups who threaten elites" (p. 56). That being said, there is no reason to think that ethnic diversity should influence the likelihood of prescribing the death penalty for same-sex sexual intercourse. Thus, if it has any influence, it would be a significant effect on the selection equation but not in the outcome equation in our model, as elaborated below. We also control for religious diversity and for world regions.

Religion and Death Penalty for Gays: The Empirical Test

If one thing is clear from the discussion thus far, it is that the phenomenon of death penalty for same-sex sex is particularly complex, with various variables interacting in the theoretical framework explaining it. Thus, we opt for a multivariate analysis, which would provide us with a best approximation and would match the theoretical framework proposed. Such an approach would allow us to accurately test the hypotheses developed above. To examine the factors that are thought to influence the death penalty in general and the factors that influence the likelihood of death penalty prescribed for homosexual acts, we employ a variation of Heckman's selection bias framework (1979).

The dependent variables in both the selection and outcome equations are dichotomous. We, therefore, estimate the sample selection probit model described by van de Ven and van Praag (1981), which allows for a dichotomous outcome variable. The selection equation predicts the likelihood that the state has death penalty prescribed on the books. The independent variables in this equation include the region of the world, government-imposed restrictions on the freedom of religious exercise, democratic and economic conditions, globalization, type of legal system, and cultural diversity. The outcome equation includes as predictors the level of religious freedom, levels of democratic rule and economic development, globalization, the type of legal system, and ethnic diversity. For the purposes of the multivariate analysis, we use data for all states for which data are available for the years 1972–2002, to a total of 2,909 observations in the selection equation and 995 observations in the outcome equation. In sum, the model's two equations are presented as follows:

Selection: P(Death Penalty General=1) = f(	*Outcome: P(Death Penalty Gays=1) = f(*
Government Restrictions on Religious Practices,	Government Restrictions on Religious Practices,
Democratic conditions,	Democratic Conditions,
Economic conditions,	Economic Conditions,
Ethnic Fractionalization,	Ethnic Fractionalization,
Globalization,	Globalization,
Common Law,	Common Law,
Cultural Diversity,	Cultural Diversity)
World Region)	

Our independent variables were drawn from the Quality of Government database (Teorell, Holmberg, & Rothstein, 2008), which aggregates a wide variety of data. The specific predictors used in the model are listed in Table 3.1 along with their original source datasets and their descriptive statistics. *Government Restriction on Religious Practices* is coded 0 if there are restrictions and 1 if there are none. This variable measures the extent of freedom to exercise religion free of government restrictions on belief, worship, proselytization, and advocacy by clergy as it relates to partisan politics and political participation broadly defined. *Common Law* is coded 1 for systems of Common Law and 0 otherwise. *Globalization* indicates on a range of 0–100 the degree of political, economic, and social globalization (see Chapter 1 for a detailed discussion of the components of the globalization measure). Higher values for cultural diversity and ethnic fractionalization indicate higher levels of those variables. *Democratic Conditions* are based on the Polity Score. The different variables for regions of the world are dummies coded 1 if the country is from that region and 0 otherwise, with Caribbean being the excluded category.

Table 3.1. Variables and Data Sources

Descriptive Statistics: Death Penalty for Same-Sex Relations

Variable	Mean	Standard Deviation	Minimum	Maximum
Death Penalty for Homosexuality	0.033	0.179	0	1
Death Penalty	0.563	0.496	0	1
Democracy Score (Polity/FH combined)	5.502	3.503	0	10
Real GDP per capita	6815.204	7814.842	170.55	84408.23
Ethnic Diversity	0.478	0.261	0.001999	1
Globalization	48.518	16.987	8.802876	93.45989
Common Law	0.307	0.461	0	1
Cultural Diversity	0.310	0.208	0	0.732836
East Europe	0.145	0.352	0	1
Latin America[i]	0.098	0.297	0	1
Middle East[ix]	0.104	0.305	0	1
Africa[ix]	0.244	0.429	0	1
South East Asia	0.063	0.244	0	1
South Asia	0.044	0.205	0	1

Note; [i]Ottoson (2008); [ii]Ottoson (2008); [iii]Teorell, et al. (2008); [iv]Gleditsch (2002); [v]Fearon (2003); [vi]Dreher (2006); [vii]La Porta (1999); [viii]Fearon (2003); [ix]Hadenius & Teorell (2005).

Table 3.1 provides information about the different variables and their data sources. Data for the dependent variable in the selection equation, *Death Penalty, General*, are taken from the website of Amnesty International.[3] Data for the dependent variable in the outcome equation, *Death Penalty for Gays*, are drawn from the *State-Sponsored Homophobia: A World Survey of Laws Prohibiting Same Sex Activity between Consenting Adults* (Ottoson, 2008). The report codes seven countries—either the whole country or parts of it—as currently having laws that make homosexual acts punishable by death. The unit of analysis is country-year and the values are 1 for death penalty prescribed for homosexual acts in that country in that year and 0 otherwise. The country-year is coded as 1 even when the death penalty for homosexuality is prescribed only in certain territories of that country.

Table 3.2 presents the results of the selection model. The selection equation is for the prescription of capital punishment in general. The outcome

Table 3.2. Results of the Selection Model

Heckman Selection Model: Death Penalty for Same-Sex Relations

Variable	General death penalty equation (selection)		Death penalty for gays equation (outcome)	
	Coef.	Std. Err.	Coef.	Std. Err.
Government Restrictions on Religious Practices	-0.058	0.09	-1.79 ***	0.22
Democracy	-0.13 ***	0.017	-0.19 ***	0.038
GDP	0.000016	0.00001	0.000005	0.00001
Ethnic Fractionalization	-0.46	0.3	0.17	0.49
Globalization	-0.03	0.004	-0.01	0.006
Common Law	0.98 ***	0.1	0.95 ***	0.15
Cultural Diversity	1.08 **	0.32	0.83	0.62
East Europe	0.21	0.17	-	-
Latin America	-1.2 ***	0.18	-	-
Middle East	2.3 ***	0.33	-	-
Africa	0.45 *	0.23	-	-
South East Asia	0.58 **	0.22	-	-
South Asia	-1.1 ***	0.27	-	-
Intercept	2.1 ***	0.36	-0.4	.4
Observations	2909 (Death Penalty General)		995 (Death Penalty for Same-sex Sex)	
Wald Test of Ind. Equations: $\chi^2(29)$	140.19***			

Note: Standard errors are robust. Caribbean is the excluded category for World Regions.
* $p < 0.05$ ** $p < 0.01$ *** $p < 0.001$ (two-tailed). LR test of Independent Equations: Prob > χ^2 = 0.25.

equation then tests the predictors that in those countries where there is death penalty, there is also the death penalty prescribed specifically for same-sex sex.

The value for Rho indicates that we are unable to reject the null hypothesis that there is no selection problem. In other words, the estimation procedure selected here is the appropriate one, since failing to take into consideration the selection procedure would lead to bias in the results. This lends support to our choice of a Heckman model. The selection equation indicates that as cultural diversity increases, so does the likelihood of capital punishment being on the books. This is also true for countries with Common Law as the legal system. While globalization and GDP per capita do not have a statistically significant effect, the more democratic the country, the less likely it is that its legal system prescribes capital punishment. Certain world regions, such as the Middle East and Africa, are more likely to have countries that have this penalty on the books. In other regions, such as Latin America, countries are less likely to prescribe this kind of punishment. Given that the countries in Latin America are almost uniformly Civil Law countries, this is hardly surprising in light of the theoretical framework developed here.

As for the outcome equation, which estimates the predictors of death penalty for gays in countries that have death penalty on the books, three of the predictors are statistically significant. Government restrictions on religious practices are a strong predictor of death penalty for gays, and so is having a Common Law legal system. When there are no restrictions on the freedom of religion, the likelihood of death penalty for gays decreases. Having a Common Law system increases the likelihood of having the death penalty on the books, not just in general, but also in specifically targeting gays.

Importantly, religious freedom has no influence in the selection equation. Furthermore, the predictors of the death penalty for same-sex sex are considerably dissimilar to the predictors of capital punishment in general. While similar to the selection equation in that having origins in Common Law is highly influential in the outcome equation, cultural diversity and globalization are not. Most important for our theory, though, is the fact that religious freedom is highly consequential in the outcome equation only. In other words, religion and religious freedom more specifically have little to no effect on whether a country has the death penalty on the books. Those variables, however, heavily influence whether the state prescribes such a penalty for gays.

This is the first chapter in the book that empirically addresses a specific aspect of legal treatment of LGBT by the state. In later chapters we take up issues such as decriminalization of sodomy and the guarantees of equality under the law for sexual minorities. Yet, before we examine those broader issues, in this chapter we aim to examine a more limited, yet crucially important, aspect of gay rights—the right to live notwithstanding one's sexual orientation. In the introductory chapter, we identify two major influences on the rights of gay individuals—colonial heritage, as it is reflected in the legal system that is in place and is carried over the years due to legal path dependence, and the influence of religion. The main goal of the current chapter is to identify the key factors that account for the prescription of the death penalty for same-sex sexual relations as a part of the legal code in the nation. Of those two key predictors, while a Common Law legal system proved to influence the likelihood of death penalty being on the books in general, it was the influence of religion that was directly and exclusively tied to the death penalty for members of sexual-minority groups.

We argued that countries where the government involves itself in restricting religious practices would be more likely to punish sodomy with capital punishment, if they already have such a punishment on their law books. Our analysis largely buttresses this hypothesis. For the death penalty in general, our analysis supports the body of knowledge in the existing literature. When it comes to which of the countries that have the death penalty prescribe this penalty for gay sexual relationships, however, our findings tell a different story; predictors of the death penalty for homosexual activity do not fit neatly into a story of wealth or democracy. Globalization and wealth are not statistically related to the application of the death penalty for consensual homosexual sex. What appear to matter the most when it comes to the death penalty for consensual same-sex relations are the involvement of the state in limiting religious practices and the nature of the legal system—whether the legal system is Common Law.

In strong support for the first hypothesis stated above, the estimation of the Heckman selection model suggests that states that restrict religious practices are more likely to punish homosexuality with death. The judgment of sexuality is intimately tied to religious cultural norms (Inglehart & Norris, 2003; Inglehart et al., 2002) and the results, as far as punishment is concerned, can be deadly (Sarat & Boulanger, 2005). One causal relationship may be that when sex ceases to serve reproduction and the preservation of the traditional heterosexual family, it challenges not only the standard views of gender but also the interests and values embraced by governments promoting a certain religious view. As several religious approaches, especially in their original forms, have embraced the prescription of capital punishment in cases of sodomy, this kind of penalty is more probable in countries that embrace such views and limit religious practices.

When religion plays a major role in state affairs—and in particular religion in its traditional forms—it is likely that its morals and perceptions would trickle down into state institutions. If the dominant faith perceives the family unit as uniquely heterosexual, or if it has moral claims for reproduction, the religiously prescribed perception of homosexuality may influence how the state itself perceives this behavior, which is sinful within the religious framework. This conduct that is identified as sinful by the state on religious grounds because of the challenges it poses to traditionally religious views of family, sex, and reproduction, may not only be judged by religious standards but also punished by the same standards. The kind of punishment prescribed by the faith to what is perceived as a sin often carries over to the penal system in those cases where the penal system is controlled by the state.

The disparity between the predictors of the death penalty in general and the death penalty as it is prescribed for sodomy is instructive. Having death penalty in general on the books, our analysis indicates, has sources other than religious ones. The likelihood that a country will continue to maintain the death penalty that is prescribed generally is instead a function of the democratic conditions there and the world region of that country. With improved democratic conditions, the death penalty is less likely. This story fits directly into a modernization narrative of tolerance (Inglehart, 1997; Inglehart & Norris, 2003; Inglehart et al., 2002). We also find that Common Law tradition that emanated from the British colonial empire makes the practice of the death penalty more likely in general and specifically in the case of death prescribed for homosexual acts (Greenberg & West, 2008).

The findings in this chapter are important for our understanding of the death penalty for same-sex relations and serve as the basis for later discussions developed in this book. Divine proscriptions and prescriptions still have an impact in many countries in the world (Simon & Blaskovich, 2007). Although the number of countries that currently have mandated the death penalty for same-sex sexual intimacy is limited, our findings are important not just from a historical perspective. Those findings increase our analytic leverage as far as the relations between an individual agent and the state are concerned.

An anti-homosexuality bill that was defeated in Uganda is being reconsidered by that country's legislature while this book is going to press. The consideration of this bill takes place at the same time that a leading opponent of the bill, David Kato, lost his life after he was identified by a Ugandan newspaper as someone who should be killed. The reason why his killing was justified was his stance on homosexuality. The framing of the arguments, both for the killing of David Kato and for the bill, is based on religious elements (Gettleman, 2011). It is true that Kato himself did not die because of a state-sponsored execution. Yet, in deeply conservative Uganda, bills that propose the death penalty for gay men or for HIV-positive homosexuals have been drawn up. In 2009, for instance, a member of parliament by the name of David Bahati proposed such a bill, riding the new wave of homophobia, vigilantism, and religious conservatism in his country.

Katherine Fairfax Wright and Malika Zouhali-Worrall in their 2012 documentary, *Call Me Kuchu*, recorded the anti-gay propaganda in the country, which was driven to a large extent by religious figures (some of which came from outside of the country). It is this type of propaganda that not only led to the death of Mr. Kato but also yielded various bills proposed to prescribe death for homosexual men for a range of reasons and in various conditions. While these legislative efforts have so far been in vain, the largely religiously motivated movement in this direction may eventually prove successful.

Our analysis suggests that the key role of religion in allowing the state to infringe on individuals' private spheres, and particularly on the private sphere of LGBTIQ individuals by threatening to take their lives if they pursue their sexual desires, is true beyond Uganda. The findings of the multivariate analyses indicate that the prescription of the death penalty for gay individuals is systematically related to the influence of religion on state affairs.

4

Sodomy Provisions and Their Repeal

As the second and third pillars of legal path dependence outlined in Chapter 2 suggest, both legislation by legislatures and rulings rendered by courts were means by which legal path dependence led to the persistence of sodomy laws. In this chapter we focus on how this path dependence persevered and how it ended. We further develop the theoretical framework and then offer empirical analyses of cases where sodomy provisions were not on the books. By construction, the move towards repeal had to happen in those very same institutions—courts and legislatures. Since law is made, morphs, and changes in legislatures and judiciaries, it was action in these institutions that also led to the nullification of sodomy provisions in various countries. We further develop the argument about the circumstances under which repeal may happen in courts compared to other cases where repeal takes place in legislatures. But before we do that, let us examine empirically the notion of legal path dependence and how it influences the likelihood of sodomy provisions as a function of the legal system determined by colonial heritage.

The set of multivariate models estimated below examines the systematic effects of legal path dependence and religion on the likelihood that sodomy laws are on the books. Before we examine the effects of legal systems and religion, however, let us first list the alternative influences on sodomy laws. After all, we attempt to provide proof for *systematic* effects for our key predictors—legal system and religion—while *controlling for* alternative possible influences. These alternative effects include the state of democracy in the country, globalization, economic development, modernization, and political inclusion. Let us first briefly examine those alternative explanations.

Democratic Conditions and Political Opportunity Structure for Minorities

Based on the democratic understanding of consensual sexual activities between adults as a human right (Mertus, 2007), we expect the spread of democracy to enhance this right (Davenport, 1999; Gurr, 2000). Along the same lines, there is a great deal of empirical analysis to support the contention that established democracies are more likely to make greater legal provisions for historically marginalized populations (Davenport, 1999; Gurr, 2000). Most variations of democracy include some notion of protection for minority groups. While historically minority groups were defined by gender or ethnic group, in recent decades, sexual orientation has been increasingly recognized as defining another type of minority group. This classification of minority group is increasingly deemed worthy of protection by the state, particularly in democratic states (Wilensky, 2002). In sum, the more democratic the polity, the more we would expect to see same-sex sexual relations acceptable by the legal standards set by the state.

The notions of political equality, equality under the law, and even more so—political inclusion—are critically important to our discussion. An examination of political inclusion and political-opportunity structures is essential to understanding the legal prohibitions on same-sex sexual activity. We look to the inclusion of women in the political process (Grey, 2002; Meyer, 2003; Swers, 2001, 2002; Vega & Firestone, 1995). Women's inclusion is a good proxy for the political inclusion of the "other"—particularly in relation to the issues of gender and sex (Robinson & Spivey, 2007). Thus, beyond the positive effect that we expect to find for the democratic conditions in the state, we also expect to see women's inclusion leading to a decreased likelihood that sodomy remains criminalized. It follows that as the number of women in the legislature increases, the likelihood of legal prohibition on same-gender sexual activity decreases.

The State of Economic Development and Modernization

As economic conditions improve, we expect the decriminalization of homosexual activity to be more likely. Political inclusion and political-opportunity structures are related to changes in the economic composition of a state. Economic development and modernization thus lead to political inclusion. In a variety of ways, such as through literacy, education, and cultural change, modernization can change the view of who should be accepted in society as equal. Modernization has been shown to act as a causal variable in increasing levels of democracy generally (Doorenspleet, 2004; Huntington, 1991; Lipset, 1960; Przeworski et al., 2000; Ramirez et al., 1997), and specifically enhancing the rights of women (Inglehart & Norris, 2003) and minorities (Gurr, 2000).

Accordingly, in order to demonstrate a statistically significant effect for our key independent variables, it is important to control in the multivariate analyses presented below for the effects of economic conditions. Such economic modernization may account for the variance between states and, over time, in the legal treatment of gays. Failing to control for this effect may erroneously enhance the effects of legal systems or religions on our dependent variable. Such spurious effects may result from under specification of the model. We use the standard measure of GDP per capita and expect that as GDP per capita increases, the likelihood that homosexual activity is criminalized decreases, *ceteris paribus*.

Globalization

Conventional theories of sovereignty have emphasized the nation-state as the guarantor of rights and liberties (Anderson, 1983). Yet, some have argued that globalization erodes the nation-state and leads to porous national boundaries in terms of legal arrangements, capital flow, immigration, and other ways (Grewal, 2005). Globalization reduces transaction costs across a range of human interactions, opening up new opportunities and exposing social systems to new ways of thinking (Hollingsworth, 1998). In relation to the issue of the rights of sexual-minority groups worldwide, information about alternative legal arrangements should be more readily available in a globalized state. Subsequently, it becomes easier to identify alternative legal frameworks; and domestic actors are exposed to the way civil rights and liberties in general, and gay rights in particular, are organized in other jurisdictions. Political entrepreneurs, the public (Lax & Phillips, 2009), political organizations, and social movements (Barclay et al., 2009) are then able to more easily recognize alternative legal arrangements within which to settle gay rights. While in this book we do not delve into the mechanisms underlying these processes, this in turn would increase the likelihood of decriminalization of sodomy.

In addition, the world-culture and normative-diffusion literature argue that the strengthening of links between countries allows for the diffusion of new human rights and norms of tolerance (Boli & Thomas, 1997, 1999; Finnemore, 1996; Meyer et al., 1997; Ramirez & McEneaney, 1997). Furthermore, literature about the regulation of sexuality worldwide underscores the importance in this context of global trends (e.g., Frank et al., 2010). We thus expect higher levels of globalization to increase the likelihood of decriminalization. In sum, increased levels of globalization increase the likelihood that homosexual activity is decriminalized.

The first set of analyses presented below examines the influences on the likelihood of sodomy provisions being on the books. We are primarily interested in the systematic effects of our two key predictors: legal system and the effects of religion. Once we unequivocally establish the notions that a Common Law system and religious influences increase the likelihood of sodomy laws in the first half of this chapter, we move on to examine the notion of legal path dependence more in depth. Legal path dependence, as elaborated in Chapters 1 and 2, suggests that legal evolution is influenced by institutional platforms. After we discuss the results for sodomy laws, at the theoretical level we elaborate how and under what circumstances different institutions (judicial compared to non-judicial) would repeal sodomy laws. We then examine a set of empirical tests for those different institutional paths. But first, let us examine the empirical tests for the hypothesized effects on sodomy laws.

Dependent Variable: Sodomy Provisions

The dependent variable in the first set of analyses offered here is whether the state has sodomy provisions on the books. The criteria determining the values for this dependent variable include (a) whether consensual homosexual intercourse is legal or illegal within the nation; and (b) if legal, in what year legality was attained. Accordingly, the dependent variable is coded 1 for country-years where sodomy was not a criminal offence. The coding is 0 otherwise. We used the ILGA State Sponsored Homophobia Report for 2009 and more recent updates to code this variable.

The pertinent sections of the legal code in each country are examined to determine whether same-sex sexual relations were legal or not in each country-year. In Lebanon, for instance, the Penal Code of 1943 states that "any sexual intercourse against nature is punished with up to one year of imprisonment" (Article 534). As same-sex sexual relations are interpreted in Lebanese law as "sexual intercourse against nature," the coding for the outcome variable was coded 0 for all country-years for Lebanon in our database. Along the same lines, the Sudanese Penal Code of 1991, Section 148 (as mentioned earlier in this book) states under Article 1, "Any man who inserts his penis or its equivalent into a women's or a man's anus or permitted another man to insert his penis or its equivalent in his anus is said to have committed Sodomy." Depending on the number of convictions on the sodomy count, the Sudanese code may lead to punishment with death or life imprisonment. As the legal code in Sudan had criminalized sodomy even before 1991, the dependent variable was coded 0 for all observations in the database for Sudan. The coding for France, where—as mentioned in Chapter 3—sodomy had been decriminalized in the Napoleonic Code more than two centuries ago, is 1 for all country-years in the dataset.

Unlike the cases for Lebanon and Sudan (where sodomy is criminal throughout the period of time we study) or France (where it is not), there are other countries where the coding changes over time within the time frame of our study. As our data are compiled for different countries (a comparative framework) and over time (a time-series component), the dependent variable may show variance not only between nations (e.g., France where sodomy provisions were not on the books for the duration of the timespan covered by our data, as opposed to Iran where such provisions are still a part of the legal code) but also over time.

As the various examples in the case studies mentioned in previous chapters clearly illustrate, variance over time within the same country reflects changes in both pro- and anti-gay rights directions. Change, in other words, is not always in a progressive direction toward decriminalization that enhances legal protections. Rather, change may move in the opposite direction as well (see the case of India discussed in Chapter 2). The United States has seen a change in the coding of this variable, which took place in the first decade of the 21st century. Until 2003, some of the states criminalized same-sex sexual relations. Indeed, the Supreme Court of the United States had deemed these laws constitutional in its own ruling in *Bowers v. Hardwick* (478 U.S. 186) in 1986. Yet, in 2003, the same court decided to strike down any and all sodomy provisions as unconstitutional (*Lawrence v. Texas* [539 U.S. 558]) and effectively overruled this part of the decision in *Bowers*. As such, the coding for all the country years for the United States prior to 2003 is 0 and changes to 1 after that year.

Another issue concerning the coding of the outcome variable relates to the structure of government. Some countries have a federal system, where different governing units may have dissimilar policy provisions. The coding scheme, however, considers federal jurisdictions as a whole. Thus, if even some of the federal units had sodomy provisions on the books, the country-year was coded as a jurisdiction with sodomy laws in effect. Thus, the coding for the dependent variable for the United States reflected criminalization until 2003 (since in parts of the United States sodomy was criminal) and changed to decriminalization after that year for all country-years, due to the ruling of the Supreme Court in *Lawrence v. Texas*. Accordingly, all federal units uniformly repealed sodomy laws and thus the coding changed.

Explanatory Variables

As for our predictors, in Chapters 2 and 3 we identified two key predictors. The first was the legal system as determined in many cases by the country's colonial heritage. Empirically, this is the *Common Law* dummy variable, which equals 1 for nations with a Common Law system. The value is 0 otherwise. The influence of religion, which is the second key predictor in the theoretical framework discussed above, is trickier to measure. We thus measure this variable in various ways—using data from different and independent sources—to make sure our coding strategy is not only theoretically sound but is also one that yields empirically robust findings. One measure that we use is for the size of the religious constituency in the country. Based on the CIA *World Factbook*, *Percent Catholic* indicates Catholics as percentage of the population and *Percent Muslim* provides the same statistic for the Muslim population. *Percent Protestant* measures the percentage of members of this faith in the country.

Yet, as we deem the influence of religion to be critical, we employ another set of measures to empirically test the influences of this variable. While data from this database are available for only a subset of the years in our data (1990–2003), we use the Religion and State database (Fox, 2003), as it is widely recognized as one of the most reliable and accurate databases concerning state and religion issues. In particular, we take advantage of two variables. The first, *Restrictions on Interfaith Marriage*, is coded as "Cases where marriages are performed only by clergy—which effectively restricts interfaith marriages." The second variable, which we use to ensure the accuracy of our coding strategy and to increase the overall robustness of our results concerning the effects of religion on sodomy provision is *Religious Court with Broad Jurisdiction*. This variable measures the "Presence of religious courts, which have jurisdiction over some matters of law other than family law and matters of inheritance." In the specification strategy we use for the different models in this and later chapters we interchangeably take advantage of those various measures for religion.

To measure *Democratic Conditions*, we utilize the Polity score, which was imputed using Freedom House data where it was missing. The scale ranges from 0 (least democratic) to 10 (most democratic) (Hadenius & Teorell, 2005). To measure the political inclusion of women, we use the Inter-Parliamentary Union Women in National Parliaments data (Inter-Parliamentary Union, 2005). We use the data for the legislative body as a whole in unicameral systems, and where there exists more than one legislative chamber, we use only the percentage of women in the upper house.[1] To measure *Economic Development* (and the associated shift towards modernization), we use GDP per capita in constant US dollars at base year 2000; missing data were imputed by using the CIA *World Factbook* (Gleditsch, 2002), and logged GDP values are used for estimation.

To measure international connections we use the KOF Index of Globalization (Dreher, 2006; Dreher et al., 2008). The indexes for the globalization variables range from 0–100, with higher values indicating increased levels of globalization. The overall index of *Globalization* is the weighted average of *Economic Globalization, Social Globalization,* and *Political Globalization* (Teorell et al., 2009). The measure for economic globalization is defined as the long distance flow of services, goods, capital, information, and perceptions that accompany market exchanges. This index measures not only actual flows of trade and investments but also trade restrictions, such as tariff rates (Dreher, 2006; Dreher et al., 2008). The index of political globalization is measured by the number of embassies and high commissions in a country, the number of memberships the country has in international organizations, participation in UN peace-keeping missions, and the number of international treaties signed since 1945 (Dreher, 2006; Dreher et al., 2008). Lastly, the social globalization measure includes three categories of indicators: personal contacts (e.g., telephone traffic and tourism), information flows (e.g., number of Internet users), and cultural proximity (e.g., trade books and number of warehouses of IKEA per capita) (Dreher 2006; Dreher et al., 2008).

We also control for measures of the effects supranational institutions have on our dependent variable—ratification of the International Labor Organization's C111, ratification of the International Covenant on Civil and Political Rights (ICCPR), and ratification of the Convention Against All Forms of Discrimination Against Women (CEDAW). Those predictors are not critical for the theoretical framework in this chapter but appear as predictors in

Chapters 5 and 6. In order to maintain similar model specifications across the different chapters of this book, we include them here as well. The exclusion of those variables yields results that are substantively indistinguishable. Date of ratification of C111 of the *International Labor Organization* was coded according to data on the ILO's official website.[2] Dates of ratification of the *ICCPR* and *CEDAW* were coded according to website for the United Nations Human Rights Treaties.[3]

We use time-series cross-sectional data, listing all states in the aforementioned data sets for which data are available from 1972 to 2002. To test Hypotheses 1–7, we employ a generalized estimating equation (GEE) model (Zorn, 2001). A marginal approach, such as the GEE, is appropriate in this case since we are interested generally in what variables influence decriminalization of homosexual acts, rather than the propensity to do so in a particular nation, for which a conditional approach would suffice (p. 475). Since the dependent variable *Legal* is dichotomous (1=homosexual acts are legal; 0=homosexual acts are illegal), and due to the data structure described above, we employ a GEE model with first-order autoregressive component and logit as the link function.

There are various examples that show how decriminalization can be overturned. One of them is the recent case in India discussed in detail in Chapter 2. Another is Russia. Criminalizing homosexuality has a long history in Russia; homosexuality was first banned in the military in 1716 and then banned for all men in 1835 (Sanders, 2009, p. 23). After the revolution, the new legal code instituted in 1922 had no provision prohibiting homosexuality. Even so, Soviet courts worked to repress homosexuality during this period; conversely Soviet academics pushed for reform related to sex and spoke out against criminal punishment for private behavior. The bifurcated nature of government attitudes towards homosexuality changed when Stalin took full control of the country, and in 1934 sodomy was once again banned (Engelstein, 1995). With the fall of the Soviet Union, homosexuality was legalized in Russia in 1993 as part of an attempt to cater to Western Europe (Noble, 2012). However, the situation in Russia has since become worse for homosexuals. The Russian Orthodox Church has taken an emphatic stance against homosexuality and has characterized it as a threat to "the Russian Christian Civilization" (Zorgdrager, 2013).

Since Vladimir Putin's second term as president, the situation has gotten much worse. Whereas sodomy has not been made illegal, gay "propaganda" has been (Bartholomew, 2014). In 2013, President Putin signed into law a prohibition on adoption by singles or same-sex couples from countries that have legalized same-sex marriage (Pinknews, 2013). As late as in 2014 it was reported: "Russian authorities are putting pressure on all kinds of institutions—banks, landlords, employers—not to do business with LGBT people and LGBT organizations" (Michaelson, 2014).

The Russian and Indian cases discussed here are but two examples of the fact that decriminalization can turn around, and repealed provisions can be recalled. Development in the area of decriminalization of sodomy provisions is not necessarily linear. This nature of the data-generation process lends further support to our choice to employ a GEE model with a logistic link function. Finally, we use robust standard errors clustered on the country.

Results

What factors influence the likelihood that consensual same-sex sexual acts are legal? Before we delve into the multivariate analyses, let us examine some descriptive statistics. In our time-series cross-sectional data, which covers 150 nations for a period of over two decades, only 8% of the observations where Common Law is the legal system do not have sodomy provisions on the books. Conversely, in the non-Common Law data points, roughly 50% of the observations have no sodomy provisions on the books. This gap is highly statistically significant.

As for the components of the theory concerning the effects of religion, the descriptive statistics are quite encouraging here as well. For instance, of the observations in our data where there is a presence of religious courts that have jurisdiction over some matters of law beyond family law, nearly 97% have sodomy laws on the books. Conversely, slightly fewer than 45% of the observations where such courts are not present have legally valid sodomy prohibitions. Along the same lines, when there are restrictions sanctioned by the state on interfaith marriage, the likelihood that this state at this point in time also prohibits same-sex sexual relations is over 82%. This number drops precipitously to less than a half (41.7%) when such restrictions are not in place. In sum, when religious prohibitions of various sorts are imposed by the state, the likelihood that this state also prohibits sodomy more than doubles. Let us now examine the multivariate models estimated to test our hypotheses for our key variables, while controlling for the range of alternative effects described above.

Table 4.1 presents the results of the first generalized estimating equation model. This multivariate analysis corroborates several of our hypotheses. The

Table 4.1. Analyses of the Predictors of Repeal of Sodomy Laws (GEE Models)

Variable	Model I (robust standard errors)
Common Law	**-0.43 *** (0.065)**
% Catholic	0.0001 (0.001)
% Muslim	**-0.004 *** (0.001)**
% Protestant	-0.0019 (0.0014)
Religious Court with Broad Jurisdiction	n/a
Restrictions on Interfaith Marriage	n/a
GDP per capita	**0.000011 * (0.000005)**
Democratic Conditions	0.0003 (0.005)
Globalization	**0.0025 ** (0.0010)**
Political Inclusion	-0.0006 (0.002)
CEDAW	**0.045 * (0.023)**
ILO	.063 (.045)
CCPR	.024 (.026)
Ethnic Fractionalization	-0.105 (0.135)
Constant	**0.45 *** (0.12)**

Note: N = 3471; Number of Groups = 150; Observations per group: Min = 1, Avg = 23.1, Max = 30; Wald Chi2 = 229.14; Prob > Chi2 = 0.

coefficient of -.43 on *Common Law* is not only negative—as suggested, having a Common Law legal system significantly decreases the likelihood that the nation has decriminalized homosexual acts—but is also highly significant. Likewise, some of the religion variables have a statistically significant effect. More specifically, the effect of *Percent Muslim* is highly significant and in the anticipated direction. The coefficient of -.004 on this variable indicates that as the percent of Muslims in the nation increases, so does the likelihood of finding sodomy provisions on its books. Notably, those findings hold even when we control for a range of control variables. Let us now examine some of those controls and see how their effects comport with the literature reviewed above.

Our findings lend support to the component of our theory concerning globalization. *Ceteris paribus*, nations with high levels of globalization, are significantly more likely to decriminalize homosexual activity. What is more, our theoretical contentions concerning economic conditions and modernization win support in the data. As gross domestic product (GDP) per capita increases, a nation is less likely to have anti-sodomy laws on its books. This finding is highly significant. We fail to find support for the democratic conditions component of our theory. Neither the variable measuring political inclusion of women (percent of women representatives in the legislature) nor the variable gauging the democratic nature of the polity has a statistically significant effect on the legality of homosexual acts.

Let us now examine a similar set of analyses—only this time while specifying a different test for the effects of religion. As mentioned above, the Fox (2001) dataset is widely regarded as a top-notch source for state and religion issues. Accordingly, and despite the fact that the data we have from that source are limited to the 1990–2003 period, we include two variables from this database in Table 4.2. The first of those two variables, *Restrictions on Interfaith Marriage*, is coded as "Cases where marriages are performed only by clergy—which effectively restricts interfaith marriages." The second variable is *Religious Court with Broad Jurisdiction*, which indicates the "presence of religious courts, which have jurisdiction over some matters of law other than family law and matters of inheritance." When we either replace the measures for religious constituencies with those new variables or simply add them to the specification of the model estimates, we find support for our theory regarding the relations between religion and sodomy laws. The coefficients on the two religion variables in the first model in the table are negative and statistically significant.

Table 4.2. Analyses of the Predictors of Repeal of Sodomy Laws (1990–2003)—with Alternative Measures for Effects of Religion

Variable	Model II (robust standard errors) Fox's variables replacing standard religion variables	Model III (robust standard errors) Fox's variables and standard religion variables
Common Law	**-0.33 *** **(0.08)**	**-0.34 *** (0.003)
% Catholic	n/a	-0.000097 (0.0011)
% Muslim	n/a	**-0.003 ** (0.001)
% Protestant	n/a	-0.003 (0.002)
Religious Court with Broad Jurisdiction	**-0.26 ** **(0.10)**	**-0.2 * (0.1)
Restrictions on Interfaith Marriage	**-0.22 * **(0.1)**	-0.07 (0.13)
GDP per capita	**0.000011 * (0.000005)**	**0.000010 * (0.000006)
Democratic Conditions	0.003 (0.007)	0.002 (0.007)
Globalization	**0.0037 *** (0.0011)**	**0.003 ** (0.001)
Political Inclusion	0.0008 (0.0019)	0.0008 (0.002)
CEDAW	0.06 (0.4)	0.046 (0.042)
ILO	**0.119 * (0.053)**	0.11 * (0.05)
CCPR	0.05 (0.05)	0.067 (0.059)
Ethnic Fractionalization	-0.17 (0.15)	-0.11 (0.14)
Constant	0.2 (0.14)	**0.31 * (0.15)

N = 1560; Number of Groups = 133; Observations per group: Min = 1 Avg = 11.7, Max = 13; Wald Chi2 = 205.25; Prob > Chi2 = 0.0; N = 1541; Number of Groups = 131; Observations per group: Min = 1 Avg = 11.8, Max = 13; Wald Chi2 = 197.34; Prob > Chi2 = 0.0

The findings from the descriptive statistics presented earlier in this chapter are corroborated by these multivariate analyses; controlling for alternative effects, we find that broad jurisdictions granted religious courts—similar to limitations on interfaith marriage sanctioned by the state—would significantly increase the likelihood that this state also prohibits sodomy. The second model in the table probably suffers from over-specification—as there are five different variables measuring religion—but still the effects of religion seem robust with all five predictors indicating the effects of religion, with no exception, exhibiting negative coefficients.

Now that we have established the systematic effects on sodomy provisions of both legal lineage of colonial times (i.e., legal path dependence) as well as religion, we are ready to move on to the next level. In the second half of this chapter, not only do we further develop the theory about legal path dependence to examine how it would present itself in different institutional setups but we also provide a comprehensive set of analyses to examine whether these theoretical notions hold water. Appendix C includes similar analyses separated into the different world regions. The analyses in Appendix C indicate that the findings are not unique to one specific world region. Appendix D includes analyses of sodomy provisions in different religions. The first table in Appendix D includes analyses at different levels of dominance for Muslim constituencies and in circumstances when Islam is the state religion. The second table includes analyses of observations at different levels of dominance for Catholic constituencies. The analyses in Appendix D indicate that the findings are not unique to one specific religion or religious constituency.

Decriminalization of Sodomy via Courts and Legislatures

In 1969 the Canadian parliament passed the Criminal Law Amendment Act. Among other sweeping changes to the existing criminal code, the act decriminalized consensual same-sex relations, effectively repealing sodomy laws, which had been a part of Canadian jurisprudence since its inheritance of the English buggery laws (McLeod, 1996). A mere two years earlier, the Supreme Court of Canada had upheld the conviction of Everett George Klippert, who had been sentenced to an indefinite prison term as a "dangerous sexual offender" for engaging in consensual sex with another man (*Klippert v. the Queen*, 1967). The court's decision elicited strong condemnation from the Canadian legal community, causing Justice Minister Pierre Trudeau to table legislation in the House of Commons to amend the criminal code (Kinsman,

1995). Heavily influenced by the United Kingdom's 1957 Wolfenden Report, the repeal initiative was added to a larger reform effort that called for the creation of a "zone of legal privacy . . . for acts committed between consenting adults." The combination of global trends and legal evolution led to significant policy change emanating from the Canadian legislature and culminated in passage of the 1969 Criminal Law Amendment Act. Change towards decriminalization in Canada took place in the legislature.

Three decades after those events in Canada, the South African Constitutional Court ruled in the aforementioned case of *National Coalition for Gay and Lesbian Equality and Another v. Minister of Justice and Others* (1998) that three legal provisions pertaining to sodomy were all "inconsistent with the Constitution of the Republic of South Africa." They included Section 20A of the Sexual Offences Act of 1957, which banned all sexual contact between males; Schedule 1 of the Criminal Procedure Act of 1977, which prohibited sodomy; and sections of the Security Officers Act of 1987, which excluded men found guilty of committing sodomy from employment as security officers. In this ruling, which was also mentioned in the opening of this book, the court referenced Section 9(3) of the 1996 Constitution in its opinion, which explicitly banned discrimination on the basis of sexual orientation (Jagwanth, 2004). Demonstrating the potential of a strong judiciary backed by a "modern document designed for the 21st century" (Wing, 2008), the South African court found it within its powers to repeal the sodomy provisions.[4]

The aforementioned cases relating to the rights of LGBTIQ from diverse parts of the globe resulted in policy change. Yet, the institutional route leading to change differed significantly. In the first case, repeal of sodomy laws took place in the legislature. In the second, a court of last resort altered the status quo. The theoretical framework proposed here accounts for the two key factors that influence change in sodomy policy: legal path dependence and religious constituencies (and political accountability towards those constituencies). Delving into the influences of those variables helps us to flesh out the mechanisms and institutional paths that explain the effects of religion and legal path dependence on sodomy provisions and their repeal. Let us now examine those institutions up close.

Path Dependence, Sodomy Provisions, and Courts

Courts of last resort are uniquely situated to change sodomy policy despite the path dependent nature of stare decisis (Kahn, 1999, 2006). This does not hold for legislative bodies or even lower-level judicial bodies which, compared to courts of last resort, are more constrained by precedent (Segal & Spaeth, 1996; Songer et al., 1994).[5] This logic leads to a prima facie counterintuitive conclusion that, in certain ways, courts of last resort are *less* constrained by legal status quo than other political and legal actors. In other words, while judicial rulings were identified earlier as one of three pillars supporting legal path dependence as it pertains to sodomy laws, it is a subset of this type of institutions—namely, courts of last resort—that are positioned to change such policy.

Apart from legal path dependence, we expect certain political institutions and arrangements (i.e., the electoral rules that enhance political accountability) to also have an effect, and given the context of sodomy and the discussion in Chapters 1 and 2, this should be particularly true for religious constituencies. More specifically, in the context of sodomy reform, we expect the presence of religious constituencies to influence the locus of policy change. Indeed, research has suggested that these constituencies have a significant impact on the accountability of government officials as well as on the trajectory of public-policy decisions (Adserà et al., 2003; Castles, 1995; Fox, 2001). A crucially important test for our theory, however, is the fact that religious constituencies would constrain legislators but have a more limited effect on justices on the Supreme Court who, by institutional design, are more insulated from the electorate.

Despite the relative isolation of judges from politics, courts of last resort tend to be majoritarian rather than counter-majoritarian bodies. Indeed, the American case is clear evidence to suggest that courts of last resort never stray too far from public opinion (Barnum, 1985; Flemming & Wood, 1997; McCloskey, 2010; Mishler & Sheehan, 1993), or from the views of national elites (Dahl, 1957; Whittington, 2007). The reason is, of course, that judges must compete with legislatures and executives for control over policy while protecting the court as a governing institution. Nonetheless, while judges may have to adjust their decisions to reflect the views of national majorities, their institutional position offers them a unique opportunity to initiate change in the presence of shifting political winds. Thus, the effect of religion on the persistence of sodomy law may be assuaged in the unique institutional position of justices.

Finally, in the analyses presented in this second half of the chapter, we expect globalization trends to similarly influence the introduction of sodomy policy change via judicial and non-judicial bodies. Globalization has a pervasive effect in society. Social, political, and economic globalization affect political entrepreneurs, public opinion, political organizations, as well as social movements (Frank et al., 2009). Such trends, therefore, are likely to equally impact courts, which are engaged in transnational judicial dialogues, as well as legislatures, which are immersed in the globalizing political system. Since the role of courts is seemingly the most complicated one, let us first tackle the question of policy change via courts.

Can Courts Repeal Sodomy Provisions?

Scholarship on American politics has extensively entertained questions concerning courts as policymakers and, more specifically, concerning the way in which courts as policymakers relate to and compare with other institutions (Segal et al., 2011). A common understanding is that not only do courts rarely initiate policy change against the preferences of national majorities (Barnum, 1985; Dahl, 1957; Flemming & Wood, 1997; Funston, 1975; Mishler & Sheehan, 1993), but that courts are in fact incapable of initiating such change and are therefore a "hollow hope" for those seeking social change (Rosenberg, 2008). More recent scholarship, however, has suggested that the interactions between courts and legislatures is better understood as one in which the elected branch actively seeks to involve the judiciary in the policymaking process. Specifically, Graber (1993) and Lovell (2003) have argued that when resolving controversial social issues, elected lawmakers, wary of alienating constituents with strongly held moral convictions, will defer decision-making to courts by delaying action on these issues or by intentionally inviting judicial intervention through vague and ambiguously worded statutes. Much as Dahl had 50 years earlier, Whittington (2007) suggested that courts are often used to reinforce and uphold the policies of the dominant political regime. Given the controversial nature of sodomy reform, this line of reasoning would suggest that policy change is more likely to be initiated by judges in countries where elected officials would prefer to avoid being held accountable for their stance on the issue.

To summarize, legal path dependence leads us to expect not only that the likelihood of legal prohibitions on sodomy in countries with Common Law systems is greater but also that the likelihood of those provisions is diminished in Civil Law countries (which is what we tested empirically in the first half of this chapter). How does legal path dependence, however, relate to differences in the institutional origins of policy change? As we elaborate below, legal path dependence has a divergent impact on judicial and non-judicial branches in Common Law countries.

Legal Path Dependence and Sodomy Repeal in Divergent Institutional Contexts

In the theoretical framework proffered here, legal path dependence and political accountability to religious constituencies have differential effects on policy change emanating from courts of last resort compared with change originating in non-judicial bodies. Courts, legislatures, and executives operate within a system where different institutions compete with one another over spheres of influence (Clinton, 1994; Eskridge, 1994; Shepsle, 1986). While the role of the elected branches of government in policymaking is relatively clear-cut, debates in the literature still exist concerning the extent to which courts function in the capacity of policy changers (Keck, 2009; Klarman, 2004; Rosenberg, 2008).

Yet, as the examples from South Africa and Canada (as well as other cases including Chile, the United States, Ecuador, and elsewhere) demonstrate, sodomy policy transfigures in both judicial and non-judicial contexts. The key question, therefore, is not whether courts can initiate policy change. Clearly judicial institutions are able to lead to policy change. Rather, we are interested in the difference in the *predictors of change* in sodomy provisions emanating from each type of institution. It is this comparison between repeal in different types of institutions, which provides us with an additional and important empirical test for our theory concerning legal path dependence.

To examine the alternative institutional setups for repeal of sodomy law, we first examine the motivations underlying actions of those different decision-making bodies, and then we analyze the differential effects of legal path dependence in each. In addition, we discuss the importance of political institutions insofar as political accountability dictates a differential effect of religious constituencies on decision makers in non-judicial bodies compared to judicial ones.

Motivations of judicial and non-judicial bodies differ. Reelection is a major motivation for elected officials, and their policymaking unfolds accordingly (Fenno, 1996; Jacobson, 2004; Kingdon, 1989). On the other hand, the introduction of policy change by courts may add to the court's legitimacy *as long as* such policies are respected and upheld (Lovell, 2003; McCloskey, 2010; Tushnet, 1999; Whittington, 2007).

Although a parallel argument can be made about the introduction of successful policy change by non-judicial bodies, questions about institutional legitimacy are particularly concerning for judicial bodies. This is because the judiciary lacks, as Hamilton put it, "influence over either the sword or the purse" (Federalist Paper 78). Courts therefore face potential challenges to their legitimacy both in terms of their lack of electoral accountability as well as the danger that their pronouncements either will face significant delays in their implementation (Rosenberg, 1991) or be ignored altogether. On the other hand, by embedding changing social, political, and economic realities in legal precedent, judges increase the likelihood that their decisions will be accorded respect and support by both political elites and the public (Kahn, 1999, p. 43).

Granted, active attempts at altering the status quo, as in the case of the repeal of sodomy laws, will likely be more challenging for judicial as well as non-judicial actors than a more passive affirmation of existing status quo. All of this is not to suggest that non-judicial officials are themselves unconcerned with the success or failure of their own attempts at policy change. At least in the American context, the "perpetual tension" between Congress and the president can at times lead one branch to frustrate the attempts at policy change of the other (Kahn, 1999). In addition, failed efforts at policy change by the elected branches are sometimes the result of courts striking down statutes passed by the legislature (see also Clark, 2009; Glick, 2009; Rasmusen, 1994). Finally, the judiciary has at times also challenged policy initiatives undertaken by the executive (e.g., in the context of war powers, see Fisher (2005) and Brandon (2005)). Nevertheless, the constraints on non-judicial policymaking authority are primarily political (Fenno, 1996; Kingdon, 1989; Mayhew, 1974; inter alia).

The process through which law and politics mutually construct each other, combined with the unique institutional position of courts of last resort, lead to the somewhat counterintuitive conclusion that, in some instances, courts of last resort are less constrained by the legal status quo of sodomy prohibitions (Kahn, 2006; Segal & Spaeth, 1996, 2003).[6] Key to our argument is the notion that, compared to the decision-making process in non-judicial institutions, the effects of legal path dependence on decision making in courts of last resort are commensurably *weaker*.

Despite our identification in Chapters 1 and 2 of court rulings as the third pillar of legal path dependence sustaining the longevity of sodomy provisions, upon closer inspection, the special role we ascribe to courts of last resort here in upsetting the status quo should not be surprising. It is features of these institutions that support this notion. Examine, for instance, Chief Justice Marshall's view in the opinion he delivered for the court in *Marbury v. Madison*: "It is emphatically the province and duty of the Judicial Department to say what the law is." Justices in a court of last resort are in a position to recognize changes taking place in society and, by institutional design, are free to act accordingly. These justices have the (often exclusive) privilege to interpret constitutional and statutory law, typically enjoy long tenures (life appointments in many cases), have no superior court to overrule their decisions, and in certain cases can even set their own agenda (Segal & Spaeth, 2003; Sommer, 2014).

Furthermore, legal decision making does not amount to a dry application of legal principle. To justify a change in policy, judges must show that existing precedents are unreasonable or mistaken. In *Lawrence v. Texas*, for instance, the United States Supreme Court announced that it had misapprehended the liberty claim presented in *Bowers v. Hardwick*, as well as overstated the historical premises upon which the decision had been based. Consequently, the court ruled that *Bowers* amounted to an invalid interpretation of the constitution and was thus subject to reversal.

The readers may want to return to the quotation from the South African Supreme Court, found at the opening of this book, to observe something similar. What is more, scholars have argued that, unlike lower courts, a Supreme Court is not always bound by its own decisions (Cooper, 1988; Hathaway, 2003). The unique institutional position enjoyed by courts of last resort, combined with judicial detachment from the vagaries of day-to-day political reality, enable judges to recognize when competing claims in the polity make social change possible (Kahn, 1999).

The way we conceptualize the legal status quo is not as black-letter law but rather as the set of rules that comprehensively organizes and constitutes the political, social, and economic spheres (Brigham, 1999; Ewick & Silbey, 1998, 1999; Kahn, 2006). Constitutional separation of powers and checks and balances work to ensure that precedent operates as a significant constraint on legislative bodies. For instance, this principle forbids elected officials from ignoring precedent just for the reason that they disagree with the court's decision.

The argument developed here goes deeper; since the legal status quo is entrenched in various aspects of the political, social, and economic systems, path dependence operates as a significant constraint on legislative bodies, rather than on courts. Introducing a controversial policy game changer that would lead to the repeal of the state's sodomy provisions may be prohibitively costly for legislators who operate in a political system and in a society that are organized according to the existing legal state of affairs. Constituencies, interest groups, social organizations, parties, economic bodies, and financial institutions all work within the framework of existing policy and thus typically favor the status quo. In turn, elected officials are held accountable to such groups via the institution of elections, which maps performance onto reelection.

Due to sunk costs, vested interests, and path dependence, constituencies, interest groups, and organizations would resist change and make the introduction of legal reform prohibitively costly for legislators. In a country where sodomy provisions have been on the books, justices in the court of last resort may under certain circumstances be at greater liberty to introduce policy change than are elected officials in the legislature. This is a counterintuitive proposition that is derived from our theory concerning legal path dependence and that later in this chapter is subject to an empirical test.

It is in the context of a contentious issue such as sodomy reform, that introducing a controversial policy change may prove particularly costly for elected officials. Such officials may seek to avoid the public pursuit of controversial policy goals (Graber, 1993). In the context of sodomy reform, it is no wonder that many elected officials have refused to come out in support of "a group of people despised by virtually everyone . . . condemned by every significant religious tradition, and pathologized by scientific experts" (D'Emilio, 2006). In contrast, courts are more autonomous when it comes to ordinary politics. Indeed, under certain circumstances, their independence leads judicial decision makers, particularly in courts of last resort, to "ignore, resist and even disregard robust political pressure" (Kahn & Kersch, 2006, p. 18).

The theory canvassed thus far lends itself to two interesting empirical tests. The paths to policy change in Common Law compared to Civil Law countries will not be the same, and the institutional web supporting this legal path dependence not only is critical for its understanding but also offers us an interesting empirical test (Merryman & Perez-Perdomo, 2007, pp. 46–47).

First, we expect that having a Common Law system would decrease the likelihood of legislative repeal of sodomy because elected officials are confined to work within the boundaries of existing precedent. Second, a system of Common Law would not have the same effect on courts of last resort as they are less constrained by path dependence and by the legal status quo. In Common Law systems, the constraints generated by legal path dependence on change in sodomy law tend to limit non-judicial rather than judicial institutions, thereby increasing the likelihood of judicial repeal. Since their operation is closely intertwined with the political, social, and economic systems, non-judicial institutions in Common Law systems are more constrained by the legal state of affairs than the somewhat autonomous judicial bodies. This would translate empirically into a differential effect of the legal system.

Testing the Effects of Institutional Settings on the Repeal of Sodomy Laws

To test whether these theoretical notions hold water, we offer here two sets of regression models. First is a GEE time-series cross-sectional analysis and then a multinomial logistic regression with year dummies. The dependent variable for the multinomial logit, *Repeal Type*, has three levels—0 for no repeal, 1 for non-judicial repeal, and 2 for judicial repeal. For the GEE analyses, three dependent variables are coded. *Legal* indicates whether a country decriminalized sodomy (1 if sodomy is legal, 0 otherwise).[7] The second dependent variable for the GEE models is *Court Repeal*, which is coded 1 for countries where repeal happened in court in the three decades following 1972, and 0 otherwise. *Non-Judicial Repeal*, which is equal to 1 when non-judicial institutions repealed sodomy, and 0 otherwise, is the third dependent variable for the GEE models. Similar to the models presented earlier in this book, data for all outcome variables are taken from the May 2009 report of the International Lesbian, Gay, Bisexual, Trans and Intersex Association.[8]

The original data collected indicate that from 1972 to 2002, nine countries repealed their sodomy provisions via judicial institutions while 35 countries repealed such statutes via non-judicial institutions. Other than in Fiji, where repeal originated with the executive, the legal measure against sodomy was revoked by the legislature in all other such cases. All countries are listed in Table 4.3 with an indication of the institutional location of change where policy was altered.

Given common wisdom about policy emanating from the political branches, the fact that over 20% of the repeals in the three decades under examination here were via the judicial path further underscores the significance of the closer look we take at the *institutional mechanisms* explaining legal path dependence and the effects of religion. The predictors in the multivariate models that follow are coded the same way as in the models presented earlier in this chapter.

Results

Table 4.4 offers a first insight into the way legal path dependence operates within disparate institutional setups. The first two models examine court repeal as the dependent variable. The difference between the two is the specification of the predictors pertaining to the effects of religion. In the first model,

Table 4.3. Institutional Contexts of Sodomy Provisions (1972–2008)

Sodomy provisions

Change from illegal to legal status (institutional path for policy change)	*No policy change*

Albania (legislative repeal in 1995)
Armenia (legislative repeal in 2003)
Australia (judicial repeal in 1994)
Austria (legislative repeal in 1971)
Azerbaijan (legislative repeal in 2000)
Bahamas (legislative repeal in 1991)
Bahrain (legislative repeal in 1976)
Belarus (legislative repeal in 1994)
Bosnia and Herzegovina
    (legislative repeal in 1998)
Cape Verde (legislative repeal in 2004)
Chile (legislative repeal in 1999)
China (legislative repeal in 1997)
Colombia (legislative repeal in 1981)
Croatia (legislative repeal in 1977)
Cuba (legislative repeal in 1979)
Cyprus (judicial repeal in 1998)
Ecuador (judicial repeal in 1997)
Estonia (legislative repeal in 1992)
Fiji (executive repeal in 2005)
Finland (legislative repeal in 1971)
Georgia (legislative repeal in 2000)
Ireland (judicial repeal in 1993)
Israel (legislative repeal in 1988)
Kazakhstan (legislative repeal in 1998)
Kyrgyzstan (legislative repeal in 1998)
Latvia (legislative repeal in 1992)
Liechtenstein (legislative repeal in 1989)
Lithuania (legislative repeal in 1993)
Macedonia (legislative repeal in 1996)
Malta (legislative repeal in 1973)
Moldova (legislative repeal in 1995)
Nepal (judicial repeal in 2007)
New Zealand (legislative repeal in 1986)
Nicaragua (legislative repeal in 2008)
Norway (legislative repeal in 1972)
Portugal (legislative repeal in 1983)
Romania (legislative repeal in 1996)
Russian Federation (legislative
    repeal in 1993)
	Homosexual Intercourse has been illegal at least since 1972:
	
	Afghanistan; Algeria; Andorra; Angola; Antigua and Barbuda; Bangladesh; Barbados; Belize; Bhutan; Botswana; Brunei Darussalam; Cameroon; Comoros; Djibouti; Dominica; Egypt; Eritrea; Ethiopia (-1992); Ethiopia (1993-); Gambia; Ghana; Grenada; Guinea; Guyana; India; Iran; Iraq; Jamaica; Kenya; Kiribati; Lebanon; Lesotho; Liberia; Libya; Malawi; Malaysia; Maldives; Mauritania; Mauritius; Micronesia; Morocco; Mozambique; Myanmar; Namibia; Nauru; Nigeria; Oman; Pakistan; Palau; Papua New Guinea; Qatar; Samoa; Sao Tome and Principe; Saudi Arabia; Senegal; Seychelles; Sierra Leone; Singapore; Solomon Islands; Somalia; Sri Lanka; St Kitts and Nevis; St Lucia; St Vincent and the Grenadines; Sudan; Swaziland; Syria; Tanzania; Tibet; Timor-Leste; Togo; Tonga; Trinidad and Tobago; Tunisia; Turkmenistan; Tuvalu; USSR; Uganda; United Arab Emirates; Uzbekistan; Vanuatu; Vietnam; Vietnam, South; Yemen; Yemen, North; Yemen, South; Zambia; Zanzibar; Zimbabwe
	
	Homosexual Intercourse has been legal at least since 1972:
	
	Argentina; Belgium; Benin; Bolivia; Brazil; Bulgaria; Burkina Faso; Cambodia; Canada; Central African Republic; Chad; Congo; Congo, Democratic Republic; Costa Rica; Cote d'Ivoire; Czech Republic; Czechoslovakia; Denmark; Dominican Republic; El Salvador; Equatorial Guinea; France; Gabon; Germany, West; Greece; Guatemala; Haiti; Honduras; Hungary; Iceland; Indonesia; Italy; Japan;

Table 4.3. (continued)

	Sodomy provisions
Change from illegal to legal status (institutional path for policy change)	No policy change
Serbia (legislative repeal in 1994)	*Homosexual Intercourse has been legal at least since 1972 (continued):*
Slovenia (legislative repeal in 1977)	
South Africa (judicial repeal in 1998)	Jordan; Korea, North; Korea, South; Laos;
Spain (legislative repeal in 1979)	Luxembourg; Madagascar; Mali; Mexico;
Tajikistan (legislative repeal in 1998)	Monaco; Mongolia; Netherlands; Niger; Paraguay; Peru; Philippines; Poland; Rwanda; San Marino; Slovakia; Suriname; Sweden; Switzerland; Taiwan; Thailand; Turkey; Uruguay; Venezuela; Vietnam, North
Ukraine (legislative repeal in 1991)	
United Kingdom (judicial repeal in 1982)	
United States (judicial repeal in 2003)	
Yugoslavia (legislative repeal in 1994)	

Note: [i]Republika Srpska in 2000. [ii]Homosexual acts are also legal in all Chinese associates; Hong Kong (1991) and Macau (1996). [iii]The sodomy statutes were declared unconstitutional and unenforceable by Supreme Court Justice Gerard Winter on 26 August 2005, but they are still on the books. [iv]Sodomy decriminalized by a Supreme Court decision on 21 December 2007. [v]England and Wales (1967), Northern Ireland (1982), Scotland (1981). [vi]There is no general prohibition on homosexual acts in the penal code. However, statutes on offences against the religion, morality and debauchery are used to prosecute homosexual and bisexual men in particular. [vii]East Germany (1968) and West Germany (1969). [viii]Homosexual acts are also legal in Aruba and the Netherlands Antilles.

the sizes of the different religious constituencies are specified. The two variables from the Fox (2003) database, which were mentioned above, replace them in the specification of the second model.

Legal path dependence in Common Law countries have no significant effect on the likelihood of judicial repeal. Indeed the coefficient on *Path Dependence* is positive, which is the opposite of what was hypothesized. Likewise, we expected that religion would have no effect on cases where courts engage in repeal of sodomy laws, since the nature of judicial institutions is such that in the lack of accountability, popular pressure is minimized. As expected, based on extant literature, however, GDP per capita and previous political inclusion of other minority groups (e.g., women) significantly increase the likelihood of repeal of sodomy provisions via courts.

The story is distinctly different in the third and fourth models, where the dependent variable is repeal via non-judicial institutions. The difference between those two models, similar to the difference between the first and second models, is the specification of the variables tapping into the effects of religion on the likelihood of repeal of sodomy laws. The third model shows a very strong effect for legal path dependence; the coefficient is negative (-.3) and highly significant. Legal path dependence strongly depresses the likelihood of non-judicial repeal. The same is evidently true in the fourth model, where the coefficient on *Path Dependence* is still highly significant and of comparable magnitude (-.25). The other interesting story is that of the effects of religion. In the third model, we find that having a large Muslim constituency significantly decreases the likelihood of repeal via non-judicial institutions. Such institutions are less likely to upset religious constituencies that deem same-sex sexual relations illegitimate because of the religious instructions of their faith.

Corroborating this finding, the effect of an alternative measure for the effects of religion on the likelihood of non-judicial repeal in the fourth model in the table is also negative and highly significant. *Restrictions on Interfaith Marriage* has a coefficient of -.21, which is statistically significant. This is an indication for the influence of religion on the state, which ultimately yields pressure on legislators not to reform sodomy laws in a way that would violate religious commandments.

In sum, the path dependent nature of legal development in Common Law systems influences non-judicial institutions when they attempt to reform policy related to sodomy law. Furthermore, the electoral link hypothesis wins support. The coefficient on *Percent Muslims* is negative and significant. GDP per capita significantly increases the likelihood of repeal in both judicial and non-judicial settings. Whereas democratic conditions do not seem to have an effect, globalization significantly increases the likelihood of legislative repeal. Political inclusion of women, on the other hand, increases the likelihood of judicial repeal while it decreases the likelihood of non-judicial measures. Certain international effects seem to also be in place. In particular, CEDAW decreases the likelihood of repeal measures emanating from judicial institutions. Yet, repeal via the non-judicial path seems to be more likely when a country is a CEDAW signatory. We go into great detail in discussing such international effects in the next chapter.

As for the robustness check using a multinomial logistic regression model, *Repeal Type* is the outcome variable in Table 4.5. Similar to the GEE models estimated above, the predictors for repeal by non-judicial institutions (presented at the top of the table) are largely in support of our hypotheses. Legal path dependence in Common Law countries decreases the likelihood of repeal via the legislature. Religious constituencies have a similar effect—the larger those constituencies are, the less likely would legislative repeal be. Globalization increases the likelihood of legislative repeal. Lastly, democratic conditions increase the likelihood of legislative repeal.

Table 4.4. Repeal of Sodomy Provisions via Judicial and Non-judicial Institutions

Variable	Model I (robust standard errors) court repeal	Model II (robust standard errors) court repeal + Fox's variables replacing standard religion variables	Model III (robust standard errors) legislative repeal	Model IV (robust standard errors) legislative repeal + Fox's variables replacing standard religion variables
Common Law	0.021 (0.025)	-0.007 (0.023)	**-0.3 *** (0.06)	**-0.25 *** (0.07)
% Catholic	0.00003 (0.0006)	n/a	0.00009 (0.0013)	n/a
% Muslim	-0.0001 (0.0003)	n/a	**-0.0020 * (0.0009)**	n/a
% Protestant	-0.0007 (0.0008)	n/a	0.001 (0.001)	n/a
Religious Court with Broad Jurisdiction	n/a	-0.005 (0.019)	n/a	-0.11 (0.09)
Restrictions on Interfaith Marriage	n/a	-0.05 (0.03)	n/a	**-0.21 * (0.11)**
GDP per capita	**0.000013 * (0.000007)**	**0.000016 * (0.000009)**	**0.00001 * (0.000005)**	0.00001 (0.000007)
Democratic Conditions	0.001 (0.003)	0.0002 (0.003)	0.012 (0.008)	0.002 (0.01)
Globalization	0.0002 (0.0008)	0.001 (0.001)	**0.002 * (0.001)**	**0.005 *** (0.001)**
Political Inclusion	**0.0048 * (0.0025)**	**0.005 * (0.002)**	-0.003 (0.003)	**-0.0037 * (0.0020)**
CEDAW	-0.011 (0.011)	**-0.033 * (0.018)**	**0.09 ** (0.03)**	0.071 (0.052)
ILO	0.019 (0.025)	0.038 (0.025)	0.04 (0.06)	0.036 (0.05)
CCPR	0.028 (0.023)	0.04 (0.04)	0.02 (0.03)	0.091 (0.084)

Table 4.4. (continued)

Variable	Model I (robust standard errors) court repeal	Model II (robust standard errors) court repeal + Fox's variables replacing standard religion variables	Model III (robust standard errors) legislative repeal	Model IV (robust standard errors) legislative repeal + Fox's variables replacing standard religion variables
Ethnic Fractionalization	0.05 (0.07)	0.07 (0.06)	-0.07 (0.11)	-0.15 (0.14)
Constant	-0.14 (0.09)	**-0.23 * (0.12)**	0.11 (0.12)	-0.05 (0.14)

N = 1743
Number of Groups = 85
Observations per group: Min = 1
Avg = 20.5
Max = 30
Wald Chi2 = 17.1
Prob > Chi2 = 0.1459

N = 739
Number of Groups = 71
Observations per group: Min = 1 Avg = 10.4
Max = 13
Wald Chi2 = 12.16
Prob > Chi2 = 0.3518

* data limited to the period from 1990–2003
* the variable for interfaith marriage is coded in the Fox database as: "Restrictions on interfaith marriages, 1990 or earliest (Cases where marriages are performed only by clergy - which effectively restricts interfaith marriages - are also coded"
* the predictor for religious courts is coded in the Fox database as: "Presence of religious courts, which have jurisdiction over some matters of law other than family law and matters of inheritance"

N = 1995
Number of Groups = 93
Observations per group: Min = 1
Avg = 21.5
Max = 30
Wald Chi2 = 62.56
Prob > Chi2 = 0.0

N = 927
Number of Groups = 84
Observations per group: Min = 1
Avg = 11
Max = 13
Wald Chi2 = 72.58
Prob > Chi2 = 0.0

* data limited to the period from 1990–2003
* the variable for interfaith marriage is coded in the Fox database as: "Restrictions on interfaith marriages, 1990 or earliest (Cases where marriages are performed only by clergy - which effectively restricts interfaith marriages - are also coded"
* the predictor for religious courts is coded in the Fox database as: "Presence of religious courts, which have jurisdiction over some matters of law other than family law and matters of inheritance"

Table 4.5. Multinomial Logistic Regression Model: Analyses of Repeal of Laws Criminalizing Same-Sex Sex (1972–2002)

Variable	All Countries
Repeal by non-Judicial Institutions	
Common Law	-1.46 ***
	(0.18)
% Muslim	-0.009 ***
	(0.002)
% Catholic	-0.005 **
	(0.002)
Democratic Conditions	0.09 ***
	(0.014)
Globalization	0.037 ***
	(0.006)
GDP	-0.00002
	(0.000012)
Constant	-3.5 ***
	(0.38)
Repeal by Judicial Institutions	
Common Law	3.38 ***
	(0.31)
% Muslim	-0.018
	(0.017)
% Catholic	0.008
	(0.006)
Democratic Conditions	0.33 ***
	(0.08)
Globalization	0.05 ***
	(0.01)
GDP	0.00001
	(0.00002)
Constant	-11.1 ***
	(1.6)
	N = 4376; Wald χ^2 = 18746.6
	Prob > χ^2 = 0.0; Pseudo R^2 = 0.3

Note. Dummies for years not presented in the table.
Due to issues of data availability, the following countries were not included in the analyses: Afghanistan, Andorra, Angola, Antigua and Barbuda, Bahamas, Barbados, Belize, Brunei, Darussalam, Cape Verde, Comoros, Czechoslovakia, Djibouti, Dominica, Equatorial Guinea, Eritrea, East Germany, West Germany, Grenada, Guinea, Haiti, Iceland, Iraq, Kiribati, North Korea, Laos, Liberia, Libya, Liechtenstein, Luxemburg, Marshall Islands, Mauritania, Micronesia, Monaco, Nauru, Niger, Palau, Samoa, San Marino, Sao Tome and Principe, Seychelles, Solomon Islands, Somalia, St Kitts and Nevis, St Lucia, St Vincent and the Grenadines, Suriname, Taiwan, Tibet, Timor-Leste, Tonga, Tuvalu, USSR, Uzbekistan, Vanuatu, North and South Vietnam, North and South Yemen, Yugoslavia, Zanzibar. Values for the globalization variables are not available for these countries.
***$p < 0.001$; **$p < 0.01$; *$p < 0.05$; #$p < 0.1$; one-tailed tests where directionality hypothesized.

As for judicial repeal, a Common Law legal system increases the likelihood of repeal. Political accountability to religious constituencies does not have a statistically significant influence. Judicial repeal is more likely when the country is more democratic and more globalized. The effect of GDP is not significantly different from zero.

Overall, legal path dependence decreases the likelihood of repeal in Common Law countries and increases this likelihood in systems of Civil Law; this finding is well established given the empirical tests presented in the first half of this chapter. Yet, this finding, which supports our theoretical framework, is complemented by the findings in the second half of the chapter, which delves more deeply into the predictions derived from our theory concerning the effects of legal path dependence. We hypothesize and then find support for the notion that legal path dependence is considerably more substantial where the legislative path is concerned.

Between the multinomial logit analyses and the GEE models, the results lend robust support for this theory. Tables 4.4 and 4.5 confirm that judicial and non-judicial institutions introduce policy change under dissimilar circumstances. In Common Law systems, the juxtaposition of the two tables indicates legislatures are less likely to be the venues for policy innovation. Courts of last resort, on the other hand, are either more likely or as likely to introduce policy change.

An overwhelming majority of Civil Law countries repealing sodomy laws between 1972 and 2002 saw those provisions rescinded in non-judicial institutions; in 97% of the cases, when a sodomy provision was repealed in a Civil Law country, the decision was non-judicial. Conversely, courts have been considerably more popular as venues for repeal in Common Law countries where, in 64% of the cases, the institutional path to policy change was judicial. The influence of religion has a statistically significant effect on legislative repeal but no significant effect on judicial repeal. There is an impact on the likelihood of the introduction of policy change in legislatures; conversely, courts as initiators of policy innovation in the realm of sodomy laws are largely unaffected by the influence of religion in state matters.

5

Equalization of Rights

In this chapter we move on to the next level of gay rights—namely, equality under the law. In Chapter 3 we examine death penalty for sodomy, in Chapter 4 the repeal of sodomy provisions, and in this chapter we examine equality under the law in the context of employment rights. More broadly, rights are codified in a variety of ways in different countries. Yet, only some have banned discrimination on the basis of sexual orientation in court rulings or by statutory or constitutional provisions (Greenberg et al., 1993; Moustafa, 2003; Sartori, 1994; Sathe, 2004; Songer & Johnson, 2007; Stone Sweet, 2000; Widner, 2001). Legislation passed in Costa Rica, for instance, prohibits discrimination against gays in the workplace and elsewhere (Lester, 2012). Likewise, certain constitutions, such as the South African constitution, which we mention several times in this book, ban discrimination on the basis of sexual orientation (Gibson, 2004; Gloppen, 2005; Haynie, 1994, 2003; Schmid, 2000). What is more, according to a 2013 report on the BBC, "nearly 90% of Fortune 500 companies already have their own policies prohibiting discrimination based on sexual orientation" (Alsop, 2013). While such a trend in the corporate world may have far-reaching implications, in this book we focus on the higher level of states and their legal and political institutions.

Whereas Costa Rica, South Africa, and other nations have those rights on the books, the general picture for gay individuals worldwide is rather bleak. The majority of countries, including some established democracies, have yet

Figure 5.1. Distribution of Sodomy Laws around the World and over Time (1975–2005)

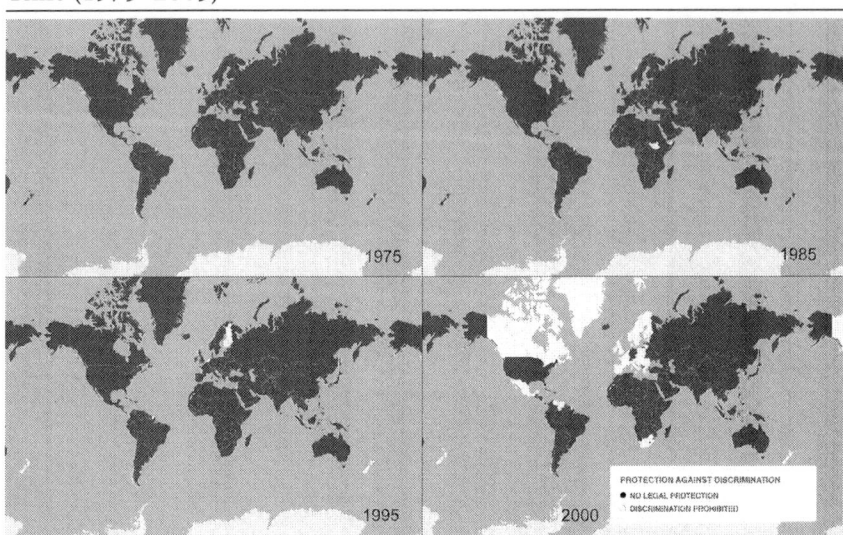

to include in their legal code a prohibition against discrimination on the basis of sexual orientation in the workplace. Figure 5.1 shows the progression over time of legal provisions prohibiting discrimination in the workplace based on sexual orientation. The countries in grey are those where no such provisions are on the books. The territories in white, on the other hand, are places where discrimination on the basis of sexual orientation is prohibited by law. The panels from the top left show the state of affairs in 1975, 1985, 1995, and 2005. While there was virtually no change at all between 1975 and 1985, by 1995 some countries in Europe (e.g., the Netherlands) prohibited discrimination based on sexual orientation. This number increases quite considerably by the middle of the following decade.

This chapter makes several important contributions to our discussion of gay rights and further develops the overall story we tell. At the level of theory, equality under the law is crucially important for the political inclusion, recognition, and empowerment of a minority group. In fact, some argue that basic rights, such as the right not to be discriminated against in employment, are stepping-stones for full equality under the law in all aspects of life (for instance, in marriage (Merin, 2002) and otherwise (Waaldijk, 2000)). Sanders (1996) also identifies stages in state practices towards LGBT individuals, where following decriminalization, which entails the repeal of legal prohibitions against same-sex sex, "enactment of antidiscrimination laws" comes next (p. 18). Sanders's formulation goes hand in hand with our own conceptualization in this book of LGBTIQ rights and their progression.

This chapter focuses on legal guarantees against discrimination. In line with some of the more recent literature on this topic, in order to explain this next level of gay rights, we are in need of explanatory variables that go beyond colonial legal heritage or the effects of religious constituencies. In fact, recent scholarship suggests that in order to explain equalization of legal rights for sexual minorities, one should examine influences that go beyond the nation-state (Lester, 2012, inter alia). In his influential work Kirby (2013), for instance, discusses several international influences that may lead in this direction. Those include, but are not limited to, international organizations such as UN agencies, international courts, and other transnational organizations and bodies such as commonwealth organizations. Simply put, equalization of rights for LGBT (for instance, in the workplace) requires global and external powers in addition to internal influence.

Accordingly, in this chapter we expand our theoretical framework into one that identifies two groups of variables predicting equality—domestic as well as global. Let us start with the group of domestic predictors. The key variable in this group is political inclusion spillover from one minority group to another. The impact of supranational institutions (such as the International Labor Organization) and globalization belong in the second group. Accordingly, our work extends the "norm cascade" argument (Finnemore & Sikkink, 1998) both to the global field, as it relates to the rights of the LGBT community, and to the domestic playing field of rights, where it has been explored much less.

The findings in this chapter highlight the importance—in the context of gay rights—of how inclusion of one group can influence the inclusion of another as well as the impact a commitment to international treaties and institutions can have on the legal protections sexual minorities enjoy. Our findings suggest that this *combination* of domestic and international factors influences the likelihood that a government would protect LGBT individuals from sexual orientation discrimination in the workplace.

Explaining Rights

The right not to be discriminated against in employment is fundamental to the ability to sustain oneself and to support a family as much as it is critical for the realization of one's dreams and aspirations. While not always analyzed in a quantitative, systematic fashion, discrimination has been studied in a variety of contexts (e.g., marriage in Merin, 2002; Waaldijk, 2000; and Rayside, 2008). We focus on discrimination in employment (Wintemute, 1995, p. 13). It is important to recognize at the outset that legal recognition may not always translate into equality on the ground (Epp, 1996).[1] Still, we argue, the legal codification of rights is often meaningful and worth focusing on (Wintemute, 1995; Graupner & Tahmindjis, 2005). While a court decision or a legal measure prohibiting discrimination may fail to translate into full equality for the minority it aims to protect, having the right etched into law has a declaratory value, is educational, and provides members of the minority group with venues to claim redress (McCann, 1994; Sanders, 1996).

Although de jure changes are not the same as de facto practices, focusing on the former helps map the first steps in potential improvements in the latter. As Justice Kennedy of the United States Supreme Court noted in *Lawrence v. Texas* (539 U.S. 558 [2003]), if "homosexual conduct is made criminal by the law of the State, that declaration in and of itself is an invitation to subject homosexual persons to discrimination both in the public and the private spheres."

What might be intuitively considered the predictors of guarantees of rights may in fact be only somewhat accurate. Indeed, assumptions about which countries would be on the cutting edge of equality under the law for sexual minorities are often incorrect. It might be expected that the Netherlands, a country that has a history of political inclusion, would be one of the first countries in 1992 to prohibit employment discrimination based on sexual orientation. Yet, on the other hand, a country such as the United States that has been at the forefront of laws against discrimination since the 1960s is yet to enforce laws protecting sexual minorities in employment.[2] To further examine the systematic influences on the guarantees of rights, we now turn to discuss the two groups of sources of rights—domestic and global—and their causal mechanisms.

Domestic Forces

The first group of predictors of rights relates to the level of domestic politics. In the theoretical framework developed here, the key predictor in this group is a spillover effect due to past political inclusion of other minority groups. In addition, we examine the effects of religion and culture as systematic predictors.

Political Inclusion and Domestic Norm Spillover

The inclusion of other previously excluded groups has a spillover effect, wherein existing legal prohibitions on discrimination are extended to additional groups (gays in our case). In this study we focus on the spillover effect created by the inclusion of women, which is another area where law and politics intertwine in the context of gender and sexuality. As more women are elected members of parliament, the passage of laws taking women's concerns into account increases (Meyer, 2003; Swers, 2001, 2002; Vega & Firestone, 1995). This is particularly true, when the presence of women legislators is substantial (Berkman & O'Connor, 1993; Grey, 2002) and has implications for other branches of government as well (Deitch, 1993; Manfredi, 2004).

Key to our argument, thus, is the notion that when women are included as active participants in the political process, they can serve as a reference group to other types of minorities. Political inclusion and legal equality for women would spur sexual minorities to become more active, mobilize, and eventually form a support structure of organized political activity and advocacy. Such a support structure is a key condition for the legal protection of the rights of those minority groups (Baird, 2004, 2007; Epp, 1996, 1998).

As more groups are included, the likelihood of inclusion generally increases. Elements of the very same support structure that had been conducive to women rights may in fact be instrumental in the context of LGBT rights. If we take the American case as an example, certain groups such as the American Civil Liberties Union (ACLU), which had been pivotal in the fight for women's equality, became also heavily involved in efforts to guarantee LGBT rights (see for instance, the ACLU involvement in the decision of the Supreme Court in *Romer v. Evans* as a friend of the court as well as in earlier campaigns for women's rights. This case is discussed in greater detail in the next chapter).

In addition to mobilization of other minority groups, the inclusion of women is likely to either be a part of a general trend in the direction of inclusion of underrepresented minorities or facilitate such a trend. Robinson and Spivey (2007) indicate that women's inclusion is an exceptionally good proxy for the political inclusion of the other in the context of gender and sex. In sum, the support structure for the inclusion of women and the trend towards inclusion more generally are likely to serve as the infrastructure for the political inclusion of sexual minorities. Hence, the inclusion of women would cause a spillover effect and would thus be a predictor of guarantees of rights for LGBT individuals (Sommer & Asal, 2014).

The Effects of Culture and Religion

Beyond the effect of political inclusion spillover from women to sexual minorities, we identify culture and religion as predictors as well. This, we believe, is true beyond certain cases where it has been shown to be the case (e.g., in Costa Rica in Lester, 2012), but rather more systematically. Frank and McEneaney (1999) do not find effects of the nation's religiosity on policies pertaining to sexual minorities. However, the research question in Frank and McEneaney (1999) concerns decriminalization rather than equality under the law. On the other hand, according to Wald et al. (1996), due to "communal protest" against social practices that threaten tradition, groups will react to potential changes in the political status quo. In the context of rights for LGBT individuals, this is true in particular for religious groups (Wald et al., 1996, p. 1161). Indeed, Wald and his colleagues examine the effect of Protestant communities and find a significant effect.

While that study pertained to the American context, ours is placed within a comparative framework. Thus, examination of the effects of additional religious groups is in place. While its origins are Judeo-Christian, the proscription on sexual relations between people of the same sex is found in other religions as well. Islam condemns same-sex intercourse. Not all nations with a Muslim majority treat same-sex related activity as a crime. For instance, no prohibitions against same-sex intercourse exist in certain nations with a large Muslim constituency because these countries are relatively secular in nature (Indonesia), are multi-religious, or because tolerance of same-sex related activity has been entrenched in the system for years (Turkey). Yet, we do expect that there is considerable pressure on public officials not to advance gay rights in nations with a strong Muslim constituency.

Akin to Islam, Catholicism also condemns sexual relations between members of the same sex as sinful. Therefore, we predict that the higher the percentage of Catholics in the population, the greater the likelihood that the country will fail to prohibit discrimination in employment against gays. We examine the effect of the dominance of religions with Judeo-Christian origins in countries worldwide, and we expect the likelihood of discrimination to increase with the size of the religious group. As in other chapters in this book, the hypothesized effect of religion on the legal status of homosexuals is probabilistic.

Global and International Influences

In the theoretical framework developed here, we recognize that while politically consequential, domestic forces could not fully account for the guarantees of rights (Kirby, 2013; Lester, 2012). As global influences permeate numerous aspects of political life (Tsutsui & Wotipka, 2004), the realm of rights and equality is no exception. To complement the domestic influences in the theoretical framework developed here, we also include global forces.

International bodies and broader processes of globalization are likely to influence rights at the domestic level. This is true in particular to agencies or covenants of the United Nations pertaining to rights in general (human rights covenants) and more specifically to employment (International Labor Organization). Ceteris paribus we expect regulation by international bodies and the broader processes of globalization to influence minority rights in general but in particular the legal circumstances for sexual minorities.

Scholarship indicates a relationship between international law in the form of UN conventions and rights in general. What is more, provisions of international law have also been linked to LGBT rights specifically. Certain human rights conventions and covenants were used in decisions related to gay rights (e.g., the decision handed down by the Human Rights Committee of the United Nations in *Toonen v. Australia*[3]). As the above subsection concerning political inclusion of women indicates, it is the protection of women's rights in particular that we deem instrumental to the evolution of gay rights. Therefore, it is ratification of the international UN convention that pertains particularly to the rights of women that we think should be consequential for the kinds of protections the country offers LGBT individuals. Let us now examine those international institutions more closely.

Human Rights Covenants

Adopted by the United Nations General Assembly on December 16, 1966, the International Covenant on Civil and Political Rights (ICCPR) came into force on March 23, 1976. Along with the International Covenant on Economic, Social and Cultural Rights (ICESCR), which in almost all cases was ratified jointly with the ICCPR by the different countries, the ICCPR sets standards for a range of rights and liberties including issues of discrimination. The relationships, in the realm of rights, between the ratification of the covenant and national politics are well studied. In fact, some understandings of gay rights see them as human rights (Beger, 2004, Ch. 4; Graupner & Tahmindjis, 2005). For instance, processes of decriminalization in Europe were first, according to Waaldijk (2000), a function of gay rights becoming a civil rights issue. Later on, this turned into a human rights issue. The implications of the International Covenant on Civil and Political Rights for rights at the domestic level were also demonstrated in the aforementioned decision in *Toonen v. Australia*.[4] In this particular case, the covenant was used to find Tasmanian laws prohibiting same-sex sex between men in violation of the privacy provision in Article 17.

We code for date of ratification by the country of the International Human Rights Covenants, which include the International Covenant on Civil and Political Rights and the International Covenant on Economic, Social and Cultural Rights (Cole, 2005). As international law has been shown to influence national politics in this sphere, the theoretical framework developed here suggests that ratification would increase the likelihood of inclusion of rights in the country's legal code; ratification of the ICCPR and the ICESCR will make it more likely that the country prohibits discriminatory practices against gays.

Adopted by the United Nations General Assembly in 1979, the Convention on the Elimination of All Forms of Discrimination against Women (CEDAW) came into force on September 3, 1981. Over 50 counties, with all developed countries but the United States included, have ratified the convention. The definition of discrimination against women appears in the convention as:

> Any distinction, exclusion or restriction made on the basis of sex, which has the effect or purpose of impairing or nullifying the recognition, enjoyment or exercise by women, irrespective of their marital status, on a basis of equality of men and women, of human rights and fundamental freedoms in the political, economic, social, cultural, civil or any other field.

Ratification of the convention entails a commitment on the part of the signatories to repeal any discriminatory legal provisions, create legal guards against discrimination, and ensure gender equality via legislation.. Likewise, the convention requires the prohibition of human trafficking and forced prostitution (also regarded as forms of discrimination). The legal provisions should protect against discrimination against women by individuals, organizations, and enterprises. The Committee on the Elimination of Discrimination against Women is the United Nations organ charged with convention oversight.

We expect that those countries that become signatories to the CEDAW would also show higher levels of protection of gay rights in their laws. When women's rights are protected not only because of political inclusion but also due to legal protections afforded by provisions of international law, we expect a spillover effect. Equality under the law should then apply to other minorities, and in particular to minority groups in the context of gender and sex. Thus, CEDAW should increase equality afforded not only women but also, by ways of proxy, sexual minorities. We code for date of ratification by the country of CEDAW (Cole, 2005).

As international law has been shown to influence national politics in this sphere, our theory suggests that ratification would increase the likelihood of inclusion of gay rights in the country's legal code; signatories to CEDAW should be more likely to legislate equality for gay individuals into their laws. In sum, ratification of CEDAW should increase the levels of legal protection for gays afforded in the country.

International Labor Organization

While we control for covenants pertaining to human rights, which may affect rights generally, some agencies of the United Nations, and specifically the International Labor Organization (ILO), are concerned with issues of labor and employment directly. Covering a wide range of issues, from discrimination in employment to child labor, and from work safety to forced labor, the ILO seeks to set an international labor code.

The United Nations inherited the ILO from its predecessor, the League of Nations. With the adoption of conventions and recommendations by the International Labor Conference and the ratification by the national governments of the member states, the ILO sets such standards for an international code. Ratifying the convention amounts to an obligation by the state to apply it by law. According to its website (ilo.org), almost all states are members of the ILO.

The ILO has adopted 188 conventions to date.[5] Of particular interest to our project for both its timing and its content is Discrimination (Employment and Occupation) Convention, 1958 (C111). The convention defines discrimination, states the obligation of each of the member states to prevent discrimination using their legal codes, and sets a comprehensive and high standard for the application of the principles put forth. We expect the ratification of the convention to increase the likelihood of anti-discriminatory legal measures in employment regulation.

Cross-Country Norm Cascade—Globalization

Beyond the effects of international institutions and laws, more general processes of globalization may also influence the likelihood of the legal entrenchment of rights. Tsutsui and Wotipka (2004) discuss a "norm cascade" between countries. Finnemore and Sikkink (1998) posit that norm entrepreneurs push norms domestically and then internationally until the number of countries that have accepted these norms reaches a tipping point. Once this tipping point has been reached, the new norm becomes expected behavior. Indeed, in their empirical analysis of women's suffrage, Ramirez et al. (1997) see such a pattern. Along the same lines, we argue that in the case of employment discrimination there is a norm diffusion that happens not only between minority groups (that is, domestically from women to sexual minorities) but also between countries.

In the post-World War II period, the embrace of human rights becomes the right, proper, and legitimate thing for the state to do. In a globalized nation, political entrepreneurs, public opinion (Lax & Phillips, 2009), political organizations, and social movements (Barclay et al., 2009; Bernstein, 2002; Patternote & Kollman, 2010) are able to recognize alternative legal arrangements within which to settle gay rights. This in turn would increase the likelihood of a legal prohibition on discrimination in employment based on sexual orientation. A more globalized political sphere is more likely to set such processes in motion. With more globalization, public opinion, political entrepreneurs, and social movements are more likely to push in that direction. And thus, with higher levels of globalization, the likelihood is greater for a norm cascade influencing domestic politics to incorporate rights into the legal code.

The logic of global norm spillover, as presented here, draws simultaneously from constructivist and rationalist understandings of international learning, which are generally thought to be different. Yet, in line with recent scholarship that argues that there is room for synthesis across these different approaches to international learning, we combine the two. In sum, we expect a greater likelihood of prohibitions on discrimination in states that are more politically globalized and are thus more likely to be part of the cross-country norm cascade.

We include as control variables in our model the democratic conditions in the nation and modernization. Political inclusion is more likely to take place in democracies, and thus democratic conditions facilitate legal equality (Wilensky, 2002). "The distribution of political and economic rights depends largely on characteristics of the political regime. A democratic regime will normally accord greater political and economic rights to the people" (Olzak & Kiyoteru, 1998). We argue that the same kind of encouragement of inclusion that has been observed for ethnic and class issues in democracies, should be true as well for sexual minorities. Hence, laws that prevent discrimination based on sexual orientation are more likely when the polity is more democratic.

Studying gay rights at the local community level within the United States, Wald et al. (1996) control for political opportunity structure. Wald et al. (1996) measure political-opportunity structure, such as civil rights for sexual minority groups, and identify it as an important predictor. The national-level equivalent to political-opportunity structure at the local level is democratic conditions; as our unit of analysis is the country, the measure of democratic conditions accounts for the extent to which the political climate allows for new rights claims. The presence of democratic political institutions, for instance, is crucial for the success of campaigns in favor of passing anti-discrimination measures (Tarrow, 1988, 1991). We thus control for democratic conditions in the country.

Lastly, an additional control variable is modernization. In a variety of ways, such as through literacy, education, and cultural change, modernization can change the view of who should be accepted in society and who should be protected by the state. Modernization has been shown to act as a causal variable in increasing levels of democracy generally (Doorenspleet, 2004; Huntington, 1991; Lipset, 1960; Przeworski & Limongi, 1997; Ramirez et al., 1997) and specifically enhancing the rights of women (Inglehart & Norris, 2003) and ethnic minorities (Gurr, 2000). More closely related to the effects of modernization on issues of sexuality in the society, Lienemann (1998) argues that "[with modernization] come removal of sexuality from the realm of taboo and a new respect for the private sphere" (p. 8). Inglehart (1997) explicitly argues that a shift to postmodern values puts the rights of women and sexual minorities in the center of political conflict. We therefore expect modernization to increase the likelihood of legal measures against discrimination.

Empirical Analyses of Equality Under the Law for Sexual Minorities

As in previous chapters of this book, the dependent variable in the following analyses is coded based on the May 2009 report of the International Lesbian, Gay, Bisexual, Trans and Intersex Association[6] (Teorell et al., 2009) as well as later updates of this document. The data are time-series cross-sectional and the dependent variable, *Legal Prohibition*, is equal to 1 if the state prohibited discrimination against gays in the workplace that year, and 0 otherwise. The coding of the dependent variable is based on the standards set by Teorell et al. (2009). The coding scheme considers cases where prohibitions consist of specific employment non-discrimination rules and in cases that consist of broad lesbian and gay non-discrimination rules. Furthermore, Teorell et al. (2009) also deal with cases where some highly decentralized countries (e.g., the United States and Australia) prohibit employment discrimination in some jurisdictions (states and provinces respectively) and not in others, in which case the coding scheme considers changes that apply to the jurisdiction as a whole. Thus, the United States, for instance, is not coded as protecting gays against discrimination as long as no legal provision to that effect is passed at the federal level. This coding scheme also considers court resolutions and constitutional prescriptions and proscriptions. Since the prohibition on discrimination can be overruled, every year in which it is on the books (due to legislation, judicial ruling, or constitutional proscription) is coded 1 for this country.

To measure domestic norm spillover, *Political Inclusion* is operationalized as the inclusion of women in the political process; as a measure of political inclusion we examine the percentage of women representatives in the national legislative body. To measure this we use the Inter-Parliamentary Union, Women in National Parliaments data (Inter-Parliamentary Union 2005).[7] The religious constituencies predictors are coded the same way they were coded in Chapter 3.

We use three measures to examine the effects supranational institutions have on our dependent variable—ratification of the International Labor Organization's C111, ratification of the International Covenant on Civil and Political Rights, and the ratification of CEDAW. Date of ratification of C111 of the *International Labor Organization* was coded according to data in the ILO's official website.[8] Date of ratification of the *International Covenant on*

Civil and Political Rights was coded according to the website for the United Nations Human Rights Treaties.[9] Measures for globalization, democracy, and GDP are the same as in previous chapters. To save space we do not recite them here.

Our data indicate that, as clear from Figure 5.1, we observe little to no change in our dependent variable up until relatively recently. As previously mentioned, only in the 1990s do we see the first countries moving in the direction of disrupting the legal status quo under which no provision guaranteed the rights of sexual minorities against discrimination in any country in the world. For the period studied, the coding was 1 in 103 of the 3782 observations, with a mean of .03 and a standard deviation of .16. Given the percentage of events compared to nonevents (2.7%) and the size of the sample (3782), an alternative estimation approach, a rare-events logit is possible. However, a rare-events logit would not make a considerable improvement on the accuracy of the coefficients (King & Zeng, 1999, p. 15–17) and would bar us from accounting for auto-regressive effects.

Results

What factors influence the likelihood of having legal guarantees of rights on the books? And more specifically, what variables affect the likelihood that a country has a prohibition on discrimination in employment based on sexual orientation in its legal code? The overall goodness of fit measures of the models in Table 5.1 is notable. Furthermore, the results lend strong support to most of our key hypotheses.

The effects of both domestic and global components of the theoretical framework proposed here are substantiated in the analyses. As expected, the effect of domestic norm spillover is positive and significant. As the percent of women representatives in the legislature increases (that is, the more politically included women are), the more likely is a legal prohibition on discrimination against LGBTIQ. Two of the three supranational institutions studied here have a positive and statistically significant effect on rights at the state level. Ratification of the ILO convention and of CEDAW each independently increases the likelihood of equality of the type studied here. These effects are either significant or highly significant and with coefficients of substantial magnitude.

Conversely, the hypothesis concerning a broader effect for globalization in the form of a global norm cascade fails to win support in the data. It is

Table 5.1. Analyses of the Predictors of Prohibitions on Legal Discrimination

Variable	Model I (robust standard errors)
Common Law	0.33
	(0.87)
% Catholic	-0.014
	(0.016)
% Muslim	-0.08
	(0.05)
% Protestant	**-0.029 ***
	(0.016)
GDP per capita	**0.00010 ***
	(0.00005)
Democratic Conditions	0.46
	(0.31)
Political Inclusion	**0.097 ***
	(0.041)
Globalization	0.01
	(0.02)
CEDAW	**3.98 ***
	(1.95)
ILO	**2.74 ****
	(1.1)
CCPR	-0.72
	(0.48)
Ethnic Fractionalization	2.6
	(2.08)
Constant	**-16.03 *****
	(2.72)

Note: N = 3471; Number of Groups = 150; Observations per group: Min = 1, Avg = 23.1, Max = 30; Wald Chi2 = 50.92; Prob > Chi2 = 0.0.

via international institutions and international law (the ILO and the human rights covenants) that global influences lead to guarantees of rights in national legislation (Kirby, 2013). In sum, we find support for the effects of a subset of the variables in each of the two groups of predictors. In the group of domestic forces, norm spillover is significant and in the anticipated direction, while only one of the culture and religion variables has a significant effect. In the group of global forces, two of the three international bodies and institutions studied systematically affect the likelihood of equality. As far as our research question is concerned, degree of globalization, however, is inconsequential.

Final Thoughts about Discrimination Against the LGBT Community

Two stories are often told in the context of right guarantees—a transnational-international account and a domestic one. Told separately, however, none is complete. As we clearly demonstrate in our analyses of equality under the law for sexual minorities, a focus on one or another would be myopic. As this chapter indicates, the best way to understand why some countries outlaw discrimination on the basis of sexual orientation is by taking into consideration both the international and the domestic perspectives.

At the level of domestic politics, we present evidence that previous widening of the circle of power to a formerly excluded group may start a cascade leading to protection of other groups. Indeed, a crucially important domestic force is the spillover of norms from the inclusion of one minority group to another. When women are politically included, they serve as a reference group to LGBT groups, which in turn mobilize and eventually form a support structure—a key condition to win legal protections (Epp, 1996, 1998). Elements in the support structure for the equality of certain minorities in the past (e.g., interest groups involved in the campaign for women equality), may be instrumental in the fight for equality of additional minorities (e.g., sexual minorities).

On the global level, our findings underscore the consequentiality of supranational institutions. The International Labor Organization and international law have a robust and substantively meaningful effect as predictors of right guarantees. Ratifications of C111 of the ILO or the CEDAW increase the likelihood of having guarantees of rights on the books.

While some accounts in the literature claim that in Europe, for instance, the mere decriminalization of same-sex sex inexorably leads to the introduction of anti-discrimination measures (e.g., Waaldijk, 2000), the theory proposed here offers an alternative analysis that is richer and more complex. In Sanders (1996), considering domestic influences side by side with global effects provides for a useful theoretical framework for the study of the second stage of legal guarantees for gays—namely, guarantees against discrimination.

6

THE GAY RIGHTS INDEX

"[T]he State of Colorado, through any of its branches or departments . . . shall [not] enact, adopt or enforce any statute . . . whereby homosexual, lesbian or bisexual orientation . . . shall . . . be the basis . . . [for a] claim of discrimination." Over 53% of Coloradoans casting their vote in the November 1992 elections supported a ballot measure that contained this language. A ballot measure is a form of direct democracy common in state-level politics in the United States. The measure is a vote originating from popular initiative to force a public vote on proposed statutes, ordinances, or constitutional amendments. Winning the support of the majority of voters, the measure, which later became known as Amendment 2, expressed popular refusal to recognize gays as a group that should win legal protections against discrimination.

Alarmed by the potential political ramifications of Amendment 2, Richard Evans, a gay employee in the office of the mayor of Denver, as well as other citizens and local governments in Colorado took Governor Roy Romer and the state of Colorado to court. When the case reached the Supreme Court of the state of Colorado, the judges accepted the claim that the amendment was repugnant to the Equal Protection Clause of the Fourteenth Amendment to the Federal Constitution of the United States. Notably, the judges applied to discrimination on the basis of sexual orientation the same legal standard traditionally used in cases of racial discrimination against African Americans. Four years after the majority of Colorado voters approved the contested ballot measure, the highest court of the land was asked, on appeal from the Colorado Supreme Court, to evaluate the measure's constitutionality.

In the opinion he delivered for the court in *Romer v. Evans*, Justice Kennedy contended that Amendment 2 imposed a "special disability upon those persons alone. Homosexuals are forbidden the safeguards that others enjoy or may seek without constraint." Thus, the Supreme Court decided in a 6–3 ruling to strike the amendment unconstitutional under the Equal Protection Clause. However, what the court failed to do in *Romer* was to create new rights or protections for homosexuals. More specifically, the court rejected the strict scrutiny interpretation of the Equal Protection Clause applied in the ruling of the Colorado Supreme Court in this case. Sexual minorities were not granted the same profound constitutional protections that African Americans win in court rulings.

In the American system, the absence of a legal guarantee preventing discrimination against LGBTIQ individuals goes beyond the court. Attempts to pass comprehensive federal legislation against employment discrimination on the basis of sexual orientation have repeatedly failed. In 1996, a proposal to extend the protections against employment discrimination under the Civil Rights Act of 1964 to individuals discriminated on the basis of sexual orientation failed in Congress. The Employment Non-Discrimination Act (ENDA) has been unsuccessfully proposed in all but one Congress since.

Yet, the rights of LGBT individuals in the United States were limited not only because of the lack of legal guarantees for equality (e.g., in employment). As discussed in great detail earlier in this book, until 2003 several of the states in the United States had prohibitions against same-sex sexual activity. Those legal provisions were not only de jure provisions, but were actually enforced. It was not until the ruling of the Supreme Court in *Lawrence v. Texas* in 2003 that the justices ruled all state sodomy laws unconstitutional. The decision in *Lawrence* effectively granted individuals in the United States the legal protection to engage in same-gender sexual activity. However, pursuant to the *Romer* ruling, their rights not to be discriminated against at the workplace, in housing, or in education have yet to win legal protection.

As we discuss in great detail in Chapter 5, the absence of firm legal prohibitions on discrimination against gays (mandated either by the court or legislatively) is not unique to the United States. While rights creation happens in a variety of ways in different nations (Sartori, 1994; Sathe, 2004), only some nations have banned discrimination on the basis of sexual orientation. Even in established democracies, the equal protection under the law, won by racial minorities, certain ethnic groups, and women, is often still a matter of political struggle for gay individuals.

Figure 6.1. Distribution of Gay Rights around the World and over Time (1975–2005)

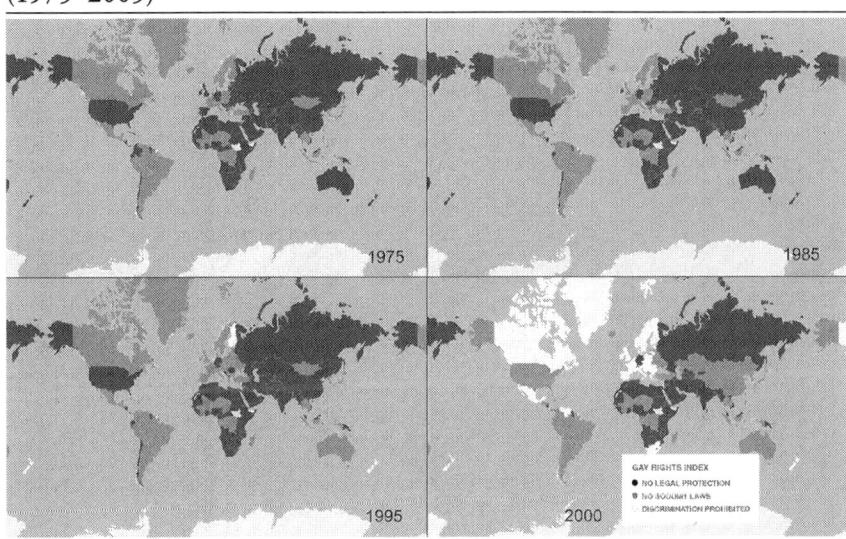

In this chapter, we aim to explain the variation in the protection of gay rights in different countries and over time as it is reflected in Figure 6.1.[1] This figure contains four maps from top left for 1975 to bottom right for 2005. The maps indicate the entire scale of gay rights that we seek to evaluate, from no legal protections, to decriminalization, and finally equality under the law. Countries in dark grey are those where sodomy is legally prohibited at the particular time. Light grey countries are places where same-sex sexual relations are allowed under law, but there are no legal clauses protecting sexual minorities against discrimination. Finally, the territories in white indicate countries that at that time prohibited discrimination based on sexual orientation.

This is the final empirical chapter in this book. After covering extensive grounds concerning various types of rights for sexual minorities, their origins and their antecedents, in this chapter we develop the Gay Rights Index (GRI). The discussion in this book culminates to a comprehensive analysis of all different types of gay rights studied, as they are reflected in the same single scale, the GRI. We use this original index to describe and then analyze the variance in rights enjoyed by sexual-minority groups around the world.

As with other chapters in this book, the GRI concerns de jure legal conditions. The absence of legal protections against discrimination, as with the existence of sodomy laws, are significant on cultural and symbolic grounds; and even if they are never enforced or rarely enforced with any consistency, they justify or potentially legitimize forms of political and socio-legal discrimination. Largely in line with the theoretical framework developed thus far in the book, the GRI consists of three levels. We first explain and describe those levels. Then we turn to use multivariate analyses to explain variance between countries and over time in the GRI.

In the GRI framework, the highest level of protection is provisions prohibiting discrimination against individuals based on their sexual orientation (countries in white in Figure 6.1). The next level of countries (in light grey in Figure 6.1) has no prohibitions on sodomy but also does not provide legal guarantees of rights for LGBT individuals. The lowest level, shown in dark grey in Figure 6.1, consists of countries where individuals may stand trial because they engaged in same-gender sexual activity; not only do LGBT individuals lack legal protections against discrimination in those countries, their actions are also restricted due to sodomy laws.

Apart from presenting a comprehensive theory that accounts for the degree to which sexual minorities are being discriminated against in a certain country, we also seek to demonstrate the advantages of our framework in explaining cross-sectional variance as well as temporal change. Lastly, we seek to provide a systematic analysis of the variance in levels of discrimination against sexual minorities, explaining the differences in the protection of gay rights between countries and over time. As the last empirical chapter in this book, this chapter aims not only to summarize but also innovate at the level of theory, measurement strategy, and empirical findings.

Levels of Legal Protection for Sexual Minorities

We think of legal provisions as granting members of minority groups with protections at various levels. Those different levels are not unrelated, and reaching one level may be critical for reaching the next. Sanders (1996) identifies several stages in state practices towards LGBTIQ. At the bottom level are states where no legal protections are afforded. In such places, engaging in same-gender sexual activity may lead to criminal prosecution. Chapters 1, 2, and 4 in this book, as well as some of Chapter 3, deal with different aspects of the legal circumstances in countries where these restrictions exist.

The first important step in Sanders's theory is decriminalization. At this level, the state repeals prohibitions against same-gender sexual activity by passing statutes, amending its constitution, or issuing judicial fiat. "[R]epeal of criminal prohibitions," according to Sanders, allows then for the "enactment of antidiscrimination laws" (p. 18). Thus, the removal of prohibitions against same-gender sexual activity may pave the way to anti-discrimination laws and for additional provisions, such as same-gender marriage. In Chapter 5 we examine the conditions that increase the likelihood that states would guarantee equality under the law for members of sexual-minority groups. The framework in this chapter covers those various levels of legal protections and taps the contingent nature of how those protections evolve.

While we continue to focus on the actions of elected branches, the judiciary, and constitutional clauses, in the current chapter we do not distinguish between those different institutions. Largely along the lines of some of the literature on gay rights, the way they evolve, and the contingent nature of the different levels of legal protections afforded members of sexual minority groups (Sanders, 2009), we identify three levels of protections. The highest level of protection is afforded when there is in place a prohibition on discrimination in the workplace based on sexual orientation, in the form of a statute, a constitutional provision, or court-mandated policy. While the highest level of protection could also be measured as protection against discrimination in housing for instance, we found the employment yardstick to be useful theoretically and empirically as it serves a standard that is set by international bodies and regulation particularly concerned with this issue (e.g., the ILO). It thus lends itself more easily to comparisons between countries and over time.

The intermediary level of protection applies when the state has decriminalized sodomy. In federal systems only when all sub-national units repeal sodomy provisions, do we think of the state as one where sodomy is decriminalized. For instance, as described above, the United States has yet to protect LGBT individuals against discrimination in the workplace. Yet, since 2003, due to the aforementioned ruling of the Supreme Court in *Lawrence v. Texas*, the United States falls into the intermediate level of protection in our theoretical framework. At the lowest level of protection, neither protection against discrimination nor decriminalization of sodomy is in place. In such country-years, sexual minorities do not enjoy any type of legal protection described in our theoretical framework.

The Gay Rights Index

We code the Gay Rights Index (GRI) based on the May 2009 report of The International Lesbian, Gay, Bisexual, Trans and Intersex Association (Teorell et al., 2009).[2] The data are time-series cross-sectional. The three levels of the

Figure 6.2. Distribution of Levels of Gay Rights

GRI correspond to the three levels of legal protections in our theory. The GRI equals 2 for country-years where employment discrimination on the basis of sexual orientation is prohibited. The index is 1 if sodomy is not considered criminal by the state, but there exists no legal protections in employment. Lastly, the GRI is coded 0 for nations with sodomy laws. In states where sodomy had never been prohibited, the coding is 1 for all country-years in the database and changes to 2 if this country includes a prohibition against discrimination. Unless the employment provision was rescinded, the coding remains the same for all subsequent years after the passage of the provision. In countries with a federal system, we code based on decisions at the federal level. Thus if only some of the sub-national units ban discrimination, but others do not, the county would not be coded at the highest level of rights. The range of GRI is thus 0 to 2, and its mean and standard deviation are .38 and .53 respectively.

Figures 6.2 and 6.3 give a general overview of the distribution of the protection of gay rights. In Figure 6.2, the light grey slice in the pie diagram is the percent of observations in our data where sodomy is criminalized. As the figure indicates, in 61% of all country-years, sodomy laws are on the books. The grey slice in the diagram indicates the share of observations where

Figure 6.3. Variation in Gay Rights in Different World Regions (Percent of countries in Region with GRI Score)

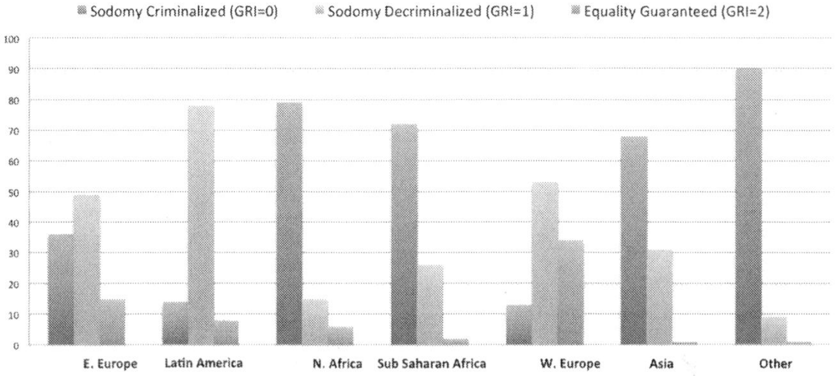

■ Sodomy Criminalized (GRI=0)   ■ Sodomy Decriminalized (GRI=1)   ■ Equality Guaranteed (GRI=2)

[Bar chart with regions on x-axis: E. Europe, Latin America, N. Africa, Sub Saharan Africa, W. Europe, Asia, Other; y-axis 0–100]

sodomy is not considered criminal, either because it has never been a crime or because of the repeal of sodomy laws. In slightly over a third of the cases, sodomy is not considered criminal. Lastly, the dark grey slice indicates that in approximately one in every 25 observations in our data, gay individuals win equality under the law.

As Figure 6.3 illustrates, the variance in the legal protections afforded gay individuals is not a uniquely Western story. Rather, countries in different world regions demonstrate considerable variance in the level of rights they guarantee gay individuals. As the plot for Western Europe and North America indicates, countries in these parts of the world are much more likely to decriminalize sodomy—if not guarantee legal equality—than they are to criminalize same-sex sex. Yet, the plots for Latin America, Asia, and Eastern Europe and the Former Soviet Union republics also show considerable variation in the protection of gay rights. For instance, while nearly four in every ten Eastern European countries have outlawed sodomy, over 50% have decriminalized it. Moreover, nearly 20% of the countries in this region provide equality under the law to members of their sexual-minority groups.

Beyond the cross-sectional perspective provided by the framework developed here, our work also allows us to conceptualize and then examine changes over time. This additional advantage is important for the description and analyses of temporal trends. Figure 6.4 provides an illustration. Time is denoted by the years on the x-axis, and on the y-axis is the percent of

Figure 6.4. Criminalization and Legal Equality (Change over Time)

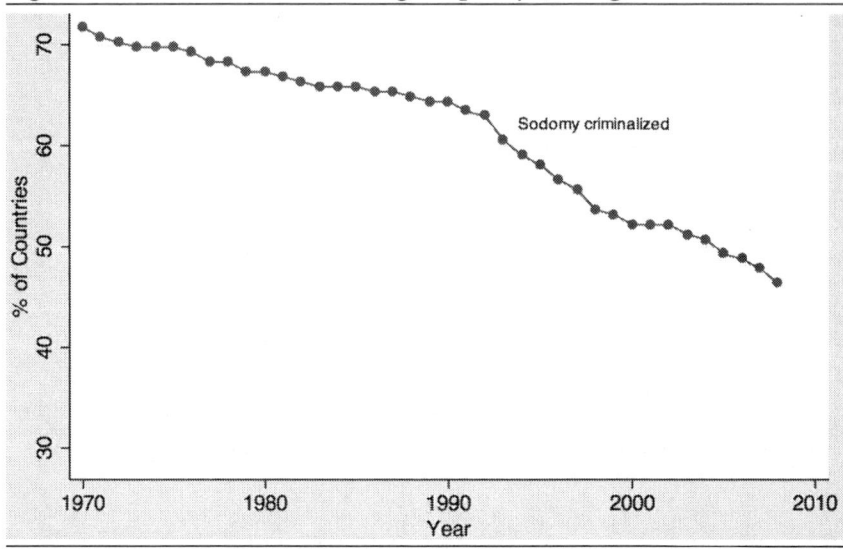

countries where sodomy laws are on the books (GRI=0). The plot indicates how this figure changes over time. While the two decades following the early 1970s saw a minor decrease of less than 10% in the share of countries where sodomy was criminalized, the mid-1990s brought about a sea change. A precipitous decline of nearly 20% in the number of countries where same-sex sex is a criminal offence occurred over the course of approximately a decade and a half.

The three levels in our theory are critical to decipher this trend. The top plot in Figure 6.5 is identical to the plot in Figure 3. As indicated in the legend at the bottom, those are the countries where no legal protections are afforded (GRI=0). Yet, the additional two plots, the hollow diamonds one for countries where sodomy is not criminal but no legal equality is guaranteed (GRI=1), and the Xs one for countries where gays enjoy legal equality (GRI=2), help us explain the trend. For instance, a good amount of the sharp decline since the mid-1990s is accounted for not just by countries that decriminalized sodomy but also in equal measure by countries where LGBT individuals won equality under the law. In terms of the literature reviewed (e.g., Sanders, 2009) and the theory developed earlier, the trend in a liberal

Figure 6.5. Variation in Levels of Legal Protection for Gays (Change over Time)

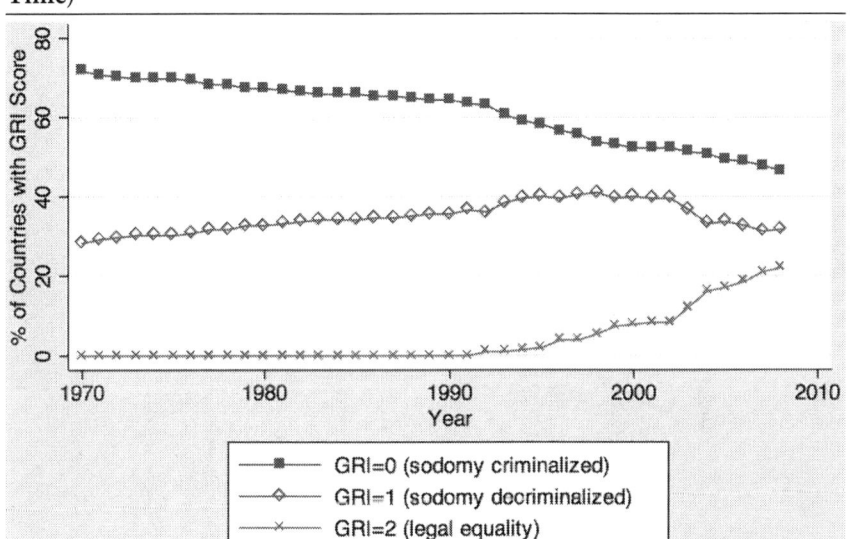

direction happened not just because countries made the move from criminalizing sodomy to decriminalizing it (switching from GRI=0 to GRI=1). Granted, there were quite a few countries where this has happened. Yet, a good number of countries also continued moving up the level of legal protection and beyond decriminalization also prohibited discrimination (switched from GRI=1 to GRI=2). In Romania, Article 200 of the Romanian criminal code was repealed after the European Union strong-armed Romania to lift its sodomy prohibitions. However, a good number of countries also made the next step by putting legal equality for gays on their law books. For instance, Estonia, which had decriminalized sodomy in the early 1990s, guaranteed legal equality for gays approximately a decade later in 2003.

Figures 6.2 to 6.5 illustrate the advantages of the framework we developed here; and the index is derived from this framework in explaining variance in gay rights across countries and over time. We now turn to the empirical measures for the variables discussed earlier as affecting this variance. Similar to our approach in Chapter 5, to measure domestic norm spillover, political inclusion is operationalized as the inclusion of women in the political

Figure 6.6. GDP Protection of Women under International Law (CEDAW) and Levels of Protection for Gay Rights

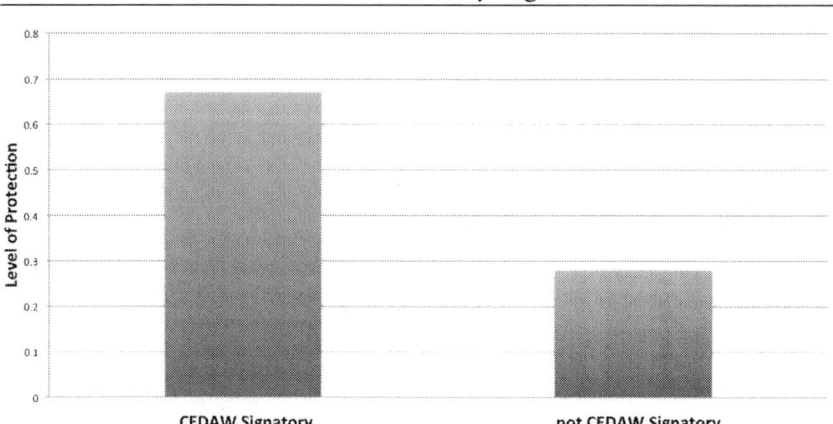

process (*Women in Parliament*); as a measure of political inclusion we examine the percentage of women representatives in the national legislative body. To measure this, we use the Inter-Parliamentary Union, Women in National Parliaments data (Inter-Parliamentary Union, 2005).[3] CEDAW is coded 1 for country-years when the country was a signatory and 0 otherwise. Figure 6.6 indicates that the difference between CEDAW signatories and countries that do not fall into this category is meaningful. The column on the left indicates that on a range of 0–2, the mean for GRI is .27 in non-CEDAW signatories. Conversely, this figure for countries that are signatories is more than twice as large at .66. This difference is extremely statistically significant with a p-value of less than 0.0001.

GDP per capita is measured in constant US dollars at base year 2000 (Gleditsch, 2002). Based on the theory presented in previous chapters in this book, we would expect levels of legal protections for gay rights to be highly correlated with trends in GDP per capita. Figure 6.7 shows this to be exactly the case, which lends considerable face validity to the new index we are introducing here. On the x-axis in Figure 6.7 are six categories ranging from countries where GDP per capita is less than $3,500 a year, to countries where the values for this variable surpass $50,000 annually. The dark grey columns indicate the share of countries in each GDP category where sodomy is criminal. The share of countries where sodomy is not criminal is indicated by the

Figure 6.7. GDP Per Capita and Levels of Protection for Gays

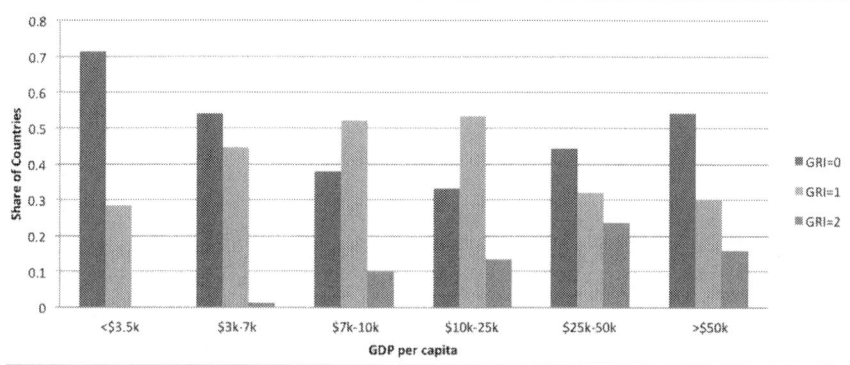

columns in red. Finally, the yellow columns show the share of countries where gays win legal equality.

Categories with higher GDP may seem to have decreased levels of countries where sodomy is decriminalized, but this is mostly due to the fact that the countries where discrimination is prohibited by law in those categories are more numerous. The coding scheme for the dependent variable is such that the score is 2 when not only does sodomy cease to be criminal, but there is also legal equality in the country. In this category of high GDP per capita, legal protection against discrimination compensates for the slight decline in the category of decriminalization of sodomy compared to categories with lower GDP. One exception is the *increase* in the share of countries where no legal protections are offered to gays in the two highest categories of GDP (i.e., where GDP per capita is greater than $25,000). This trend is accounted for by such countries as the oil-producing nations in the Middle East, where GDP per capita is high, while the legal proscription of same-gender sex is oftentimes still in place.

Let us now quickly examine other explanatory variables used here and which readers are already well familiar with based on the frameworks developed throughout this book. *Common Law* is equal to 1 when the country's legal origins are in Common Law, and 0 otherwise. *Religion Based Banning of Parties* equals 1 for country-years where religious affiliation determines the banning of parties, and 0 otherwise (Teorell et al., 2010). To measure *Democratic Conditions*, we utilize the Polity score, which was imputed using Freedom House data where it was missing. The scale ranges from 0 (least democratic) to 10 (most democratic) (Hadenius & Teorell, 2005).

Figure 6.8. Democratic Conditions and Variation in Legal Protection for Gays

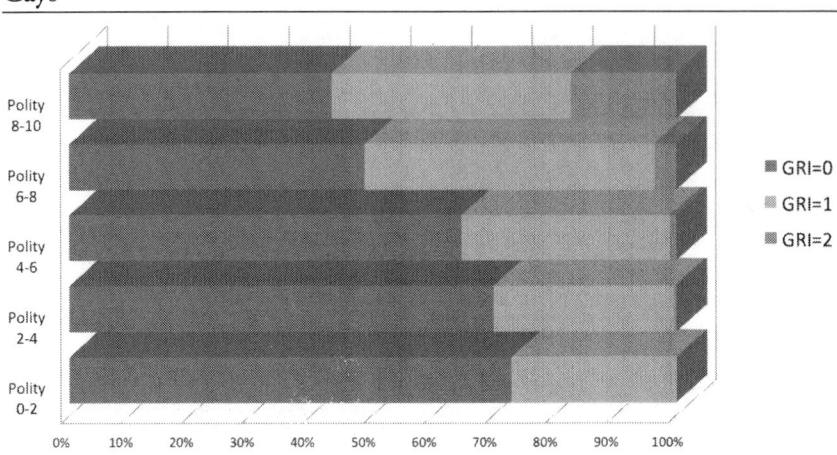

Figure 6.8 has the distribution of rights afforded sexual minorities at different levels of democracy. The dark grey portions of the bars indicate the share of countries out of the total number of countries with the indicated Polity score that offer no legal protection for gays. The light grey portion indicates the share of countries where sodomy is decriminalized, but there is no legal provision in place prohibiting discrimination against gays. Finally, the grey portions of the bars indicate the share of countries within the indicated range of Polity scores that prohibit discrimination on the basis of sexual orientation. As the bottom three bars indicate, hardly any country where the Polity scores are below 6 guarantees legal equality for gays. Furthermore, approximately two thirds of such countries criminalize sodomy. As democratic conditions improve, the share of countries where sodomy is decriminalized grows.

Where democracy is established (Polity scores from 8–10), almost one in every six countries has made the additional step beyond decriminalization, guaranteeing legal equality for gays. That said, Figure 6.8 also introduces a conundrum. While it is to be expected that more than 70% of the most non-democratic countries in the world have sodomy laws on the books, more than four out of ten of the most democratic countries also present the same conditions. It is clearly a question worth the attention of future researchers. See the appendix for descriptive statistics of the different predictors.

Multivariate Analyses of the Predictors of the Gay Rights Index

Similar to the empirical tests we used in earlier chapters, for the purposes of the multivariate analysis of the predictors of the GRI, we use time-series cross-sectional data, listing all states for which data are available for the years 1975–2002. After discussing the cross-sectional advantages of the theoretical perspective developed here, as well as the leverage it provides for temporal analysis, we now turn to an examination of some of the key independent variables explaining variance in gay rights between nations and over time.

What explains the variance in equality for LGBT individuals in different countries and over time as reflected in the GRI developed here? The Ordered Logit model estimated with data for 3471 country-year data points lends support to our hypotheses. As Table 6.1 indicates, the model performs reasonably well in terms of the goodness of fit measures, including the McFadden's pseudo R^2 at 0.36. The first model in the table is estimated with the effect of religion measured as the percent of different religious constituencies. Those are replaced in the second model with the measures from Fox (2003) discussed extensively above.

A *Common Law* legal system has a depressing effect on the rights afforded LGBT individuals. Compared to other systems of law, a Common Law system decreases the ordered log-odds of higher levels of legal protection for gays in the first model by 3.1, ceteris paribus. In line with the findings in Chapters 3 and 4, Common Law countries are considerably less likely to address issues of gay rights in legislation either with respect to the decriminalization of sodomy or as far as equality under the law is considered. The effect of *Women in Parliament* is positive in both models, but is significant in the second model only. With increasing numbers of women representatives in the parliament, the level of legal protections afforded gay individuals increases. Ceteris Paribus, an increase of *Women in Parliament* by one unit would increase the ordered log-odds of a bump of one unit on the dependent variable by .04.

Largely in line with the findings in Chapter 5, protection of women's rights under international law has a similar effect; when a country is a signatory to the CEDAW, the level of legal protections for gays increases in a statistically significant manner. Becoming a signatory to the CEDAW increases the ordered log-odds of a higher level on the outcome variable for the country by .51 (in the first model), holding all other variables constant. In support of the preliminary results in Figure 6.7, as the gross domestic product of the nation increases, so does the level of legal protections for sexual minorities. This finding is along the lines of the empirical findings in Chapters 4 and 5

Table 6.1. Analyses of the Predictors of Gay Rights Index (Ordered Logistic Regression Models)

Variable	Model I (robust standard errors)	Model II (robust standard errors) Fox's variables replacing standard religion variables
Common Law	-3.1 ****	-2.1 ***
	(0.15)	(0.21)
% Catholic	**-0.0032 ***	n/a
	(0.0016)	
% Muslim	-0.028 ***	n/a
	(0.002)	
% Protestant	-0.002	n/a
	(0.002)	
Religious Court with Broad Jurisdiction	n/a	-15.9 ***
		(0.3)
Restrictions on Interfaith Marriage	n/a	-.005
		(.308)
GDP per capita	0.000046 ***	0.00005 ***
	(0.000007)	(0.00001)
Democratic Conditions	0.11***	0.27 ***
	(0.01)	(0.02)
Globalization	.021 ***	0.006
	(0.002)	(0.004)
Political Inclusion	0.009	**0.036 ***
	(0.006)	**(0.007)**

in the book. Similar to what we would expect given the descriptive statistics in Figure 6.8, as democratic conditions improve, so does the legal protection for gays. This finding is highly statistically significant and is sensible given the empirical results presented earlier in this book. The findings in Table 6.1 indicate that beyond the effects in the basic crosstabs described above, the effects of variables such as international institutions, GDP, and democracy are not only systematic, but they also remain standing when simultaneously tested with alternative hypotheses.

As for the cut points, in the second model country-years with a value of 2.73 or less on the latent variable underlying GRI would be those where sodomy is legally prohibited, given that all predictors are set at 0. Furthermore, country-years with a value of at least 6.9 on the latent variable underlying GRI would be classified as progressively protecting gay rights, assuming all

Table 6.1. (continued)

Variable	Model I (robust standard errors)	Model II (robust standard errors) Fox's variables replacing standard religion variables
CEDAW	0.51 ***	1.11 ***
	(0.13)	(0.27)
ILO	0.17	0.48 *
	(0.11)	(0.18)
CCPR	-0.6 ***	-0.67 ***
	(0.1)	(0.16)
Ethnic Fractionalization	-0.54 **	-0.7 **
	(0.17)	(0.26)
Cut1	-0.03	2.73
	(0.32)	(0.42)
Cut2	5.008	6.9
	(0.342)	(0.44)
	N = 3471	N = 1560
	Wald Chi2 = 1004.52	Wald Chi2 = 9141.64
	Prob > Chi2 = 0.0	Prob > Chi2 = 0.0
	Pseudo R2 = 0.36	Pseudo R2 = 0.31

Note: Dummies for years not presented in the table.
* data limited to the period from 1990–2003
* the variable for interfaith marriage is coded in the Fox database as: "Restrictions on interfaith marriages, 1990 or earliest (Cases where marriages are performed only by clergy—which effectively restricts interfaith marriages—are also coded"
* the predictor for religious courts is coded in the Fox database as: "Presence of religious courts, which have jurisdiction over some matters of law other than family law and matters of inheritance"

regressors' values are 0. Naturally, country-years with values between 2.73 and 6.9 in the second model in the table are those where sodomy is not considered criminal, yet there is no equality under the law for sexual minorities.

For robustness in Table 6.2 we report the results of GEE models, similar in terms of estimation to the ones reported in Chapter 4. The results in Table 6.2 are substantively indistinguishable. See also Appendix E for additional analyses of the Gay Rights Index at varying levels of dominance for various religions such as Islam and Catholicism.

The predicted probabilities in Table 6.3 shed more light on the substantive interpretation of our findings. The effect of legal path dependence is unmistakable. The likelihood of legal provisions against discrimination drops by nearly 2% in Common Law systems. Contrariwise, the likelihood of antisodomy prohibitions being on the books surges by 58% in Common Law.

Table 6.2. Analyses of the Predictors of Gay Rights Index (GEE Models)

Variable	Model I (robust standard errors)	Model II (robust standard errors) Fox's variables replacing standard religion variables
Common Law	-.0.43 ***	-0.35 ***
	(0.072)	(0.10)
% Catholic	-0.0003	n/a
	(0.0011)	
% Muslim	**-0.004 *** **	n/a
	(0.001)	
% Protestant	-0.0032 *	n/a
	(0.0017)	
Religious Court with Broad Jurisdiction	n/a	**-0.21 ***
		(0.11)
Restrictions on Interfaith Marriage	n/a	**-0.25 ***
		(0.13)
GDP per capita	0.000023 **	0.00005 ***
	(0.000008)	(0.00001)
Democratic Conditions	0.006	0.0008
	(0.008)	(0.011)
Globalization	0.003 **	0.0046 *
	(0.001)	(0.0017)
Political Inclusion	0.005	0.005
	(0.004)	(0.003)
CEDAW	**0.067 ***	0.065
	(0.028)	(0.053)

As Figure 6.6 illustrated, being a CEDAW signatory increases the level of protection the state affords gays. This finding holds even when we switch to a multivariate analyses. What is more, the multivariate analysis provides us with a more accurate measure for this effect. As Table 6.3 indicates, being a CEDAW signatory decreases the likelihood of having anti-sodomy laws on the books by nearly 20%. On the other hand, it increases the likelihood of sodomy repeal by 19%.

The GRI is based on the theoretical frameworks developed throughout this book. Its advantages for descriptive purposes are clear. It not only organizes gay rights along a reasonable scale where repeal of sodomy prohibitions comes first and the guarantee of equality comes last. What this original scale does as well is provide us with a powerful tool to describe those legal conditions as they fluctuate over time and between nations. Finally, as the

Table 6.2. (continued)

Variable	Model I (robust standard errors)	Model II (robust standard errors) Fox's variables replacing standard religion variables
ILO	0.083	**0.16 ***
	(0.067)	**(0.07)**
CCPR	0.004	0.041
	(0.039)	(0.057)
Ethnic Fractionalization	0.035	0.26
	(0.16)	(0.23)
Constant	0.24	-0.35
	(0.16)	(0.26)
	N = 3471	N = 1560
	Number of Groups = 150	Number of Groups = 133
	Observations per group: Min = 1, Avg = 23.1, Max = 30	Observations per group: Min = 1, Avg = 11.7, Max = 13
	Wald Chi2 = 204.48	Wald Chi2 = 152.03
	Prob > Chi2 = 0.0	Prob > Chi2 = 0.0

* data limited to the period from 1990–2003
* the variable for interfaith marriage is coded in the Fox database as: "Restrictions on interfaith marriages, 1990 or earliest (Cases where marriages are performed only by clergy—which effectively restricts interfaith marriages—are also coded"
* the predictor for religious courts is coded in the Fox database as: "Presence of religious courts, which have jurisdiction over some matters of law other than family law and matters of inheritance"

Table 6.3. Predicted Probabilities

Variable	Average change	Sodomy provisions on the books (DV = 0)	No sodomy provisions (DV = 1)	Prohibitions against legal discrimination (DV = 2)
Common Law	38.6	58.0	-56.2	-1.7
CEDAW Signatory	13.3	-19.9	19.3	0.6
Women in Parliament	25.9	-38.9	36.6	2.3
GDP per capita	37.2	-55.7	47.0	8.7
Democratic Conditions	30.8	-46.1	44.5	1.7

Note: All numbers are in percentages.

multivariate analyses presented at the end of the current chapter illustrates, our theory concerning the influences on sexual minority rights is largely supported with the measurement strategy of the GRI.

Indeed, we find that the range of legal circumstances of sexual minorities is influenced by the key predictive variables we had identified. Legal path dependence, religion, international law, political inclusion, GDP, and conditions of democracy all *systematically* influence the rights enjoyed by LGBT. This variance is not only described well by the GRI, but it is also captured and explained comprehensively using the range of predictors we identified as critical in the theoretical framework we develop. We believe the Gay Rights Index can contribute to additional scientific breakthroughs in the study of minority rights, and we hope it will be adopted and used in future research into these topics.

7

Conclusions

The last 40 years have seen some of the biggest advances in the legal rights and protections of sexual minorities possibly ever in the history of humankind. Even in states that have both elements of a religious state and the Common Law, there have been tremendous improvements. For example, in 1989, a flight attendant by the name of Jonathan Danilovich, took El Al, Israel's national airline and his employer, to court. Founded in 1948, Israel adopted the Common Law system from the British, who, during their mandate in Palestine, had established a system of law imaging the one in the motherland. Thus, Common Law is the principal system of law in Israel (Edelman, 1995). In addition, with specialized courts with a unique religious jurisdiction as well as other forms of entanglement of state and religion, the influence of religion on the state has been substantial in Israel since its very founding (Arian, 1998). Yet, the ruling in *Danilovich* is an illustration for how—despite bleak conditions for sexual minorities in the early years of the republic—Israel has made great strides in legally protecting its LGBT citizens.

Danilovich was incentivized to petition the Supreme Court when his male partner was denied a discounted flight ticket, a benefit offered employees' spouses or companions. Five years later, when the case made it to the Israeli Supreme Court, the question before the justices was whether El Al's different policy for same-sex companions was legal. Delivering the opinion for the Court in *El Al v. Danilovich*, Justice Aharon Barak argued that "[e]quality is a fundamental value in Israeli law . . . [and] discrimination is a plague." El Al's policy amounted to discrimination on the basis of sexual orientation and was thus ruled illegal.

Whereas the court in this case ruled in favor of Danilovich, the legal protections and judicial remedies offered to members of the gay community in Israel have not always been that expansive. While largely unenforced throughout the nation's history, Section 351(3) of the Israeli Criminal Code outlawed "unnatural sexual relations." What was essentially a sodomy law was inheritance from the British, very similar to the cases of the various forms of legal codification extensively discussed in Chapter 2. Similar to the legal system in many former British colonies, the Israeli legal system inherited an incarnation of sodomy provisions originating in the Buggery Act of 1533.

That said, prima facie, this provision had little real influence—in the 1960s the Israeli Supreme Court ruled that due to the legal right for privacy, the section could not be enforced. Still, it remained on the books for four of the nation's six decades, to be repealed as late as 1988 (see discussion of unenforced provisions in Leslie (2000) as well as earlier in this book). Indeed, it was this legal change introduced by the Knesset, the Israeli parliament, that allowed shortly thereafter for several far-reaching judicial decisions extending rights and privileges to individuals of all sexual orientations. One of those landmark decisions was the ruling in *Danilovich*.

While there have been enormous advances for the LGBT community around the world, the challenge of legalized discrimination continues to be present in many countries. In the second decade of the 21st century, we are still seeing states execute men for homosexual activity (Dehghan, 2011); and people are in jail around the world for being gay (76crimes.com, 2014). As we finish writing this book, the president of Uganda has criminalized HIV transmission—putting another law on the books that can be used against homosexuals and creating another obstacle to fighting AIDS in the country (Feder, 2014). In academia and in the media there is a continuing debate around the causes of this governmental discrimination.

In 2014, Mark Joseph Stern, in response to an article by Decca Aitkenhead from almost a decade before (2005), argued that blaming Common Law and the legacy of colonialism for homophobia today is a mistake. While recognizing that many of these laws are the legacy of British colonialism, he denies that we should put the onus any longer on the imposition of these laws but should place it on the homophobia in these countries. As Aitkenhead (2005) points out though, laws shape values. As we analyze in great detail in this book, there is an inextricable link between those laws and the various countries that had experienced a period of British colonialism.

The theoretical frameworks, historical evidence, case studies, illustrations, and large-N analyses presented throughout this book contradict this argument and point directly to the pernicious impact of a decision made by a king and a chief minister almost five centuries ago and the colonial enterprise that followed. Furthermore, we find that the long arm of the religious state greatly influenced the legal circumstances under which sexual minorities find themselves today in various corners of the world. The impact of the religious state is underlined further perhaps by the efforts of those who are trying to establish new religious states today. There is a growing record of religious militia killing members of the LGBT community in Iraq, for example (Long & Moumneh, 2009; Siegel, 2014).

The goal of writing this book is to develop a theoretical framework explaining the variation in gay rights and to show its advantages in explaining discrepancies between countries as well as changes over time. The book examines a range of questions, all of which center one way or another on the extent to which LGBT individuals can live their life free of abuse of their rights and free of limitations on their way of life. We understand those rights as contingent in nature, with sodomy repeal potentially leading, over time, to full equality under the law, such as in the cases of Estonia or Israel.

Thus, countries where prohibitions on discrimination against gays are on the books are understood to be the ones where legal protections for sexual minorities are at their highest levels. Next are those countries, which while not guaranteeing equality under the law, did not prescribe a criminal prohibition on sodomy. Lastly, countries where sodomy is criminal and equality for sexual minorities is not protected by law are those with no law on their books protecting gays. This theory is based on understandings in the literature of gay rights, and of the way those rights evolve, and the contingent nature of the different levels of legal protection afforded members of sexual-minority groups (Sanders, 2009).

As is clear throughout the book, we do not purport to argue that an identical set of processes and institutions leads to all changes in the legal status of sexual minorities. This book examines a range of such rights—from the right not to lose one's life because of one's sexual orientation, through the right to freely live one's sexual orientation, to the right not to be discriminated against based on sexual preferences. While there are several common threads running between the frameworks that we offer to analyze those different legal rights, those frameworks are not identical.

For instance, as we show in Chapter 3, religion plays a major role in explaining the variance between whether or not countries prescribe the death penalty to individuals violating a sodomy prohibition. Religion is still critical for explaining the mere presence of such provisions on the books.

Furthermore, when we examine issues of equality under the law in Chapters 5 and 6, the importance of international law and international institutions come into the fore. Those explain a good part of the variance in legal equality for LGBTI. Thus, while it makes a whole lot of sense to examine different types of gay rights in the same book—it is a set of legal provisions that pertain to a minority group that is present in each and every country and is defined by sexual orientation—there are aspects of those political phenomena that differ. Put another way, the dependent variables in all chapters are clearly related to each other; they pertain to the rights denied or granted sexual-minority groups. Yet, the sets of predictors offered to explain variance in those different outcome variables are dissimilar.

In sum, the first valuable insight from this book is probably the notion that while the political and legal issues examined all fall into the category of gay rights—and while obviously there is a prima facie hierarchy where abolition of death penalty for sodomy is at the most basic level, sodomy repeal is next, and right guarantees are at the top—in fact, moving up this apparent ladder of rights is a result of a combination of legal and political processes. No one set of political and legal institutions and agents could satisfactorily account for all.

The two key independent variables, which we focus on and where we find the innovation in this book, are legal path dependence and the influence of the religious state. Just as in the case of Israel mentioned at the beginning of this chapter, colonial heritage has played a major role in the legal conditions for sexual-minority groups in different parts of the world. As a result of the breakaway from Rome and the passage of the Buggery Act in the times of Henry VIII, sodomy entered the civil legislation in the kingdom. Through codification of British law when it was transported to the colonies and through legislative and judicial rulings (the Three Pillars in Chapter 2), legal path dependence means that Common Law jurisdictions have been more likely to have sodomy prohibitions on the books.

As the French had repealed such provisions after the Revolution, never to insert them back into the legal codes, we observe a different story of path dependence in Civil Law jurisdictions. The French first codified (e.g., in the Napoleon Code) and later exported this system of law to their territories and colonies. The upshot was that Civil Law jurisdictions were considerably less likely to have sodomy provisions on their law books. Common Law systems tend to be less favorable environments for the protection of the rights of LGBT individuals.

This story of legal path dependence wins considerable support when we juxtapose different institutions that may serve as venues for sodomy repeal. Our findings lend support to the notion that political actors are more constrained by legal status quo than their judicial counterparts and, accordingly, that the effects of path dependence on decision making in supreme courts are commensurably weaker. More broadly, this finding addresses a major criticism leveled against path-dependence scholars concerning their inability to explain policy change. We contend that under certain circumstances the judicial hierarchical structure *enables* courts of last resort to produce policy change. Indeed, as Kahn (2006) suggests, such courts may serve as important mechanisms of change, a relief valve of sorts, in theories of path dependence. We observe this clearly in the case of repeal of sodomy provisions.

A testament to the link between criminalization of gay behavior and religion comes from what is surely one of the most influential texts addressing that issue. Recommending substantial modifications to homosexual offences in Britain, the Wolfenden Report suggests: "Unless a deliberate attempt is made by society, acting through the agency of the law, to equate the sphere of crime with that of sin, there must remain a realm of private morality and immorality which is, in brief and crude terms, not the law's business" (pp. 187–188). We find that when religion is a basis for political exclusion, the rights afforded gay individuals suffer. The religious sources of prohibitions on sodomy account, at least partly, for this effect.

In addition, we find that the inclusion of women in the political system is associated with higher levels of protection of sexual minorities within the legal system. We argue that when other minorities are incorporated into the political system, sexual minorities win more legal protection. This spillover effect is boosted by international law. More specifically, when a country becomes a signatory to the CEDAW, it is also likely to improve legal protections for gays. In fact, the effect of international law in this context is so substantial, that such a country may repeal sodomy laws, if those are on the books, or pass legislation prohibiting discrimination on the basis of sexual orientation if, at the time of ratification, sodomy is already decriminalized. We also find effects in certain cases for other international and global effects such as membership in the ILO and levels of globalization. Better economic conditions as reflected in the country's GDP per capita, and improved democratic conditions also increase levels of protection for sexual minorities.

While this book sheds important light on the impact of the religious state and legal path dependence as they impact the legal rights of the LGBT community, we believe it is just a first step in better understanding the human rights of the LGBT community and the way discrimination and protection of this community has changed over time. The next big step would be to examine how and why social discrimination against sexual minorities changes over time. This is both a major data-collection challenge that needs to be addressed but also a burning concern, given that for many countries, it is social rather than legal discrimination that is the next big hurdle that needs to be addressed. Understanding why legal restrictions against the LGBT community were put in place in the first place and why they were removed is important and covers enough topics and areas for (as we have seen) a book. Yet, it is only the first part of the story.

We chose not to cover issues of societal discrimination in this book for length reasons—but not only for such reasons. Coding societal discrimination is a much greater challenge than coding legal persecution or legal protection. It is one thing to code laws that protect against violations of employment rights against the LGBT community than it is to code the level of such discrimination itself—particularly when one is attempting to do this cross-nationally and outside the West where there are fewer efforts to keep track of such discrimination. We will end this chapter and this book by pointing out what we believe to be the key road ahead in the study of advances in LGBT rights cross-nationally.

While coding a country for societal discrimination might be fairly easy in a country such as Jamaica where sodomy is still illegal (Itaborahy & Zhu, 2014) and homophobia is extremely high across much of the population (Padgett-Kingston, 2006), for many other countries it becomes much more complicated. In a recent piece in *The New York Times* titled "A Sea Change in Less Than 50 Years as Gay Rights Gained Momentum," Harwood (2013) points out that there truly has been a vast change in the legal rights of the LGBT community but also in their treatment societally. It was less than 30 years ago that the first US congressman came out of the closet and less than 20 years ago that a liberal president signed the Defense of Marriage Act. In 2013 a "Gallup poll found that 53 percent of respondents favored legal recognition of same-sex marriages" (Harwood, 2013). More and more politicians are openly out of the closet, and a growing number of positive representations of LGBT members can be found on TV and in Hollywood movies.

Despite this sea change in acceptance and legal status, there are still states that allow discrimination against the LGBT community, and there are still high levels of discrimination against the LGBT community across the United States (Itaborahy & Zhu, 2014). The National Coalition of Anti-Violence

Programs released a report (Ahmed &Jindasura, 2013), which identifies 2001 incidents of violence and an increase of the severity of violence against members of the "Lesbian, Gay, Bisexual, Transgender, Queer and HIV-Affected Communities." The report also identifies 18 hate-crime homicides against members of the community. The United States raises the hard question of how to code societal discrimination given the wide range of behaviors on display towards the LGBT community in the United States today. This challenge is underlined when we look at other countries that send out mixed messages when it comes to the rights and acceptance of their LGBT communities.

In Brazil for example, sodomy has been legal since 1831. Yet, there has been an ongoing trend of violence against the LGBT community, which has risen over the last decade despite a well-organized LGBT community (Jebsen, 2012). Jebsen reports in 2012 that:

> Attacks against gays have climbed steadily for most of the last decade, with 272 murdered in 2011—one every 36 hours, according to Grupo Gay da Bahía, a leading gay-rights group that tracks antigay violence. This year, GGB reports, it's even worse, with 75 murders in just the first 10 weeks. That's one every 24 hours.

The same Grupo Gay da Bahía, which is the oldest LGBT human rights organization in Brazil, reports that "between 1980 and 1998, over 1600 gays, lesbians and transvestites were killed in Brazil (GGB, 2014)." Our next efforts focus on how we might usefully code the different dimensions of societal discrimination against the LGBT community so we can continue our work and build on the theory and findings in *Legal Path Dependence and the Long Arm of the Religious State* to better understand the political inclusion and exclusion of the LGBTIQ community around the world.

APPENDIX

Appendix A. Descriptive Statistics

Variable	Observations	Mean	SD	Min	Max
% Catholic	6732	31.13	35.58	0	99.1
% Protestant	6624	13.19	21.2	0	97.8
% Muslim	6732	23.2	35.68	0	99.9
Women in Parliament	3943	9.9	8.8	0	42.7
Democracy	6173	5.5	3.4	0	10
GDP	5625	7711.3	8330.7	170.55	84408.23
Globalization	6245	49.2	24.5	1.55	98.78
ILO	7380	.54	.49	0	1
ICCPR	7380	.47	.49	0	1

Appendix B: A Correlation Matrix

Variable	Women in Parliament	Democracy	GDP	Globalization	% Catholic	% Protestant	% Muslim	ILO
Democracy	.14							
GDP	.24	.52						
Globalization	.18	.49	.49					
% Catholic	-.03	.28	.11	.23				
% Protestant	.38	.35	.34	.18	-.15			
% Muslim	-.03	-.41	-.17	-.12	-.46	-.32		
ILO	.12	.11	.05	.355	.2	.007	.07	
ICCPR	.21	.27	.09	.35	.15	.1	-.1	.4

Appendix C: Supporting Analyses and Robustness Tests

GEE Models: Sodomy Analyses in Different World Regions

Variable	Eastern Europe and Post-Soviet Union	Latin America	North Africa and the Middle East	Sub-Saharan Africa	Western Europe and North America
Common Law	omitted	omitted	-.14	**-.486 *****	**-.43 ****
			(.28)	**(.118)**	**(.16)**
% Catholic	.004 *	.004	-.024	-.0007	**-.002 ***
	(.002)	(.003)	(.017)	(.0043)	**(.001)**
% Muslim	**-.004 ***	**-.18 *****	-.001	-.0021	.08
	(.002)	**(.03)**	(.004)	(.0031)	(.07)
% Protestant	**.009 *****	.007	.73	-.0004	-.003
	(.002)	(.016)	(.46)	(.0051)	(.002)
GDP per capita	-.000016	**.00003 ***	.000009	.000001	.000005
	(.000016)	**(.00001)**	(.000007)	(.000003)	(.000015)
Democratic Conditions	-.008	-.017	-.01	.009	**.094 *****
	(.015)	(.01)	(.01)	(.008)	**(.019)**
Globalization	**.007 ****	.0018	.001	**.0031 ***	.003
	(.002)	(.0014)	(.003)	**(.0018)**	(.003)
Political Inclusion	-.006	.0046	.006	.0016	.003
	(.004)	(.0042)	(.007)	(.0047)	(.007)
CEDAW	.1	.123	.055	-.026	.07
	(.08)	(.085)	(.057)	(.023)	(.07)
ILO	**.3 ***	**-.08 ***	.009	.047	.15
	(.13)	**(.04)**	(.038)	(.035)	(.14)
ICCPR	.027	-.083	.124	-.008	.04
	(.13)	(.057)	(.133)	(.009)	(.04)
Ethnic Fractionalization	.46	-.34	-.23	.077	.36
	(.37)	(.34)	(.48)	(.276)	(.26)

Appendix C (continued)

GEE Models: Sodomy Analyses in Different World Regions

Variable	Eastern Europe and Post-Soviet Union	Latin America	North Africa and the Middle East	Sub-Saharan Africa	Western Europe and North America
Constant	-.07 (.24)	.37 (.35)	.29 (.49)	.3 (.3)	-.6 (.4)
	N=365 Number of Groups=26 Observations per group: Min=4 Avg=14 Max=30 Wald Chi2=291.36 Prob>Chi2=.0	N=520 Number of Groups=20 Observations per group: Min=14 Avg=26 Max=30 Wald Chi2=1872.26 Prob>Chi2=.0	N=415 Number of Groups=16 Observations per group: Min=1 Avg=25.9 Max=30 Wald Chi2=2927.33 Prob>Chi2=.0	N=883 Number of Groups=42 Observations per group: Min=4 Avg=21 Max=30 Wald Chi2=32.77 Prob>Chi2=.0011	N=579 Number of Groups=20 Observations per group: Min=12 Avg=28.9 Max=30 Wald Chi2=412.03 Prob>Chi2=.0

Appendix D: Supporting Analyses and Robustness Tests

GEE Models: Sodomy Analyses in Different Levels of Dominance for Islam

Variable	Muslims > 20%	Muslims > 35%	Muslims > 50%	Islam Is State Religion	Islam Is NOT State Religion
Common Law	-.3**	-.27*	-.109	.054	-.48***
	(.1)	(.11)	(.127)	(.18)	(.06)
% Catholic	n/a	n/a	n/a	n/a	n/a
% Muslim	n/a	n/a	n/a	n/a	n/a
% Protestant	n/a	n/a	n/a	n/a	n/a
GDP per capita	.0000014	.00000058	.00000014	.00000014	.000017**
	(.0000013)	(.0000013)	(.00000017)	(.00000016)	(.000007)
Democratic Conditions	.013	.013	-.0002	-.012	.003
	(.01)	(.013)	(.006)	(.013)	(.006)
Globalization	.003**	.0022	.001	.0015	.002*
	(.001)	(.0013)	(.001)	(.0016)	(.001)
Political Inclusion	-.008*	-.002	.002	-.002	-.001
	(.003)	(.004)	(.002)	(.002)	(.002)
CEDAW	.02	.012	-.02	-.006	.04*
	(.02)	(.026)	(.02)	(.009)	(.02)
ILO	.1	.123	.05	.048	.061
	(.07)	(.09)	(.05)	(.049)	(.045)
ICCPR	.01	.0006	.015	-.003	.02
	(.03)	(.03)	(.03)	(.006)	(.029)

Appendix D (continued)

	GEE Models: Sodomy Analyses in Different Levels of Dominance for Islam				
Variable	Muslims > 20%	Muslims > 35%	Muslims > 50%	Islam Is State Religion	Islam Is NOT State Religion
Ethnic Fractionalization	.29	.42	.045	-.01	-.17
	(.23)	(.27)	(.29)	(.16)	(.14)
Constant	-.09	-.16	.04	-.007	**.37 ****
	(.14)	(.18)	(.17)	(.127)	**(.13)**
	N=945	N=789	N=616	N=358	N=3132
	Number of Groups=48	Number of Groups=40	Number of Groups=30	Number of Groups=16	Number of Groups=136
	Observations per group: Min=1 Avg=19.7 Max=30	Observations per group: Min=1 Avg=19.7 Max=30	Observations per group: Min=1 Avg=20.5 Max=30	Observations per group: Min=1 Avg=22.4 Max=30	Observations per group: Min=4 Avg=23 Max=30
	Wald Chi2=22.71	Wald Chi2=23.18	Wald Chi2=9.33	Wald Chi2=2.6	Wald Chi2=213.79
	Prob>Chi2=.0	Prob>Chi2=.0058	Prob>Chi2=.41	Prob>Chi2=.98	Prob>Chi2=.0

	GEE Models: Sodomy Analyses in Different Levels of Dominance for Catholicism		
Variable	Catholics > 20%	Catholics > 35%	Catholics > 50%
Common Law	-.58 ***	-.56 ***	-.75 ***
	(.1)	(.13)	(.09)
% Catholic	n/a	n/a	n/a
% Muslim	n/a	n/a	n/a
% Protestant	n/a	n/a	n/a

Appendix D (continued)

GEE Models: Sodomy Analyses in Different Levels of Dominance for Catholicism

Variable	Catholics > 20%	Catholics > 35%	Catholics > 50%
GDP per capita	.000021 *	.00002 *	.00002 *
	(.0000096)	(.00001)	(.00001)
Democratic Conditions	.0003	.002	.001
	(.007)	(.009)	(.01)
Globalization	**.0018 ***	**.0025 ***	.0022
	(0009)	**(.001)**	(.0014)
Political Inclusion	.003	.001	.0038
	(.002)	(.002)	(.0027)
CEDAW	.05	.067	.09
	(.04)	(.051)	(.06)
ILO	-.023	-.017	-.028
	(.035)	(.05)	(.06)
ICCPR	-.029	-.034	-.05
	(.03)	(.041)	(.04)
Ethnic Fractionalization	-.165	-.16	-.222
	(.21)	(.2)	(.238)
Constant	.5 ***	.51 **	.52 **
	(.16)	(.17)	(.17)
	N=1559 Number of Groups=63 Observations per group: Min=9 Avg=24.7 Max=30 Wald Chi2=79.49 Prob>Chi2=.0	N=1171 Number of Groups=47 Observations per group: Min=9 Avg=24.9 Max=30 Wald Chi2=53.74 Prob>Chi2=.0	N=976 Number of Groups=39 Observations per group: Min=9 Avg=25 Max=30 Wald Chi2=199.07 Prob>Chi2=.0

Appendix E: Supporting Analyses and Robustness Tests

GEE Models: Gay Rights Index in Different World Religions

Variable	Muslims > 20%	Muslims > 35%	Muslims > 50%	Catholics > 20%	Catholics > 50%
Common Law	**-.3** ** (.1)	**-.27** ** (.11)	-.11 (.12)	**-.655** *** (.13)	**-.75** *** (.15)
% Catholic	n/a	n/a	n/a	n/a	n/a
% Muslim	n/a	n/a	n/a	n/a	n/a
% Protestant	n/a	n/a	n/a	n/a	n/a
GDP per capita	.0000011 (.0000013)	.00000058 (.0000013)	.00000014 (.00000017)	**.000041** ** (.000014)	**.00004** * (.00002)
Democratic Conditions	.013 (.011)	.013 (.013)	-.0002 (.006)	-.004 (.008)	-.004 (.012)
Globalization	**.003** ** (.001)	.0022 (.0014)	.0016 (.0011)	**.003** ** (.001)	**.004** ** (.001)
Political Inclusion	**-.008** ** (.003)	-.002 (.004)	.002 (.002)	**.008** ** (.003)	**.008** * (.004)
CEDAW	.025 (.025)	.012 (.026)	-.02 (.02)	**.083** * (.043)	**.11** * (.06)
ILO	.11 (.07)	.123 (.09)	.05 (.05)	-.026 (.06)	.002 (.1)
ICCPR	.014 (.032)	.0006 (.03)	.015 (.03)	**-.07** * (.034)	**-.095** * (.047)

Appendix E (continued)

GEE Models: Gay Rights Index in Different World Religions

Variable	Muslims > 20%	Muslims > 35%	Muslims > 50%	Catholics > 20%	Catholics > 50%
Ethnic Fractionalization	.19	.42	.04	.06	-.15
	(.23)	(.26)	(.29)	(.26)	(.29)
Constant	-.09	-.16	.04	.18	.2
	(.14)	(.18)	(.17)	(.23)	(.25)
	N=945 Number of Groups=48 Observations per group: Min=1 Avg=19.7 Max=30 Wald Chi2=22.71 Prob>Chi2=.007	N=789 Number of Groups=40 Observations per group: Min=1 Avg=19.7 Max=30 Wald Chi2=23.18 Prob>Chi2=.006	N=616 Number of Groups=30 Observations per group: Min=1 Avg=20.5 Max=30 Wald Chi2=9.33 Prob>Chi2=.4	N=1559 Number of Groups=63 Observations per group: Min=9 Avg=24.7 Max=30 Wald Chi2=67.6 Prob>Chi2=.0	N=976 Number of Groups=39 Observations per group: Min=9 Avg=25 Max=30 Wald Chi2=70.24 Prob>Chi2=.0

Appendix F: Illustrations

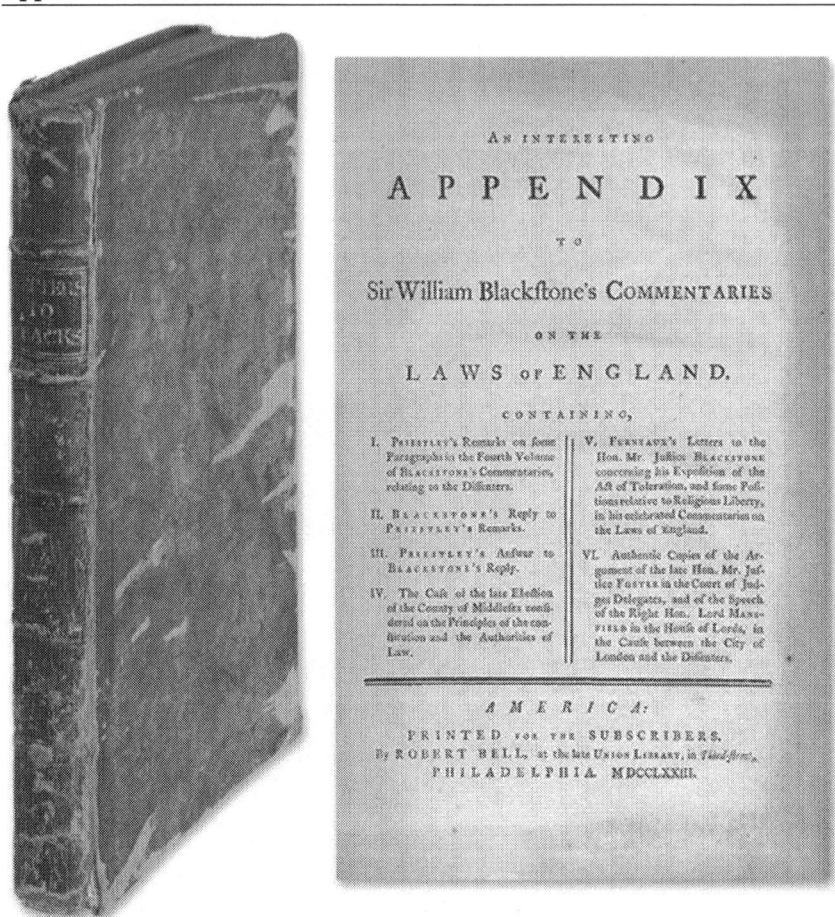

William Blackstone's *Commentaries on the Laws of England*

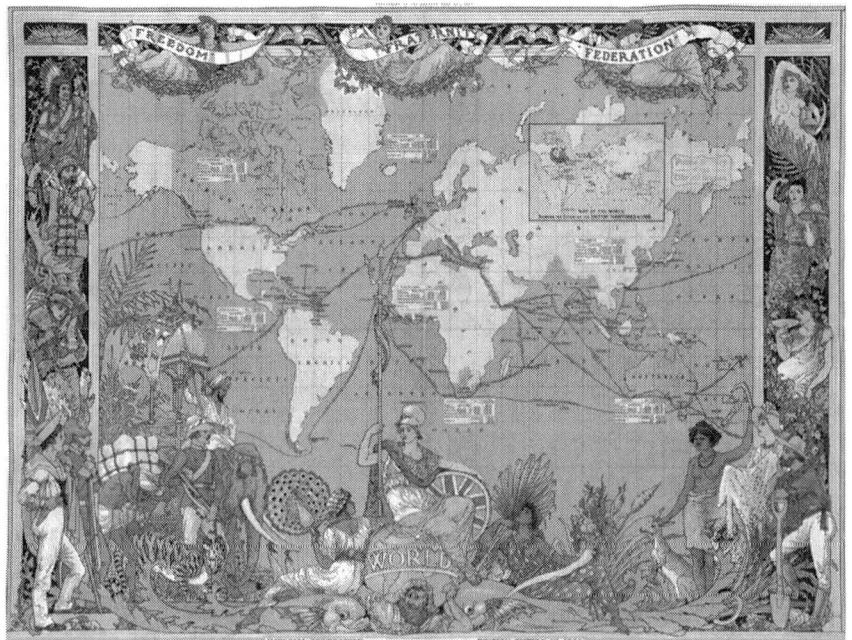

The British Empire (1886)
"Imperial Federation, Map of the World Showing the Extent of the British Empire in 1886 (levelled)" by Walter Crane. Retrieved from http://maps.bpl.org/id/M8682/. Licensed under Public Domain via Commons: https://commons.wikimedia.org/wiki/File:Imperial_Federation,_Map_of_the_World_Showing_the_Extent_of_the_British_Empire_in_1886_(levelled).jpg#/media/File:Imperial_Federation,_Map_of_the_World_Showing_the_Extent_of_the_British_Empire_in_1886_(levelled).jpg

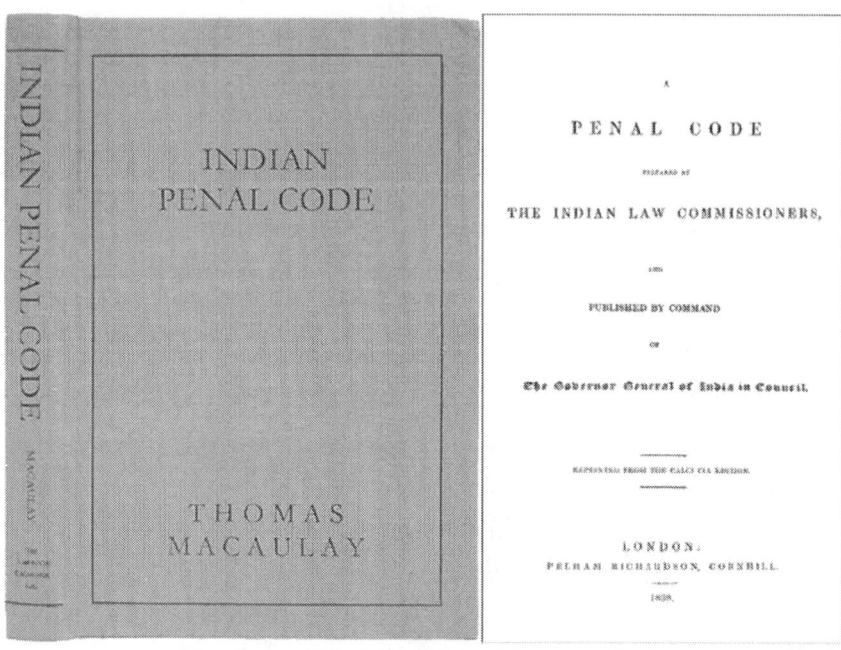

The Indian Penal Code, the Macaulay Code

King Henry VIII

NOTES

Chapter 1. Introduction

1. We do not contend here that it is particularly one denomination (e.g., Catholicism or Islam) that makes criminalization more likely. Rather, it is the role of religion in politics and the legal limitations on religious minorities that are critical. Indeed, in nations with a large Muslim population, which are also secular or multi-religious, or alternatively where there is a tradition of tolerance, Islam would not have such an effect. See for instance the cases of Turkey and Indonesia.
2. We are aware of alternative interpretations for these verses.
3. "Even as Sodom and Gomorrah, and the cities about them in like manner, giving themselves over to fornication, and going after strange flesh, are set forth for an example, suffering the vengeance of eternal fire."
4. For example, the government shut down workshops for LGBT activists, and the high court of Uganda dismissed efforts to try and stop the government from doing so. In 2014, Uganda passed legislation targeting sexual-minority groups. This was a blow to efforts to push for recognition of the rights of LGBT individuals or the LGBT community (Lowder, 2014a). The 2014 proposal—which passed eventually after the law to make homosexuality punishable by death had been tabled—includes provisions for life imprisonment for gay sex, including oral sex; life imprisonment for "aggravated homosexuality," including sex with a minor

or while HIV-positive; life imprisonment for living in a same-sex marriage; seven years for "attempting to commit homosexuality"; between five and seven years in jail or a $40,700 (£24,500) fine or both for the promotion of homosexuality; businesses or non-governmental organizations found guilty of the promotion of homosexuality would have their certificates of registration cancelled and directors could face seven years in jail (BBC, 2014). The law created an environment that proved dangerous for sexual minorities. For example, a newspaper in Uganda published a list similar to the one that led to the killing of a gay-rights activist in 2011 (BBC, 2014). Consequently, there have been people arrested for homosexual activity who are being held for trial with a possible punishment of life imprisonment (Stewart, 2014).
5. Much of the literature that does exist takes a particularly legal perspective and does not attempt to address possible larger causal mechanisms.
6. We believe that precedent is "flexible" and in some instances may be circumvented by both judges and legislators. Indeed, judges are free to choose among precedents that coincide with their own subjective interpretation of the facts. Moreover, legislators may act to overturn precedent. In the United States, for example, Congress can pass legislation (amendments) in order to reverse statutory (constitutional) interpretations, while in England legal precedents can be overruled by subsequent acts of parliament. However, precedent is not without meaning. Ultimately, lower court judges adhere to precedent to avoid being overruled (Songer, Segal, & Cameron, 1994; Segal & Spaeth, 1996, 2003), while members of courts of last resort uphold precedent in order to maintain institutional legitimacy and prestige (Epstein & Knight, 1998). At the same time, it is often difficult for legislators to reverse precedent given the majority and sometimes supermajority requirements necessary to do so and because the principle of precedent is deeply ingrained in the legal culture of many Common Law systems (Brigham, 1991; Gillman, 1999; Hathaway, 2003).
7. Section 61 of the Offences against the Person Act, 1861.
8. The act implemented some of the recommendations in the Wolfenden Report published in 1957. Thus, it took ten years of campaigning following the renowned report for only a subset of the recommendations in the report to be etched into law. With processes such as colonization, these prohibitions found their way into other countries with Common Law systems and, by ways of path dependence, influenced how laws concerning homosexuality and same-sex acts developed in those jurisdictions.

9. Though this has not occurred without controversy, as evidenced by the vocal opposition to references to foreign law in American courts led by Justice Antonin Scalia (Finkelman, 2007).
10. All original data sets are also cited.

Chapter 3. The Religious State and Death Penalty for Sodomy

1. See also Human Rights Watch (2005).
2. See also Franck & Schabas (2003); Greenberg & West (2008); Hood (2002); Mortensen (2008); Schabas (2002).
3. http://www.amnesty.org/en/death-penalty/abolitionist-and-retentionist-countries (last accessed January 2013).

Chapter 4. Sodomy Provisions and Their Repeal

1. Ideally we would use the percentage in the lower house; however, such data are not available.
2. ilo.org (accessed 25 December 2010).
3. http://www.bayefsky.com/docs.php/area/ratif (accessed 25 December 2010).
4. Throughout this chapter, we examine policy changes as they pertain to the country as a whole. Therefore, if in a federal system some of the political units decriminalized sodomy while other did not, it is not until there is a blanket decision pertaining to the entire nation that we code for policy change. As an illustration: in the case of the United States, while some states repealed sodomy laws prior to the decision of the Supreme Court in *Lawrence v. Texas* in 2003, it was not until this decision that policy in the entire country changed uniformly. For that reason, the change in this country is coded as repeal by judicial means.
5. Lower court justices do not enjoy the same type of institutional freedom as courts of last resort. This is primarily because their decisions are subject to review by higher courts and may be reversed if "incorrectly" decided (Segal & Spaeth, 1996). Lower court justices are thus unable to use their positions to affect policy change unless those changes are endorsed and actively pursued by courts of last resort.
6. Kahn (2006) explicitly makes this argument—courts of last resort sit atop a hierarchical structure that not only enables them to incorporate

changing "social facts" into law (because they are isolated from public opinion) but also relieves them from the fear of being overruled. In other words, lower courts are more constrained by law than courts of last resort because lower courts avoid making decisions they know will be overturned by a higher court (i.e., decisions that do not adhere to established precedent). See also Segal and Spaeth (2003) in that matter.
7. For our purposes, decriminalization and legalization are both considered to be instances of the repeal of sodomy laws. While there may be some difference between the two concepts, the behavior we seek to explain is policy change; and both legalization and decriminalization represent a shift in policy of the type we are interested in.
8. "State-sponsored Homophobia: A World Survey of Laws Prohibiting Same Sex Activity Between Consenting Adults."

Chapter 5. Equalization of Rights

1. Change on the ground is not always preceded by legal change.
2. In general, the United States is a laggard when it comes to the rights of sexual minorities (Barclay et al., 2009).
3. (Communication No. 488/1992) (31 March 1994) (50th Session), UN H.R. Committee Doc. No. CCPR/C/50/D/488/1992, 1.H.R.R. 97.
4. (Communication No. 488/1992) (31 March 1994) (50th Session), UN H.R. Committee Doc. No. CCPR/C/50/D/488/1992, 1.H.R.R. 97.
5. According to the website of the ILO: http://www.ilo.org/ilolex/english/convdisp1.htm (accessed 25 December 2010).
6. "State-sponsored Homophobia: A World Survey of Laws Prohibiting Same Sex Activity Between Consenting Adults."
7. We use the data for the legislative body as a whole in unicameral systems; and where there exists more than one legislative chamber, we use only the percentage of women in the upper house. Ideally we would use the percentage in the lower house; however, such data are not available.
8. Accessed 25 December 2010 at ilo.org.
9. Accessed 25 December 2010 at: http://www.bayefsky.com/docs.php/area/ratif.

Chapter 6. The Gay Rights Index

1. See Kohut (2013) but see also Spiegel Online (2013) and Strasser (2010) for additional information about recent trends.
2. "State-sponsored Homophobia: A World Survey of Laws Prohibiting Same Sex Activity Between Consenting Adults."
3. We use the data for the legislative body as a whole in unicameral systems; and where there exists more than one legislative chamber, we use the percentage of women in the upper house only. Ideally we would use the percentage in the lower house; however, such data are not available.

REFERENCES

Abiad, N. (2008). *Sharia, Muslim states and international human rights treaty obligations: a comparative study*. London: British Institute of International and Comparative Law.

Adewoye, O. (1977). *The judicial system in Southern Nigeria, 1854–1954: Law and justice in a dependency*. Atlantic Highlands, NJ: Humanities Press.

Adserà, A., Boix, C., & Payne, M. (2003). Are you being served? Political accountability and quality of government. *Journal of Law, Economics, & Organization, 19*(2), 445–490.

Ahmed, O., & Jindasura, C. (2013). *Report on lesbian, gay, bisexual, transgender, queer, and HIV-affected hate violence*. New York City Anti-Violence Project. Retrieved from http://avp.org/storage/documents/2013_ncavp_hvreport_final.pdf

Aitkenhead, D. (2005, January 5). Their homophobia is our fault. *The Guardian*. Retrieved August 24, 2014, from http://www.theguardian.com/world/2005/jan/05/gayrights.comment

Akinola, P. Why I object to homosexuality and same-sex unions. Retrieved on June 28, 2011, from http://www.anglican-nig.org/Pri_obj_Homo.htm

Alesina, A., Devleeschauwer, A., Easterly, W., Kurlat, S., & Wacziarg, R. (2003). Fractionalization. *Journal of Economic Growth, 8*(2), 155–194.

Alsop, R. (2013, June 17). Gay Employees Accepted, But Not Protected, At Work. bbc.com

Amnesty International. (2012, February 14). Amnesty International condemns "outrageous" government raid on LGBT activists' workshop in Uganda. Retrieved July 7, 2014, from http://www.amnestyusa.org/news/press-releases/amnesty-international-condemns-outrageous-government-raid-on-lgbt-activists-workshop-in-uganda

Anderson, B. (1983). *Imagined communities.* New York: Verso.

Appadurai, A. (Ed.) (2000). *Globalization.* Durham, NC: Duke University Press.

Arian, A. (1998). *The second republic—Politics in Israel.* Chatham, NJ: Chatham House.

Asal, V., Sommer, U., & Harwood, P. G. (2013). Original sin: A cross-national study of the legality of homosexual acts. *Comparative Political Studies, 46*(3), 320–351.

Ashkanasy, N. M., Trevor-Roberts, E., & Earnshaw, L. (2002). The Anglo cluster: Legacy of the British Empire. *Journal of World Business* 37(1), 28-39.

Awondo, P., Geschiere, P., & Reid, G. (2012). Homophobic Africa? Toward a more nuanced view. *African Studies Review, 55*(3), 145–168.

Bacchetta, P. (1999). When the (Hindu) nation exiles its queers. *Social Text, 61,* 141–166.

Baird, V. A. (2004). The effect of politically salient decisions on the U.S. Supreme Court's agenda. *The Journal of Politics, 66,* 755–772.

Baird, V. A. (2007). *Answering the call of the court: How justices and litigants set the Supreme Court's agenda.* Charlottesville, VA: University of Virginia Press.

Baker, J. H. (2002). *An introduction to English legal history.* London: Oxford University Press.

Barclay, S., Bernstein, M., & Marshall, A.-M. (2009). *Queer mobilizations: LGBT activists confront the law.* New York University Press.

Barnum, D. G. (1985). The Supreme Court and public opinion: Judicial decision making in the post-new deal period. *The Journal of Politics, 47,* 652–666.

Bartholomew, R. E. (2014). Beware the medicalisation of deviance in Russia: Remembering the lessons of history. *Journal of the Royal Society of Medicine, 107*(5), 176–177.

Bates, S. (2004). *A church at war: Anglicans and homosexuality.* London: I. B. Tauris.

BBC. (2014, February 25). Uganda health services "are for all." *BBC News,* 25. Retrieved from bbc.com July 7, 2014.

Bedau, H., & Cassell, P. (2004). *Debating the death penalty: Should America have capital punishment? The experts on both sides make their best case.* New York: Oxford University Press.

Beger, N. J. (2004). *Tensions in the struggle for sexual minority rights in Europe: Que(e)rying political practices.* Manchester University Press.

Bellomo, M. (1995). *The common legal past of Europe, 1000–1800.* Washington, DC: The Catholic University of America Press.

Ben-Asher, D. (1989). Legal discrimination against homosexuals in America, and a comparison with more tolerant societies. *New York Law School Journal of Human Rights, 7,* 157.

Bergel, J. L. (1988). Principal features and methods of codification. *Louisiana Law Review, 48,* 1073.

Berkman, M. B., & O'Connor, R. E. (1993). Do women legislators matter? *American Politics Research, 21*(1), 102–124.

Bernstein, M. (2002). Identities and Politics: Toward a Historical Understanding of the Lesbian and Gay Movement. *Social Science History, 26*(3), 531.

Bhan, G. (2005). *Because I have a voice: Queer politics in India.* New Delhi: Yoda Press.

Bigel, A. I. (1991). Presidential power and political questions. *Presidential Studies Quarterly, 21,* 663–672.

Boli, J., & Thomas, G. M. (1997). World culture in the world polity: A century of international non-governmental organization. *American Sociological Review, 62*(2), 171–190.

Boli, J., & Thomas, G. M. (1999). *Constructing world culture: International nongovernmental organizations since 1875.* Stanford University Press.

Bollen, K.A., & Jackman. R.W. (1985). Political democracy and the size distribution of income. *American Sociological Review,* 438–457.

Boris, K. (2004). *Same-sex desire in the English Renaissance: A sourcebook of texts, 1470–1650.* New York: Routledge.

Bosch, R. (1942). Andres Bello: The Blackstone of American Civil Law. *American Bar Association Journal, 28,* 825.

Bowers v. Hardwick, 478 U.S. 1986.

Brandon, M. E. (2005). War and the American constitutional order. In M. Tushnet (Ed.), *The Constitution in wartime: Beyond alarmism and complacency.* Durham, NC: Duke University Press, 11–38.

Brathwaite, L. F. (2013, July 24). Jamaica still "most homophobic place on earth" as cross-dressing teen "chopped and stabbed" to death. *Queerty.* Retrieved July 24, 2013, from http://www.queerty.com/in-jamaica-cross-dressing-teen-chopped-stabbed-to-death-20130724.

Brigham, J. (1991). *The cult of the court.* Philadelphia, PA: Temple University Press.

Brigham, J. (1999). The constitution of the Supreme Court. In H. Gillman & C. Clayton (Eds.), *The Supreme Court in American politics.* Lawrence, Kansas: University Press of Kansas, 15–28.

Butler, J., & Chakravorty, G. (2007). *Who sings the nation-state? Language, politics, belonging.* University of Chicago Press.

Castles, F. G. (1994). On religion and public policy: Does Catholicism make a difference? *European Journal of Political Research, 25,* 19–40.

Chu, J. (2009). One controversy, two jurisdictions: A comparative evaluation of the ultra vires and Common Law theories of judicial review. *Judicial Review, 14,* 347–358.

Clark, T. S. (2009). The separation of powers, court curbing, and judicial legitimacy. *American Journal of Political Science, 53,* 971–989.

Clemens, A. (2005). Executing homosexuality: Removing anti-gay bias from capital trials. *Georgetown Journal of Gender and the Law, 6,* 71.

Clinton, R. (1994). Game theory, legal history, and the origins of judicial review: A revisionist analysis of Marbury v. Madison. *American Journal of Political Science, 38,* 285–302.

Coke, E. (1797). Buggery or sodomy. In *The third part of the institutes of the laws of England.* London: E. & R. Brooke.

Cole, W. M. (2005). Sovereignty relinquished? Explaining commitment to the international human rights covenants, 1966–1999. *American Sociological Review, 70,* 472–495.

Collier, R. B., & David, C. (1991). *Shaping the political arena: Critical junctures, the labor movement, and regime dynamics in Latin America.* Princeton University Press.

Convention on the Elimination of All Forms of Discrimination against Women. Retrieved December 18, 1979, from http://www2.ohchr.org / english/law/cedaw.htm

Cook, T. E. (1999). The empirical study of lesbian, gay, and bisexual politics: Assessing the first wave of research. *American Political Science Review, 93*(3), 679–692.

Cooper, Charles. J. (1988). Stare decisis: Precedent and principle in constitutional adjudication. *Cornell Law Review, 73,* 401–410.

Crompton, L. (1976). Homosexuals and the death penalty in colonial America. *Journal of Homosexuality 1*(3), 277–293.

Crompton, L. (2006). *Homosexuality and civilization.* Cambridge, MA: Harvard University Press.

Day, A. (2013, July 3). Russia: Putin signs same-sex adoption ban into law. Retrieved March 3, 2016, from Pinknews.co.uk

D'Emilio, J. (1998). *Sexual politics, sexual communities: The making of a homosexual minority in the United States, 1940–1970.* University of Chicago Press.

D'Emilio, J. (2006). The marriage fight is setting us back. *The Gay and Lesbian Review*, November-December.

Dahl, R. A. (1957). Decision making in a democracy: The Supreme Court as a national policy-maker. *Journal of Public Law, 6*, 279–295.

Dahl, R. A. (1971). *Polyarchy: Participation and opposition.* New Haven, CT: Yale University Press.

Dainow, J. (1974). *The role of judicial decisions and doctrine in civil law and in mixed jurisdictions.* Baton Rouge, LA: Louisiana State University Press.

Dainow, J. (1996–1997). The Civil Law and the Common Law: Some points of comparison. *American Journal of Comparative Law, 15*(3), 419–435.

Davenport, C. (1999). Human rights and the democratic proposition. *Journal of Conflict Resolution, 43*(February), 92–117.

Hall, D. (2007, June 19). Gay, Arab, American. *The Advocate, 32.* Retrieved from http://www.advocate.com/issue_story_ektid45260.asp

Dawson, P. J. (1959). Specific performance in France and Germany. *Michigan Law Review, 57*(4), 252.

Dehghan, S. K. (2011, September 8). Iran executes three men on homosexuality charges. *The Guardian.* Retrieved August 24, 2014, from http://www.theguardian.com/world/2011/sep/07/iran-executes-men-homosexuality-charges

Deitch, C. (1993). Gender, race, and class politics and the inclusion of women in Title VII of the 1964 Civil Rights Act. *Gender and Society, 7*(2), 183–203.

Dicklitch, S., Yost, B., & Dougan, B. (2012). Building a barometer of gay rights (BGR): A case study of Uganda and the persecution of homosexuals. *Human Rights Quarterly, 34*(2), 448–471.

Dixon, R. (2010, November 3). Uganda paper declares "war" against gays; Homosexuals in the African nation report living in fear since a newspaper published their names, photos and addresses. *Los Angeles Times.*

Doorenspleet, R. (2004). The structural context of recent transitions to democracy. *European Journal of Political Research, 43*(May), 309–335.

Dreher, A. (2006). Does globalization affect growth? Evidence from a new index of globalization. *Applied Economics, 38*(10), 1091–1110.

Dreher, A., Gaston, N., & Martens, P. (2008). Measuring globalization:

Gauging its consequences. Retrieved from http://works.bepress.com/noel_gaston/14

Dudgeon v. United Kingdom, European Court of Human Rights, Appl. No. 7525/76.

Dundes, A. (2002). Much ado about "Sweet Bugger All": Getting to the bottom of a puzzle in British folk speech. *Folklore, 113*(1), 35–49.

Duran, K. (1993). Homosexuality and Islam. In A. Swindler (Ed.), *Homosexuality and world religions* (pp. 181–197). Valley Forge, PA: Trinity Press International.

Dynes, W. R. (1992). *Asian homosexuality* (Vol. 3). New York: Routledge.

Eastman, D. (1997). Homosexuality: Not a sin, not a sickness; What the Bible does and does not say. *Gay Theological Journal, 1*(1)(September–December), 12.

Edelman, M. (1995). Israel. In N. C. Tate & T. Vallinder (Eds.), *The global expansion of judicial power* (pp. 403–415). New York University Press.

El Al v. Danilovich, 48(5) P.D. 749 (Israel, 1994).

Engelstein, L. (1995). Soviet policy toward male homosexuality: Its origins and historical roots. *Journal of Homosexuality, 29*.2–3, 155–178.

Epp, C. R. (1996). Do bills of rights matter? The Canadian Charter of Rights and Freedom. *American Political Science Review, 90*, 765–779.

Epp, C. R. (1998). *The rights revolution: Lawyers, activists, and Supreme Courts in comparative perspective.* University of Chicago Press.

Epstein, L. & Walker, T. G. (2014). *Constitutional law for a changing America: Constitutional powers and constraints.* London: CQ Press.

Epprecht, M. (2009). *Heterosexual Africa: The history of an idea from the Age of Exploration to the Age of AIDS.* Athens, OH: Ohio University Press.

Eron, L. J. (1993). Homosexuality and Judaism. In A. Swindler (Ed.), *Homosexuality and world religions* (pp. 103–134). Valley Forge, PA: Trinity Press International.

Ertman, T. (1997). *Birth of the leviathan: Building states and regimes in Medieval and Early Modern Europe.* Cambridge University Press.

Eskridge, W. N. (2003). A history of same-sex marriage. *Virginia Law Review,* 1419–1513.

Eskridge, W. N. (2008). *Dishonorable passions: Sodomy laws in America, 1861–2003.* New York: Viking Press.

Eskridge, W. N. (1994). *Dynamic statutory interpretation.* Cambridge: Harvard University Press.

European Union Agency for Fundamental Rights. (May 2013). *European Union lesbian, gay, bisexual and transgender survey results at a glance.*

Retrieved July 6, 2014, from http://fra.europa.eu/en/publication/2013/eu-lgbt-survey-european-union-lesbian-gay-bisexual-and-transgender-survey-results

Ewick, P., & Silbey, S. (1998). *The common place of law: Stories from everyday life*. University of Chicago Press.

Ewick, P., & Silbey, S. (1999). Common knowledge and ideological critique: The significance of knowing that the "haves" come out ahead. *Law and Society Review, 33*, 1025–1041.

Feder, L. J. (2014, June 23). Ugandan court rules government can stop LGBT Groups. *BuzzFeed*. Retrieved July 5, 2014, from buzzfeed.com

Feder, L. J. (2014, August 19). Ugandan president signs law criminalizing HIV transmission. *BuzzFeed*. Retrieved August 19, 2014, from http://www.buzzfeed.com/lesterfeder/ugandan-president-signs-law-criminalizing-hiv-transmission#2tat52p

Fenno, R. F. (1996). *Senators on the campaign trail: The politics of representation*. Norman, OK: University of Oklahoma Press.

Finkelman, P. (2007). Foreign law and American constitutional interpretation: A long and venerable tradition. *New York University Annual Survey of American Law, 63*, 29–62.

Finnemore, M. (1996). Norms, culture and world politics: Insights from sociology's institutionalism. *International Organization, 50*, 325–348.

Finnemore, M., & Sikkink, K. (1998). International norm dynamics and political change. *International Organization, 52*, 887–917.

Fisher, L. (2005). Judicial review of the war power. *Presidential Studies Quarterly, 35*, 466–495.

Flemming, R. B., & Wood, B. D. (1997). The public and the Supreme Court: Individual justice responsiveness to American policy moods. *American Journal of Political Science, 41*, 468–498.

Fox, J. (2001). Religion as an overlooked element of international relations. *International Studies Review, 3*, 53–73.

Franck, H. N. K., & Schabas, W. (2003). *The barbaric punishment: Abolishing the death penalty*. The Hague: Martinus Nijhoff.

Frank, D. J., Camp, B. J., & Boutcher, S. A. (2010). Worldwide trends in the criminal regulation of sex, 1945 to 2005. *American Sociological Review, 75*(6), 867–893.

Frank, D. J., Boutcher, S.A., & Camp, B. (2009). Reform of sodomy laws from a world society perspective. In S. Barclay, M. Bernstein, & A. M. Marshall (Eds.), *Queer mobilizations: LGBT activists confront the law* (pp. 123–141). New York University Press.

Frank, D. J., & McEneaney, E. H. (1999). The individualization of society and the liberalization of state policies on same-sex sexual relations, 1984–1995. *Social Forces, 77*(3), 911–944.

Frank, D. J., Boutcher, S. A., & Camp, B. (2009). The repeal of sodomy laws from the perspective of world society. In S. Barclay, M. Bernstein, & A. M. Marshall (Eds.), *Queer mobilizations: LGBT activists confront the law* (pp. 123–141). New York University Press.

Fukuyama, F. (1992). *The end of history and the last man.* New York: Free Press.

Funston, R. (1975). The Supreme Court and critical elections, *The American Political Science Review, 69*, 795–811.

Gagnon, R. A. J. (2001). *The Bible and homosexual practice.* Nashville: Abingdon Press.

GayAsiaNews. (2014, April 8). Saudi police arrest 35 people for being at an alleged gay party. *GayAsiaNews.* Retrieved July 6, 2014, from http://gayasianews.com/2014/04/08/saudi-police-arrest-35-people-for-being-at-an-alleged-gay-party/

Gettleman, J. (2011, January 29). Remembering David Kato, a Gay Ugandan and a Marked Man. *The New York Times.* Retrieved from http://www.nytimes.com/2011/01/30/weekinreview/30gettleman.html

Gevisser, M. (2013). A different fight for freedom. In E. Cameron, & M. Gevisser (Eds.), *Defiant desire: gay and lesbian lives in South Africa* (pp. 14–88). Routledge.

Grupo Gay da Bahia (GGB). Retrieved October 19, 2014, from http://www.ggb.org.br/ggb-ingles.html

Gibbs, H. (2002). The Queensland criminal code: From Italy to Zanzibar. Address at opening of exhibition, Supreme Court Library. Retrieved from http://www.sclqld.org.au

Gibson, J. L. (2004). Truth, reconciliation, and the creation of a human rights culture in South Africa. *Law and Society Review, 38*, 5–40.

Gibson, J. L. (1980). Environmental constraints on the behavior of judges: A representational model of judicial decision making. *Law and Society Review, 14*, 343–370.

Giddens, A. (2002). *Runaway world: How globalization is reshaping our lives.* London: Profile Books.

Gilbert, A. N. (1976). Buggery and the British navy, 1700–1861. *Journal of Social History, 10*(1), 72–98.

Gilbert, A. N. (1981). Conceptions of homosexuality and sodomy in western history. *Journal of Homosexuality, 6*(1–2), 57–68.

Gjorgievska, A. (2014). U.S. takes action against Uganda over anti-homosexuality law. *TIME.com*. Retrieved July 5, 2014, from http://time.com/2902234/us-uganda-homosexuality

Gleditsch, K. (2002). Expanded trade and GDP data. *Journal of Conflict Resolution, 46*(5), 712.

Glick, D. (2009). Conditional strategic retreat: The court's concession in the 1935 gold clause cases. *Journal of Politics, 71*, 800–816.

Gloppen, S. (2005). Social rights litigation as transformation: South African perspectives. In P. Jones, & K. Stokke, (Eds.), *Democratising development: The politics of socio-economic rights in South Africa* (pp. 153–180). Leiden: Martinus Nijhoff.

Goodish. M. (1976). Sodomy in medieval secular law. *Journal of Homosexuality, 1*(3), 295–302.

Goodman, R. (2001). Beyond the enforcement principle: Sodomy laws, social norms, and social panoptics. *California Law Review, 89*, 643–740.

Graber, M. (1993). The non-majoritarian difficulty: Legislative deference to the judiciary. *Studies in American Political Development, 7,* 35–73.

Graupner, H., & Tahmindjis, P. (2005). *Sexuality and human rights*. New York: Harrington Park Press.

Greenberg, D., & West V. (2008). Siting the death penalty internationally. *Law and Social Inquiry, 33*(2), 295–343.

Greenberg, D., Katz, S. N., Oliviero, M. B., & Wheatley, S. C. (Eds.). (1993). *Constitutionalism and democracy: Transitions in the contemporary world*. New York: Oxford University Press.

Grewal, I. (2005). *Transnational America: Feminisms, diasporas, neoliberalisms*. Durham, NC: Duke University Press.

Grey, S. (2002). Does size matter? Critical mass and New Zealand's women MPs. *Parliamentary Affairs, 55*(1), 19–29.

Gupta, A. (2006). Section 377 and the dignity of Indian homosexuals. *Economic and Political Weekly, 41*(46), 4815–4823.

Gupta, A. (2008). *This alien legacy: The origins of "sodomy" laws in British colonialism*. New York: Human Rights Watch.

Gurr, T. R. (2000). *People versus states*. Washington, DC: United States Institute of Peace.

Habib, S. (Ed.). (2009). *Islam and homosexuality*. Santa Barbara, CA: ABC-CLIO.

Hacker, J. S. (1998). The historical logic of national health insurance: Structure and sequence in the development of British, Canadian, and U.S. medical policy. *Studies in American Political Development, 12,* 57–130.

Hadenius, A., & Teorell, J. (2005). Assessing alternative indices of democracy. In *Committee on Concepts and Methods—Working Paper Series*, (August).

Haider-Markel, D. P., & Meier, K. J. (1996). The politics of gay and lesbian rights: Expanding the scope of the conflict. *The Journal of Politics, 58*(2), (May), 332–349.

Hajjar, L. (2004). Religion, state power, and domestic violence in Muslim societies: A framework for comparative analysis. *Law and Social Inquiry, 29*(1), 1–38.

Harvey, A. D. (1978). Prosecutions for sodomy in England at the beginning of the nineteenth century. *The Historical Journal, 21*(04), 939–948.

Harwood, J. (2013, March 25) A sea change in less than 50 years as gay rights gained momentum. *The New York Times*. Retrieved October 19, 2014, from http://www.nytimes.com/2013/03/26/us/in-less-than-50-years-a-sea-change-on-gay-rights.html?pagewanted=all&_r=0

Hathaway, O. A. (2003). Path dependence in the law: The course and pattern of legal change in a Common Law system. *John M. Olin Center for Studies in Law, Economics, and Public Policy Working Papers.* Paper 270. Retrieved from hhtp://digitalcommons.law.yale.edu/lepp_papers/270

Hawley, C. (2001, August 15). Anger over Egypt gay trial. BBC News. Retrieved April 11, 2012, from http://news.bbc.co.uk/2/hi /middle_east/1493041.stm

Haynie, S. L. (1994). Resource inequalities and litigation outcomes in the Philippine Supreme Court. *Journal of Politics, 56,* 752–772.

Haynie, S. L. (2003). *Judging in black and white: Decision making in the South African appellate division, 1950–1990.* New York: Peter-Lang Publishing.

Healey, D. (2002). Homosexual existence and existing socialism: New light on the repression of male homosexuality. In Stalin's Russia. *GLQ: A Journal of Lesbian and Gay Studies, 8*(3), 349–378.

Hensle, E. (2009). Human rights and sexual orientation: An expansion of the equality doctrine. *Bologna Center Journal of International Affairs,* 12.

Hepple, J. (2012). Will sexual minorities ever be equal? The repercussions of British colonial "sodomy" laws. *The Equal Rights Review, 8,* 50–64.

Hermans, H. J. M., & Kempen, H. J. G. (1998). Moving cultures: The perilous problems of cultural dichotomies in a globalizing world. *American Psychologist, 53,* 1111–1120.

Hinsch, B. (1990). *Passions of the cut sleeve: The male homosexual tradition in China.* Berkeley, CA: University of California Press.

Hirst, P., & Thompson, G. (1999). *Globalization in question: The international economy and the possibilities of governance* (2nd ed.). Cambridge, MA: Polity Press.

Hoad, N. W. (2007). *African intimacies: Race, homosexuality, and globalization.* Minneapolis, MN: University of Minnesota Press.

Hollingsworth, J. R. (1998). New perspectives on the spatial dimensions of economic coordination: Tensions between globalization and social systems of production. *Review of International Political Economy, 5,* 482–507.

Holmes, O. W. (1897). The path of the law. *Harvard Law Review, 10,* 47.

Hood, R. (2002). *The death penalty: A worldwide perspective.* New York: Oxford University Press.

Huber, E., & Stephens, J. D. (2001). *Development and crisis of the welfare state: Parties and policies in global markets.* University of Chicago Press.

Human Rights Watch. (2005). Iran: Two more executions for homosexual conduct. Retrieved October 10, 2010, from http://www.hrw.org/en/news /2005/11/21/iran-two-more-executions-homosexual-conduct

Huntington, S. P. (1991). *The third wave: Democratization in the late twentieth century.* Norman, OK: University of Oklahoma Press.

Huntington, S. P. (1996). *The clash of civilizations: Remaking the world order.* New York: Simon and Schuster.

Inglehart, R. (1997). Modernization and postmodernization: Cultural, economic, and political change in 43 societies. Princeton University Press.

Inglehart, R., & Norris, P. (2003). *Rising tide: Gender equality and cultural change around the world.* Cambridge University Press.

Inglehart, R., Norris, P., & Welzel, C. (2002). Gender equality and democracy. *Comparative Sociology, 1,* 321.

Inter-Parliamentary Union. (2005). Women in national parliaments. Retrieved from http://www.ipu.org/

International Lesbian, Gay, Bisexual, Trans and Intersex Association (2010). Retrieved December 20, 2010, from http://ilga.org/ilga/en/article/1161

Itaborahy, L. P., & Zhu, J. (2014). State-sponsored homophobia. *ILGA—International Lesbian, Gay, Bisexual, Trans and Intersex Association* (May 2014). Retrieved July 2014, from http://old.ilga.org/Statehomophobia /ILGA_SSHR_2014_Eng.pdf

Jacobson, G. C. (2004). *Politics of congressional elections.* New York: Pearson.

Jagwanth, S. (2004). Affirmative action in a transformative context: The South African experience. *Connecticut Law Review, 36,* 725–745.

Jebsen, K. (2012, April 8). Brazil's surge in violence against gays is just getting worse. *The Daily Beast.* Retrieved June 20, 2014, from http://www.thedailybeast.com/articles/2012/04/08/brazil-s-surge-in-violence-against-gays-is-just-getting-worse.html

Johnson, C. (2013, May 4) Obama criticized for lack of LGBT cabinet appointments. *Washington Blade Gay News Washington DC LGBT.* Retrieved July

6, 2014, from http://www.washingtonblade.com/2013/05/04/obama-criticized-for-lack-of-lgbt-diversity-in-cabinet

Joseph, S. (1996). Gay and lesbian movement in India. *Economic and Political Weekly, 31*(33), 2228–2233.

Joshi, Y. (2010). The case for repeal of India's sodomy law. *South Asia: Journal of South Asian Studies, 33*(2), 304–317.

Kahn, R. (1999). Institutional norms and the historical development of Supreme Court politics: Changing "social facts" and doctrinal development. In R. Kahn, & K. Kersch (Eds.), *The Supreme Court in American politics* (pp.169–227). Lawrence, KS: University Press of Kansas.

Kahn, R. (2006). Social constructions, Supreme Court reversals, and American political development. In R. Kahn, & K. Kersch (Eds.), *The Supreme Court and American political development*. Lawrence, KS: University Press of Kansas.

Kahn, R., & Kersch, K. (2006). Introduction. In R. Kahn & K. Kersch (Eds.), *The Supreme Court and American political development* (pp. 1–32). Lawrence, KS: University Press of Kansas.

Kane, M. (2003). Social movement policy success: Decriminalizing state sodomy laws, 1969–1998. *Mobilization: An International Quarterly, 8*(3), 313–334.

Kane, M. (2007). Timing matters: Shifts in the causal determinants of sodomy law decriminalization, 1961–1998. *Social Problems, 54*(2), 211–239.

Keck, T. (2009). Beyond backlash: Assessing the impact of judicial decisions on LGBT rights. *Law and Society Review, 43*, 151–185.

Kent, S. (2010). Predicting abolition: A cross-national survival analysis of the social and political determinants of death penalty statutes. *International Criminal Justice Review, 20*(1), 56.

Khosla, M. (2011). Inclusive constitutional comparison: Reflections on India's sodomy decision. *American Journal of Comparative Law, 59*(4), 909–934.

King, G., & Zeng, L. 1999. *Logistic regression in rare events data*. Cambridge, MA: Department of Government, Harvard University. Retrieved from http://GKing.Harvard.Edu

Kingdon, J. W. (1989). *Congressmen's voting decisions*. Ann Arbor, MI: University of Michigan Press.

Kinnvall, C. (2004). Globalization and religious nationalism: Self, identity, and the search for ontological security. *Political Psychology, 25*, 741–767.

Kinsman, G. (1995). *The regulation of desire: Homo and hetero sexualities*. Montreal: Black Rose Press.

Kirby, M. (2008). Lessons from the Wolfenden Report. *Commonwealth Law Bulletin, 34,* 551.

Kirby, M. (2013). The sodomy offence: England's least lovely criminal law export. In C. Lennox & M. Waites (Eds.), *Human rights, sexual orientation and gender identity in the Commonwealth: Struggles for decriminalisation and change* (pp. 61–82). London: School of Advanced Study, University of London.

Klarman, M. J. (2004). *From Jim Crow to civil rights: The Supreme Court and the struggle for racial equality.* New York: Oxford.

Klarman, M. J. (2005). Brown and Lawrence (and Goodridge). *Michigan Law Review, 104,* 431–489.

Kligerman, N. (2007). Homosexuality in Islam: A difficult paradox. *Macalester Islam Journal, 2*(3), 8.

Kohut, A. (2013). The global divide on homosexuality: Greater acceptance in more secular and affluent countries. Washington, DC: Pew Research Center. Retrieved from http://www.pewglobal.org/2013/06/04/the-global-divide-on-homosexuality/

Kollman, K. (2010) LGBT human rights: from queers to humans. In R. A. Denemark (Ed.), *International Studies Encyclopedia* (pp. 4875–4897). Chichester: Wiley-Blackwell.

Kurth, J. R. (1979). The political consequences of the product cycle: Industrial history and political outcomes. *International Organization, 33*(1) (Winter), 1–34.

La Porta, R., López-de-Silanes, F., Shleifer, A., & Vishny, R. (2008). Economic consequences of legal origin. *Journal of Economic Literature, 46*(2), 285–332.

Lavers, M. K. (2013, July 23). Jamaican LGBT advocates condemn murder of cross-dressing teenager. *Washington Blade Gay News Washington DC LGBT.* Retrieved July 5, 2014 from http://www.washingtonblade.com /2013/07/23/jamaican-lgbt-advocates-condemn-murder-of-cross-dressing-teenager

Lawrence v. Texas, 539 U.S. 558.

Lax, J. R., & Phillips, J. (2009). Gay rights in the States: Public opinion and policy responsiveness. *American Political Science Review, 103*(3), 367–386.

Leslie, C. R. (2000). Creating criminals: The injuries inflicted by "unenforced" sodomy laws. *Harvard Civil Rights-Civil Liberties Law Review, 35,* 103–81.

Lester, T. (2012). Machismo at the crossroads—Recent developments in

Costa Rican gay rights law. *Michigan State International Law Review, 20*(2), 421–439.

Lipset, S. M. (1960). *Political man: The social bases of politics.* Garden City, NJ: Doubleday.

Llewellyn, K. N. (1960). *The common law tradition: Deciding appeals.* Boston: Little, Brown & Co.

Long, S., & Moumneh, R. (2009). "They want us exterminated": Murder, torture, sexual orientation and gender in Iraq. Human Rights Watch.

Lovell, G. I. (2003). *Legislative deferrals: Statutory ambiguity, judicial power, and American democracy.* Cambridge University Press.

Lowder, J. B. (2014a, February 24). It is now completely illegal to be gay in Uganda. *Slate Magazine.* Retrieved July 5, 2014, from http://www.slate.com /blogs/outward/2014/02/24/ugandan_president_signs_horrific_anti_gay_bill.html

Lowder, J. B. (2014b, May 23). God loves Uganda reveals how American evangelicals infected a country. *Slate Magazine.* Retrieved July 5, 2014, from http://www.slate.com/blogs/outward/2014/05/23 /god_loves_uganda_shows_how_american_evangelicals_exported_homophobia_to.html

MacKenzie, G. (2002). An enduring influence: Sir Samuel Griffith and his contribution to criminal justice in Queensland. *Queensland University of Technology Law Review, 2*(1), 53–63.

Mahoney, J. (2000). Path Dependence in Historical Sociology. *Theory and Society, 29,* 507–548.

Maioni, A. (1998). *Parting at the crossroads: The emergence of health insurance in the United States and Canada.* Princeton University Press.

Manfredi, C. P. (2004). *Feminist activism in the Supreme Court.* Vancouver: University of British Columbia Press.

Marbury v. Madison, 5 U.S. 137 (1803).

Marks, S. (2006). Global recognition of human rights for lesbian, gay, bisexual, and transgender people. *Health and Human Rights, 9*(1), 33–42.

McCann, M. W. (1994). *Rights at work: Pay equity reform and the politics of legal mobilization.* University of Chicago Press.

McCloskey, R. G. (2010). *The American Supreme Court.* University of Chicago Press.

McLelland, M. (2000). *Male homosexuality in modern Japan.* London: Curzon Press.

McLeod, D. W. (1996). *Lesbian and gay liberation in Canada: A selected annotated chronology, 1964–1975.* Toronto: Homewood Books & ECW Press.

McNeill, J. J. (1977). *The Church and the homosexual*. London: Darton, Longman & Todd.

Merin, Y. (2002). *Equality for same-sex couples: The legal recognition of gay partnerships in Europe and the United States*. University of Chicago Press.

Merryman, J. H., & Perez-Perdomo, R. (Eds.). (2007). *The Civil Law tradition: An introduction to the legal system of Europe and Latin America*. Stanford University Press.

Mertus, J. (2007). The rejection of human rights framings: The case of LGBT advocacy in the US. *Human Rights Quarterly, 29*, 1036–1064.

Meyer, B. (2003). Much ado about nothing? Political representation policies and the influence of women parliamentarians in Germany. *Review of Policy Research, 20*(3), 401–421.

Meyer, J. W., Boli, J., Thomas, G. M., & Ramirez, F. O. (1997). World society and the nation-state. *American Journal of Sociology, 103*(1), 144.

Michaelson, J. (2014, June 9). Homophobia in Russia is taking a Kafkaesque turn. *The Daily Beast*. Retrieved July 5, 2014, from http://www.thedailybeast .com/articles/2014/06/09/homophobia-in-russia-is-taking-a-kafkaesque-turn.html

Michaelson, J. (2014, July 7). How Campus Crusade for Christ exports homophobia to Africa. *The Daily Beast*. Retrieved July 7, 2014, from thedailybeast.com

Miethe, T., Lu, H., & Deibert, G. (2005). Cross-national variability in capital punishment. *International Criminal Justice Review, 15*(2), 115.

Milsom, S. F. C. (1981). Historical foundations of the Common Law. London: Butterworth and Company.

Mishler, W., & Sheehan, R. S. (1993). The Supreme Court as a countermajoritarian institution? The impact of public opinion on Supreme Court decisions. *The American Political Science Review, 87*, 87–101.

Monter, W. E. (1974). La sodomie à l'époque moderne en Suisse romande. *Annales E. S. C., 29*, 1023–1033.

Morris, H. F. (1970). How Nigeria got its criminal code. *Journal of African Law, 12*(3), 137–154.

Mortensen, A. K. (2008). *Abolition of the death penalty*. Masters thesis in the Department of Comparative Politics, University of Bergen, Norway.

Moustafa, T. (2003). Law versus the state: The judicialization of politics in Egypt. *Law and Social Inquiry, 28*(4), 883–930.

Msibi, T. (2011). The lies we have been told: On (homo) sexuality in Africa. *Africa Today, 58*(1), 54–77.

Murray, R., & Viljoen, F. (2007). Towards non-discrimination on the basis of sexual orientation: The normative basis and procedural possibilities before the African Commission on Human and Peoples' Rights and the African Union. *Human Rights Quarterly, 29*(1), 86–111.

Murray, S., & Roscoe, W. (1997). *Islamic homosexualities: Culture, history, and literature.* New York University Press.

Narrain, A. (2009). Challenging the anti sodomy law in India: Story of a continuing struggle. In G. Bhan et al. (Eds.), *Queer perspectives on the law.* New Delhi: Yoda Press.

National Coalition for Gay and Lesbian Equality and Another v. Minister of Justice and Others (CCT11/98) ZACC 15 (1998).

Naz Foundation India Trust v. Government of NCT Delhi and Others, (India). (2009).

Neapolitan, J. (2001). An examination of cross-national variation in punitiveness. *International Journal of Offender Therapy and Comparative Criminology, 45*(6), 691.

Neumayer, E. (2008a). Death penalty abolition and the ratification of the Second Optional Protocol. *The International Journal of Human Rights, 12*(1), 3–21.

Neumayer, E. (2008b). Death penalty: The political foundations of the global trend towards abolition. *Human Rights Review, 9*(2), 241–268.

Noble, B. (2012). Decriminalising sex between men in the former Soviet Union, 1991–2003. In K. E. Goodall, M. S. Malloch, B. Munro, & W. G. Munro (Eds.), *Building justice in post-transition Europe: Processes of criminalisation within central and eastern European societies* (Vol. 2) (pp. 115–136). New York: Routledge.

North, D. C. (1990). *Institutions, Institutional Change and Economic Performance.* Cambridge University Press.

Norton, R. (1977). The Biblical Roots of Homophobia and A Rejoinder. In M. Macourt (Ed.), *Towards a theology of gay liberation* (pp. 39–46, 57–60). London: SCM Press.

Norton, R. (2005). Recovering gay history from the Old Bailey. *The London Journal, 30*(1), 39–54.

Olyan, S. (1994). And with a male you shall not lie the lying down of a woman: On the meaning and significance of Leviticus 18:22 and 20:13. *Journal of the History of Sexuality, 5,* 179–206.

Olzak, S., & Kiyoteru, T. (1998). Status in the world system and ethnic mobilization. *Journal of Conflict Resolution, 42*(6), 691–720.

Ottoson, D. (2009). State-sponsored homophobia: a world survey on laws prohibiting same sex activity between consenting adults. International

Gay and Lesbian Association. Retrieved August 6, 2009, from http://ilga.org/ilga/en/index.html

Padgett-Kingston, T. (2006, April 12). The most homophobic place on earth? *Time*. Retrieved June 19, 2014, from http://content.time.com/time/world/article/0%2C8599%2C1182991%2C00.html

Patel, A. R. (2010). India's Hijras: The case for transgender rights. *George Washington International Law Review, 42*, 835.

Patternote, D. & Kollman, K. (2013). Regulating intimate relationships in the European polity: Same-sex unions and policy convergence. In *social politics: International studies in gender, state, and society.*

Pedriana, N. (2009). Intimate equality: The lesbian, gay, bisexual, and transgender movement's legal framing of sodomy laws in the *Lawrence v. Texas* case. In S. Barclay, M. Bernstein, & A.-M. Marshall (Eds.), *Queer mobilizations: LGBT activists confront the law* (pp. 52–75). New York University Press.

Penketh, A. (2008, March 6). Brutal land where homosexuality is punishable by death. *The Independent*. Retrieved from http://www.independent.co.uk/news/world/middle-east/brutal-land-where-homosexuality-is-punishable-by-death-792057.html

Peters, J. W. (2013, January 25). Openly gay, and openly welcomed in Congress. *The New York Times*. Retrieved July 6, 2014, from http://www.nytimes.com/2013/01/26/us/politics/gay-lawmakers-growing-presence-suggests-shift-in-attitudes.html?pagewanted=all&_r=0

Peters, R. (1994). The Islamization of criminal law: A comparative analysis. *Die Welt des Islams, 34*(2), 246–274.

Pierson, P. (2000). Path dependence, increasing returns, and the study of politics. *American Political Science Review, 94*(2), 251–267.

Pierson, P. (2004). *Politics in time: History, institutions, and social analysis.* Princeton University Press.

Pierson, P., & Skocpol, T. (2002). Historical institutionalism in contemporary politics. In I. Katznelson & H. V. Milner (Eds.), *Political Science: The state of the discipline* (3rd ed.). New York: W.W. Norton & Company.

Pinello, D. (2003). *Gay rights and American law.* Cambridge University Press.

Przeworski, A., & Limongi, F. (1997). Modernization: Theories and facts. *World Politics, 49*, 155–183.

Przeworski, A., Alvarez, M., Cheibub, J. A., & Limongi, F. (2000). *Democracy and development: Political institutions and well-being in the world, 1950–1990.* Cambridge University Press.

Quansah, E. K. (2004). Same-sex relationships in Botswana: Current perspectives and future prospects. *African Human Rights Law Journal, 4,* 201.

Radelet, M., & Borg, M. (2000). The changing nature of death penalty debates. *Annual Review of Sociology, 26,* 43–61.

Rahami, M. (2005). Development of criminal punishment in the Iranian post revolutionary penal code. *European Journal of Criminal Law and Criminal Justice, 13*(4), 585.

Ramirez, F. O., & McEneaney, E. H. (1997). From women's suffrage to reproduction rights? Cross-national considerations. *International Journal of Comparative Sociology, 38,* 6–24.

Ramirez, F. O., Soysal, Y., & Shanahan, S. (1997). The changing logic of political citizenship: Cross-national acquisition of women's suffrage rights. *American Sociological Review, 62*(5), 735–745.

Rankin, G. C. (2016). *Background to Indian law.* Reprinted by Cambridge University Press. (Original work published 1946).

Rasmusen, E. (1994). Judicial legitimacy as a repeated game. *Journal of Law, Economics, & Organization, 10,* 63–83.

Rayside, D. (1992). Homophobia, class and party in England. *Canadian Journal of Political Science, 25*(1), 121–149.

Rayside, D. (2008). *Queer inclusions, continental divisions: Public recognition of sexual diversity in Canada and the United States.* University of Toronto Press.

Reddy, K. (2012). Gender and sexuality in contemporary Germany. *Kiez Kieken: Observations of Berlin, 1* (Spring), 46.

Report of the Committee on Homosexual Offences and Prostitution. (1957). Wolfenden Report. (Cmnd 247, HMSO) London.

Reuters (2007, October 11). Iran clarifies leader's remark on gays. *The New York Times.* Retrieved from http://www.nytimes.com

Rimmerman, C., & Wilcox, C. (Eds.). (2007). *The politics of same-sex marriage.* The University of Chicago Press.

Robertson, S. (2006). "Boys, of course, cannot be raped": Age, homosexuality and the redefinition of sexual violence in New York City, 1880–1955. *Gender & History, 18*(2), 357–379.

Robinson, C., & Spivey, S. (2007). The Politics of masculinity and the ex-gay movement. *Gender & Society, 21*(5), 650.

Romer v. Evans, 517 U.S. 620 (1996).

Rose-Ackerman, S. (2010). Regulation and Public Law in Comparative Perspective. *University of Toronto Law Journal, 60,* 519–535.

Rosenberg, G. N. (2008). *The hollow hope: Can courts bring about social change?* University of Chicago Press.

Ruddell, R. (2005). Social disruption, state priorities, and minority threat. *Punishment & Society, 7*(1), 7.

Ruddell, R., & Urbina, M. (2004). Minority threat and punishment: A cross-national analysis. *Justice Quarterly, 21*(4), 903–931.

Saifee, S. (2003). Penumbras, privacy, and the death of morals-based legislation: Comparing U.S. constitutional law with the inherent right of privacy in Islamic jurisprudence. *Fordham International Law Journal, 27*(1), 370–454.

Sanders, D. (1996). Getting lesbian and gay issues on the international human rights agenda. *Human Rights Quarterly, 18*, 67–106.

Sanders, D. (2009). 377 and the unnatural afterlife of British colonialism in Asia. *Asian Journal of Comparative Law, 4*.1, 165–189.

Sarat, A., & Boulanger, C. (2005). *The cultural lives of capital punishment: Comparative perspectives.* Stanford University Press.

Sartori, G. (1994). *Comparative constitutional engineering: An inquiry into structures, incentives and outcomes.* New York University Press.

Sathe, S. P. (2004). *Judicial activism in India: Transgressing borders and enforcing limits.* New York: Oxford University Press.

Schabas, W. (2002). *The abolition of the death penalty in international law.* Cambridge University Press.

Schmid, H. (2000). Decriminalization of sodomy under South Africa's 1996 constitution: Implications for South African and US law. *Cardozo Journal of International and Comparative Law, 8*, 163.

Segal, J. A., Westerland, C., & Lindquist, S. (2011). Congress, the Supreme Court, and judicial review: Testing a constitutional separation of powers model. *American Journal of Political Science, 55*, 89–104.

Segal, J. A., & Spaeth, H. J. (1996). Norms, dragons and stare decisis. *American Journal of Political Science, 40*, 1064–1082.

Segal, J. A., & Spaeth, H. J. (2003). *The Supreme Court and the attitudinal model revisited.* Cambridge University Press.

Sharma, A. (1993). Homosexuality and Hinduism. In A. Swindler (Ed.), *Homosexuality and world religions* (pp. 47–80). Valley Forge, PA: Trinity Press International.

Shepsle, K. A. (1986). Institutional equilibrium and equilibrium of institutions. In H. F. Weisberg (Ed.), *Political Science: The Science of Politics* (pp. 51–81). New York: Agathon Press.

Sibalis, M. D. (1996). The regulation of male homosexuality in revolutionary and Napoleonic France, 1789–1815. In J. Merrick & B. T. Ragan (Eds.), *Homosexuality in modern France* (pp.150–167). London: Oxford University Press.

Siegel, J. (2014, July 22). An Iraqi group helping women and gays is receiving death threats. *The Daily Beast*. Retrieved August 24, 2014, from http://www.thedailybeast.com/articles/2014/07/22/an-iraqi-group-helping-women-and-gays-is-receiving-death-threats.html

Simon, R., & Blaskovich, D. (2007). *A comparative analysis of capital punishment: Statutes, policies, frequencies, and public attitudes the world over.* Lanham, MD: Lexington Books.

Skocpol, T. (1979). *States and social revolutions: A comparative analysis of France, Russia and China.* Cambridge University Press.

Skowronek, S. (1993). *The politics presidents make: Leadership from John Adams to George Bush.* Cambridge, MA: Harvard University Press.

Skyers, J. (2014, June 30). Thousands rally against tossing out Buggery Act; Shout out for clean, righteous living—news. *Jamaica Observer News*. Retrieved July 2, 2014, from http://www.jamaicaobserver.com/news/No-to-homo-agenda_17050490

Smith, M. C. (2008). *Political institutions and lesbian and gay rights in the United States and Canada.* New York: Routledge.

Sommer, U. (2014). *Supreme Court agenda setting: Strategic behavior during case selection.* New York: Palgrave MacMillan.

Sommer, U., & Asal, V. (2014). A cross national analysis of the guarantees of rights. *International Political Science Review, 35*(4), 463–481.

Sommer, U., Asal, V., Zuber, K., & Parent, J. (2013). Institutional paths to policy change. *Law & Society Review, 47*(2), 409.

Songer, D. R., & Johnson, S. W. (2007). Judicial decision making in the Supreme Court of Canada: Updating the personal attribute model. *Canadian Journal of Political Science, 40*, 911–934.

Songer, D., Segal, J., & Cameron, C. (1994). The hierarchy of justice: Testing a principal-agent model of Supreme Court-circuit court interactions. *American Journal of Political Science, 38*, 673–696.

Spiegel Online. (2013, May 17). Beaten, bullied, badgered: EU study finds widespread homophobia in Europe. *Spiegel Online*. Retrieved July 5, 2014, from http://www.spiegel.de/international/europe/eu-survey-shows-widespread-homophobia-in-europe-a-900505.html

Stein, P. (1999). *Roman law in European history.* Cambridge University Press.

Stern, M. J. (2014, July 3). Don't blame yesterday's colonialism for today's homophobia. *Slate.com*. Retrieved March 3, 2016, from http://www.slate.com/blogs/outward/ 2014/07/03/don_t_blame_homophobia_on_colonialism_cultural_relativists.html

Stewart, C. (2014, May 14). Anti-gay Ugandan tactic: Abusive, worthless anal exam. *76 CRIMES*. Retrieved July 7, 2014, from http://76crimes.com/2014/05/14/anti-gay-ugandan-tactic-abusive-worthless-anal-exam/

Stone-Sweet, A. (2000). *Governing with judges: Constitutional politics in Europe*. London: Oxford University Press.

Strasser, M. (2010). The global gay rights battlefields. *Foreign Policy*. Retrieved from http://www.foreignpolicy.com/articles/2010/12/20 /the_global _gay_rights_battlefields

Sullivan, A. (2001). This is a religious war. *The New York Times, 7*.

Swers, M. L. (2001). Understanding the policy impact of electing women: Evidence from research on Congress and state legislatures. *PS: Political Science and Politics, 34*(2), 217–220.

Swers, M. L. (2002). *The difference women make: The policy impact of women in Congress*. University of Chicago Press.

Tarrow, S. (1988). National politics and collective action: Recent theory and research in Western Europe and the United States. In W. R. Scott & J. Blake (Eds.), *Annual Review of Sociology*, (Vol. 14). Palo Alto, CA: Annual Reviews.

Tarrow, S. (1991). Comparing social movement participation in Western Europe and the United States: Problems, uses, and a proposal for synthesis. In D. Rucht (Ed.), *Research on Social Movements* (pp. 421–440). Frankfurt am Main, Germany: Campus Verlag.

Teorell, J., Charron, N., Samanni, M., Holmberg, S., & Rothstein, B. (2009). *Quality of government dataset* (version 17, June 2009). University of Gothenburg: The Quality of Government Institute. Retrieved from http://www.qog. pol.gu.se

Teorell, J., Samanni, M., Charron, N., Holmberg, S., & Rothstein, B. (2010). *Quality of government dataset* (version 27, May 2010). University of Gothenburg: The Quality of Government Institute. Retrieved from http://www.qog.pol.gu.se

Teorell, J., Holmberg, S., & Rothstein, B. (2008). *Quality of government dataset* (version 7, January 2008). University of Gothenburg: The Quality of Government Institute. Retrieved from http://www.qog. pol.gu.se

Trew, B. (2014, June 28). A Sisi's government is worse for gays than Muslim Brotherhood. *The Daily Beast*. Retrieved July 8, 2014, from http://www.thedailybeast.com/articles/2014/06/27/egypt-targets-gays.html

Tsutsui, K., & Wotipka, C. M. (2004). Global civil society and the international human rights movement: Citizen participation in human rights international nongovernmental organizations. *Social Forces, 83*, 587–620.

Tsutsui, K., & Wotipka, C. M. (2006). The Supreme Court and the national political order: Collaboration and confrontation. In R. Kahn & K. Kersch (Eds.), *The Supreme Court and American political development* (pp. 117–137). Lawrence, KS: University Press of Kansas.

Tushnet, M. (1999). The possibilities of comparative constitutional law. *Yale Law Journal, 108*, 1225–1309.

Van Caenegem, R. C. (1988). *The birth of the English Common Law.* Cambridge University Press.

van de Ven, W. P. M. M. & van Praag, B. (1981). The demand for deductives in private health insurance: A probit model with sample selection. *Journal of Econometrics, 17*(2).

Vega, A., & Firestone, J. M. (1995). The effects of gender on congressional behavior and the substantive representation of women. *Legislative Studies Quarterly, 20*(2), 213–222.

Waaldijk, K. (2000). Civil developments: Patterns of reform in the legal position of same-sex partners in Europe. *Canadian Journal of Family Law, 17*(1), 62–88.

Wafer, J. (1997). Muhammad and male homosexuality. In S. O. Murray & W. Roscoe (Eds.). *Islamic homosexualities: Culture, history and literature* (p.89). New York University Press.

Wald, K. D., Button, J. W., & Rienzo, B. A. (1996). The politics of gay rights in American communities: Explaining antidiscrimination ordinances and policies. *American Journal of Political Science, 40*(4), 1152–1178.

Wawrytko, S. A. (1993). Homosexuality and Chinese and Japanese religions. In A. Swindler (Ed.), *Homosexuality and world religions* (pp. 199–230). Valley Forge, PA: Trinity Press International.

Weeks, J. (1996). The construction of homosexuality. In S. Seidman (Ed.), *Queer theory/sociology* (pp. 41–63). London: Wiley-Blackwell.

Weeks, J. (2007). Discourse, desire and sexual deviance: Some problems in a history of homosexuality. In R. G. Parker & P. Aggleton (Eds.), *Culture, society and sexuality* (pp. 125–149). New York: Routledge.

Wejnert, B. (2005). Diffusion, development, and democracy, 1800–1999. *American Sociological Review, 70*(1), 53–81.

Wells, M. (2004). International norms in constitutional law. *Georgia Journal of International and Comparative Law, 32*, 429–436.

West, D. J., & Green, R. (1997). *Sociolegal control of homosexuality: A multination comparison.* New York: Plenum Press.

Whittington, K. (2007). *Political foundations of judicial supremacy: The presidency, the Supreme Court, and constitutional leadership in U.S. history.* Princeton University Press.

Widner, J. A. (2001). *Building the rule of law: Francis Nyalali and the road to judicial independence in Africa.* New York: W.W. Norton & Company.

Wilensky, H. L. (2002). *Rich democracies: Political economy, public policy, and performance.* Berkeley, CA: University of California Press.

Williams, S. (2009, December 6). Ugandan gay death penalty bill: Sweden threatens to withdraw aid, should the USA? *Care2.* Retrieved July 6, 2014, from http://www.care2.com/causes/ugandan-gay-death-penalty-bill-one-week-closer-to-passing-another-week-of-protest.html

Williamson, J. G. (1996). Globalization, convergence and history. *The Journal of Economic History, 56,* 277–306.

Wing, A. K. (2008). The South African Constitution as a role model for the United States. *Harvard BlackLetter Law Journal, 24,* 73–80.

Wintemute, R. (1995). *Sexual orientation and human rights: The United States Constitution, the European Convention, and the Canadian Charter.* New York: Oxford University Press.

Wright, B. (2006). Self-governing codifications of English criminal law and empire: the Queensland and Canadian examples. *University of Queensland Law Review, 26*(1), 36–65.

Young, W., & Brown, M. (1993). Cross-national comparisons of imprisonment. *Crime and Justice, 17,* 1–49.

Zorgdrager, H. (2013). Homosexuality and hypermasculinity in the public discourse of the Russian Orthodox Church: an affect theoretical approach. *International Journal of Philosophy and Theology, 74*(3), 214–239.

Zorn, C. J. W. (2001). Generalized estimating equation models for correlated data: A review with applications. *American Journal of Political Science, 45*(2), 470–490.

Zweigert, K., Kots, H., & Weir, T. (1998). *Introduction to comparative law.* Oxford: Clarendon Press.

INDEX

Amnesty International, 73
Australia, 11, 25, 51, 54, 100, 114

Banana v. the State, 8
Bowers v. Hardwick, 1, 54, 83, 97
Brazil, 26, 100, 147,
Buggery Act of 1533, 18, 34, 38–41, 49, 68, 142
Canada, 26, 50–51, 91–95, 100

capital punishment, 2, 10, 11, 14, 21, 26, 31, 63–78. *See also* death penalty
Caribbean, 72, 74
Catholicism, 112, 137, 154, 155, 161. *See also* Christianity
Chile, 25, 60, 95, 100
Christianity, 13, 20, 30, 67. *See also* Catholicism
Civil Law, 11, 16, 19, 29, 30, 38, 42, 44, 55–61, 69, 70, 75, 94, 98, 106, 144. *See also* French code, Napoleonic Code
civil rights, 23, 32, 81, 114, 117, 124

Common Law, 8–13, 16–19, 28–33, 39–50, 55, 58–63, 68–77, 82, 84, 87–90, 94, 98, 101–106, 120, 133–44, 151–56, 162
Convention Against All Forms of Discrimination Against Women (CEDAW), 85–90, 102–3, 114, 115, 118–21, 132–39, 145, 151–56
Costa Rica, 26, 100, 107, 112

database, 14, 24, 25, 72, 83, 84, 86, 89, 101, 104, 128, 137, 139
dataset. *See* database
de Facto, 110
de Jure, 7–9, 31, 56, 65, 110, 124–25
death penalty, 5–7, 1–14, 21–24, 29–30, 63–78, 107, 143–44. *See also* capital punishment
democracy, 21–23, 69–81, 117, 119, 123, 134, 136, 140, 149–50
discrimination, 3–5, 7–10, 14, 21, 24, 27–30, 32, 47, 85, 92, 107–28, 131–47
Dudgeon v. United Kingdom, 23

191

El-Al v. Danilovich, 141–42
England, 17–18, 26, 30, 33–45, 49–55, 68, 158, 162. *See also* United Kingdom
equality under the law, 6, 10, 21, 28–29, 31, 75, 80, 107–108, 112, 115, 118, 125–30, 135, 137, 143–44
Estonia, 25, 100, 131, 143
Europe, 2, 19, 29, 33, 38, 40, 44, 56–61, 73–74, 86, 114, 121, 129, 151, 152

French code 19, 55, 56, 61. *See also* Civil Law, Napoleonic Code

Gay Rights Index, 6, 20, 26–27, 31, 123–40, 156–57
GDP per capita, 28, 73, 75, 81, 85, 88–90, 101–103, 120, 132–33, 136, 138–39, 145, 151, 153, 155–56
Germany, 3, 24, 26, 56–58, 60, 100, 101, 105
Ghana, 25, 52, 100
globalization, 5, 22–24, 28, 31, 72–76, 80–82, 85, 89–93, 102,103, 105, 109, 113, 116, 119, 120, 136, 138, 145, 149–151, 153, 155, 156
GRI. *See* Gay Rights Index

Henry the VIII, 12, 18, 26, 33–39, 144
Holmes, Oliver Wendell, 43
Human Rights Watch, 13, 64

India, 7–9, 11, 17, 25, 29, 45–50, 54, 83, 86,100
interfaith marriage, 84, 87–81, 102–104, 136–139
International Covenant on Civil and Political Rights, 70, 85, 113, 114, 118
international institutions, 6, 113, 116, 120, 136, 144

International Labor Organization (ILO), 86, 88, 90, 103, 109, 113, 115, 118–121, 127, 137, 139, 145, 149–156
international law, 6, 31, 113–15, 120,121, 132, 135, 140, 144, 145
International Lesbian, Gay, Bisexual, Trans and Intersex Association, 24, 99, 118, 127
Inter-Parliamentary Union, 85, 118, 132
Iran, 25,63–65, 83,100,
Islam, 11–12, 20, 30, 64, 67–69, 91, 112, 137, 153–54, 161. *See also* Muslim
Israel, 11, 25, 51, 54, 141–44

Jamaica, 9, 25, 52, 100, 146
Japan, 26, 56, 57, 61, 70, 100
Judicial, 10, 16, 17, 27, 29, 30, 41–44, 47, 54, 56, 59, 60, 62, 64, 82, 93–106, 118, 126, 142, 144, 145, 163

Klippert v. the Queen, 91

Lawrence v. Texas, 1, 9, 23, 83, 84, 97, 110, 124, 127, 163
Lebanon, 25, 82, 83, 100
legal rights, 3, 5, 13, 23, 109, 141, 143, 145, 146
legislative, 18, 29,30, 37, 40, 54, 56, 69, 68, 78, 85, 93, 97, 98, 100–104, 106, 118, 132, 144, 164, 165

Marbury v. Madison, 96
Middle East, 73–75, 133, 151, 152
Muslim. *See also* Islam, 20, 28, 49, 68, 84, 88, 89–91, 102–105, 112, 120, 136, 138, 149–57, 161

Napoleonic Code, 18–19, 55–62, 83.

See also Civil Law, French code, Napoleonic Code
National Coalition for Gay and Lesbian Equality and Another v. Minister of Justice and Others, 2, 92
Naz Foundation India Trust v. Government of NCT Delhi and Others, 47–48
Netherlands, 19, 26, 56, 58, 101, 108, 110
Nigeria, 11, 12, 25, 51, 52, 65, 67, 100
non-judicial, 10, 27, 30, 62, 82, 93–96, 98, 99, 101–103, 105, 106
norm spillover, 31, 111, 116–120, 131
North, D. C., 15, 16, 19, 41, 42, 51,

O'Leary v. the King, 54

parliament, 14, 37–39, 44, 50, 53, 54, 78, 85, 91, 11, 118, 132, 135, 139, 142, 149, 150, 162
path dependence, 6, 10, 11, 15–21, 29–32, 33–62, 75, 79, 82, 91–102, 106, 140, 145, 147
Political Inclusion, 22, 28, 31, 80, 81, 85, 88–90, 101–103, 108–18, 120, 131, 132, 136, 138, 140, 147, 151, 153, 155, 156
political institutions, 5, 6 16, 19, 23, 30, 53, 61, 93, 95, 107, 117,
political rights, 7, 70, 85, 113, 114, 118, 119
Pope, 34–37, 40, 44

Quality of Government Database, 24, 72
Quality of Government Institute. *See* Quality of Government Database

R v. McDonald, 54
religion, 8, 9, 13–16, 18, 21–24, 29, 32–37, 63–79, 81–88, 90, 92–96, 102, 104–107, 109, 114–116, 123, 136, 138–148
Religious State, 10, 13, 17, 36, 63–78, 141, 143–147
Repeal of Sodomy Laws, 16, 17, 19, 27, 30, 39, 47, 55–57, 79–106
Roe v. Wade, 48
Romania, 25, 100, 131,
Romer v. Evans, 111, 123–24
Russia, 25, 71, 86, 87, 100

same sex relations, 6, 7, 11, 13, 16, 21, 29, 31, 55, 57, 66, 67–68, 73, 74, 76, 77, 91
sexual minority rights, 4, 6, 10, 51, 140
South Africa, 1, 7, 9, 10, 14, 23, 25, 92, 95, 97, 101, 107
Soviet Union, 24, 86, 129, 151, 152
stare decisis, 17, 41, 42, 92
Sudan, 12, 25, 65, 83, 100

Toonen v. Australia, 113, 114
Turkey, 20, 26, 101, 112, 161

Uganda, 13, 14, 25, 51, 65, 77, 78, 100, 142, 161, 162
United Kingdom, 23, 25, 38, 50, 69, 92, 101. *See also* England
United Nations, 11, 67, 86, 113–115, 119
United States, 1, 3, 4, 9, 10, 14, 17, 23, 25, 42, 44, 48, 63, 64, 66, 70, 83, 84, 95, 97, 101, 110, 114, 117, 118, 123, 124, 127, 146, 147, 162–164

Veslar v. the Queen, 54

women, 8, 22, 31, 47, 52, 80, 81, 83, 85, 89, 101, 102, 111–121, 124, 131, 132, 135, 139, 145, 149, 150, 164, 169

Zimbabwe, 8